TWAYNE'S WORLD LEADERS SERIES

EDITOR OF THIS VOLUME

Hans L. Trefousse
Brooklyn College

John Milton Hay

TWLS 69

John Milton Hay (1874)

JOHN MILTON HAY

The Union of Poetry and Politics

HOWARD I. KUSHNER
Cornell University

and

ANNE HUMMEL SHERRILL
Mills College

TWAYNE PUBLISHERS
A DIVISION OF G. K. HALL & CO., BOSTON

Library of Congress Cataloging in Publication Data

Kushner, Howard I
  John Milton Hay.

  (Twayne's world leaders series ; TWLS 69)
  Includes bibliographical references and index.
    1. Hay, John, 1838–1905.   2. Statemen — United
States — Biography.   3. United States — Foreign relations —
1865–1921.   4. United States — Politics and government
1865–1900.   I. Sherrill, Anne Hummel, joint author.
E664.H41K87   327'.2'0924   [B]   77-7955
ISBN 0-8057-7719-9

Contents

About the Authors

Concentrating in the field of U.S. foreign relations, Howard I. Kushner received his A.B. from Rutgers University, and his M.A. and Ph.D. degrees from Cornell. He currently teaches at Cornell and has previously taught at the State University of New York at Fredonia, and San Francisco State University, where he served as a visiting professor for the academic year 1973–1974. Along with numerous articles and reviews, he is the author of the book, *Conflict on the Northwest Coast: American Russian Rivalry in the Pacific Northwest, 1790–1867*, published by the Greenwood Press in 1975. His interest in psychohistory has led him to do advanced coursework in psychoanalysis at the San Francisco Psychoanalytic Institute. He is also an editorial consultant for the publishing firm of Little, Brown, and Company.

Anne Hummel Sherrill has taught History at Mills College since 1959 and been a visiting professor at SanFrancisco State University and Holy Names College. In 1977 she held the O'Connor Chair in American Institutions at Colgate University. She received her A.B. from the University of Arizona, Tucson, and her M.A. and Ph.D. degrees from the University of California at Berkeley. Studying under Carl Bridenbaugh, James D. Hart, and Armin Rappaport, her dissertation, "John Hay: Shield of Union," (1966) was the first study of Hay's intellectual development and its relationship to his literary and political career. She is the editor and coauthor with Merrill D. Peterson and Alfred Frankenstein of *Trumpets Sounding*: Essays and Discussion of Jefferson, Franklin, and Peale (1977).

Preface

Ever since Richard Hofstadter wrote the *Age of Reform* in 1955,[1] the term *mugwump* has been synonymous for downwardly mobile upper-class political reformers of the late nineteenth century. Like their social antithesis, the populists, the mugwumps, argued Hofstadter, had "apocalyptic, . . . hatred of big businessmen, bankers, and trusts. . . ." He characterized this group as "a small imperialist elite" who came from the East and "whose spokesmen were such solid and respectable gentlemen as Henry and Brooks Adams, Theodore Roosevelt, Henry Cabot Lodge, John Hay, and Albert J. Beveridge."[2]

The career of John Milton Hay, however, is a clear contradiction of Hofstadter's thesis. It demonstrates how easily historians have been misled by reading only what the subject desired posterity to read about his life. Born on the Indiana frontier, raised in a small Illinois village, and son of a country physician whose financial condition was often precarious, John Hay was most assuredly not downwardly mobile. Hay's later wealth, as did Carnegie's, Rockefeller's, or Morgan's, rested upon the rapid industrialization of post–Civil War America. His interest and activity in politics were acute. Abraham Lincoln, one of America's most successful politicians, was Hay's political mentor. Although initially attracting national attention through his reformist writings, Hay's political regularity rivaled that of his friend James G. Blaine and his enemy Roscoe Conkling. Hay did not like to admit it, but he was a member of what his father called the "ascending class."

This book is less a biography of John Hay than an essay on his life. Our purpose is to explain Hay's importance to the historian and to the general reader as well as to suggest how this son of a rural physician rose to direct the foreign policy of the United States at the turn of the last century. It is our contention that neither of these questions has been adequately answered despite the fact that Hay's varied career has attracted such eminent biographers as Henry Adams, William Roscoe Thayer, and Tyler Dennett. While Dennett's 1933 Pulitzer-Prize-winning biography remains the best full-length work and well-rounded study of Hay,[3] a fresher approach must be attempted which takes into account the archival material made available since 1933, recent interpretations of American history, and newer analytic techniques. Although we have integrated these new manuscript collections with recent approaches and historical interpretations of this period, we do not claim that this short book will supplant Dennett's as a basic biography of Hay.

Kenton J. Clymer's study, *John Hay: The Gentleman as Diplomat*, is an important addition, but it is not a definitive biography of John Hay.[4] Clymer concentrates much of his book on Hay's diplomacy, and, although he often deals in depth with particular aspects of Hay's social and intellectual development, Clymer neglects Hay's childhood, family background, and association with Abraham Lincoln. These are crucial matters not only for any biography but also for a full understanding of Hay's significance and rise to power. Thus, our emphasis and our conclusions differ from Clymer's because we begin earlier in Hay's life and attribute more importance to his childhood and relationship with Lincoln.

While most of our acknowledgment appears in our citations, we wish to thank several persons who, over the past several years, have been helpful in our preparation of this book or earlier versions of it. No doubt we have inadvertently left out some names, and others that we have included might prefer to remain anonymous. In particular, Carl Bridenbaugh, Roger Daniels, John Gleason, Nathan Hale, Jr., James D. Hart, James Kindregan, Carol R. Kushner, Walter LaFeber, Thomas J. McCormick, Armin Rappaport, Edward Saveth, Lawrence Shrader, Paul Sherrill, Hans Trefousse, and Franklin Walker have added to our understanding of John Milton Hay. The staffs of several research libraries were particularly helpful to us in our research. Stuart Sherman and John Stanley of the John Hay Library, Brown University, were especially understanding. Mary Ellen McElligot of the Illinois State Historical Society provided us with previously unnoticed manuscript material on the life of Dr. Charles Hay. Lulie Davis of the Washington County Historical Society in Salem, Indiana, was gracious and resourceful in locating Hay family material for us. Leslie Morris and Gary Barber of the Reed Library of SUNY, Fredonia provided important assistance. Also, the staffs of the Massachusetts Historical Society, the Rush Rhees Library of the University of Rochester, the University of California Libraries at Berkeley, the National Archives,

Houghton Library of Harvard University, and the Cornell University Libraries should be mentioned.

Three typists combined to complete this manuscript: to Mary Notaro, Valerie Stannard, and Gertrude Fitzpatrick, a special thanks. The preparation of this book was supported, in part, by grants from Mills College, Oakland, California, the Research Foundation of the State University of New York, and History Department Research Fund of the University of California at Berkeley.

We would like to thank the John Hay Library of Brown University and the Rush Rhees Library of the University of Rochester for permission to reprint complete versions of letters in their possession. Much of the material in Chapter 4 appeared previously in the *Journal of the Illinois State Historical Quarterly*, 67 (September, 1974) under the title " 'The Strong God Circumstance': The Political Career of John Hay."

HOWARD I. KUSHNER
Ithaca, New York

ANNE HUMMEL SHERRILL
San Francisco, California

Chronology

1838 Born October 8 in Salem, Indiana.
1841 Moved with family to Warsaw, Illinois.
1849– Sent to Pittsfield Academy, Pike County, Illinois.
1851
1852– Sent with older brother to Illinois State University,
1855 Springfield, Illinois.
1855– Attended Brown University, Providence, Rhode Island.
1858
1859 Read law with Uncle Milton Hay in Springfield, Illinois.
1860 Worked on Lincoln's nomination and election campaigns.
1861 Admitted to the Bar.
1861 Left for Washington, D.C., to serve as Lincoln's assistant
     private secretary.
1863 Traveled to Sea Islands and Florida as Lincoln's personal
     emissary.
1864 Commissioned major and appointed assistant adjutant gen-
     eral of the volunteers.
1864 Sent to Niagara Falls with Horace Greeley to meet with
     Confederate peace commissioners.
1865 Lincoln assassinated (April).
1865 Promoted to colonel (May).
1865– Secretary to the Legation at Paris.
1867
1867– Chargé d'Affaires at Vienna.
1868
1869– Secretary of the Legation in Madrid.
1870
1870 Editorial writer and night editor of the *New York Tribune*.
1871 Published *Pike County Ballads* and *Castillian Days*.
1872 Translated Emilio Castelar's *The Republican Movement in
     Europe*.
1874 Married Clara Stone of Cleveland.
1875 Resigned from *Tribune* and moved to Cleveland.
1875 Began business career under direction of Amasa Stone.
1879– Appointed Assistant Secretary of State.
1881

1881   Managing editor (temporary) of *New York Tribune*.
1882–   Toured Europe with family.
1883
1883   Became director of Western Union.
1883   Published *The Bread-winners* (anonymously).
1886   Moved to Washington, D.C.
1886–   With Nicolay, published *Lincoln, A History*.
1890
1887–   Became active in Republican party politics.
1896
1897   Appointed Ambassador to England.
1898   Appointed Secretary of State.
1899   Open Door Notes.
1900   First Hay-Pauncefote Treaty signed.
1900   Boxer Rebellion in China; issued Second Open Door Notes.
1901   Second Hay-Pauncefote Treaty signed.
1901   Deaths of McKinley, King, Nicolay, and son, Adelbert Hay.
1902   Newfoundland Fisheries Treaty negotiated.
1903   Hay-Herbert Treaty signed.
1903   Alaskan boundary settled.
1904   Hay-Bunau-Varilla Treaty ratified.
1904   Awarded Grand Cross of the French Legion of Honor.
1904   Elected to American Academy of Arts and Letters.
1905   Died on July 1 at Lake Sunapee, New Hampshire.

CHAPTER 1

The Successful Youth of John Milton Hay

I N October, 1861, Dr. Charles Hay proudly wrote to his sister
Elisabeth that his twenty-three-year-old son John had "attained
a position in a social and a political point of view never before
reached by a young man of his age in this government." John's
"arrival in a city," the father continued, is "noticed in the dalies as
much as general Jackson's would have been 30 years ago."[1]

When asked to explain how he achieved so much in life, John Hay
answered that it had been "the result of accident."[2] Hay's close
friend, Henry Adams also publicized this view of Hay's life.[3] William R. Thayer, in his two-volume biography of John Hay, agreed.[4]
So did Tyler Dennett's 1933 Pulitzer-Prize-winning biography.
Hay's successes, Dennett argued, resulted from "a chain of accidents,"[5] and recent studies of Hay's career have allowed this expla-
nation to stand.[6]

None of Hay's biographers have seen his childhood experiences
as a cause for his success. Those of Hay's biographers who have
investigated his childhood and adolescence have presented young
John Hay as a melancholy youth, tormented by indecision.[7] Even in
postadolescence Hay is pictured as a neurotic who succeeded in
spite of his neuroses. Some of the studies on Hay suggest that, if he
had only been less neurotic, he would have achieved greater fame
and fortune. Adding up Hay's record of accomplishments such a
view borders on the ludicrous.

Hay's biographers thus leave us with the picture of John Hay at
age twenty-one as an indolent and neurotic youth who somehow
successively held positions as Lincoln's assistant personal secretary
(1861–1865), Secretary of the American Legation in Paris (1865–
1867), Chargé d'Affaires in Vienna (1867–1868), Secretary of the
American Legation in Madrid (1869–1870), Assistant Secretary of

13

State (1879–1881), Ambassador to England (1897–1898), and Secretary of State (1898–1905). Given the personality disabilities attributed to him, it is no wonder that his biographers concluded that John Hay was a lucky man. This study is an attempt to reinvestigate John Hay's childhood and adolescence to discover whether other factors helped fortune along.

In 1876 John Hay's seventy-five-year-old father, Dr. Charles Hay, wrote that his goal in life had been "to found a family . . . not in any aristocratic, still less plutocratic sense; but I have hoped to leave behind me children, and children's children . . . with whom intelligence, honor, and thrift would be matters of instinct and tradition."[8] This statement, of course, says both less and more than appears. While the founding of a family may seem ambitious, this statement by a seventy-five-year-old man demonstrates how limited his ambitions were.

In a sense Dr. Hay's goals had been restricted by a life that generally would not be called successful by traditional nineteenth-century standards. As a young graduate of Transylvania University's medical school (June, 1829) Charles Hay migrated thirty miles north of his native Lexington, Kentucky, to Salem, Indiana. For twelve years Dr. Hay tried to eke out a living as a physician in the town. Almost from the first he realized that settling in Salem had been a mistake; yet only the threat of starvation persuaded him to migrate further west. After a year's attempt to build his medical practice in Salem, Dr. Hay found himself with almost no patients. "I find," he wrote his sister Elisabeth, "that although I have the confidence of the people to a considerable extent, it is like driving a wedge into the toughest oak to attain a place like this."[9] In September, 1830, Charles Hay explained to his sister that his failure to prosper was due to "the unsettled character of the emigrants to this country [which] is injurious to its improvement in every respect. It is injurious to beginners in every kind of business [such as] a mechanic, or merchant, or a physician [who] sets up in town in any part of the state." The people, he added, are "very cautious about encouraging a man until they see he has become 'settled' as they say."[10]

Charles Hay remained in Salem for eleven more years and apparently, if his fortune was any indication, the people of Salem remained cautious. As he admitted, "the word 'moving' is almost as odious to me as the term revolution is said to be in France."[11] Rather than move, in 1835 Dr. Hay became part owner of a printing office in Salem and published a newspaper, the Salem *Monitor*.[12] But within a few years both the *Monitor* and the printing office closed for lack of patronage. Next, Dr. Hay attempted land speculation, which also ended in financial disaster.[13]

At forty, after eleven years of financial failure, Charles Hay decided to move further west. Curiously, he did not choose one of the more rapidly growing western towns like Springfield or Cincinnati. Instead, he picked the village of Warsaw, Illinois, whose population (400) was half that of Salem. Dr. Hay's financial condition was so tenuous in 1841 that he was only able to resettle in Warsaw with money borrowed from his family in Springfield.[14] Once settled in Warsaw, Charles Hay, until his death in 1885, rarely left the village. His more ambitious son summed up his father: "With talents which might have gained him distinction, he was destitute of that interior spur of restlessness which goads men into the race of competition."[15]

Charles Hay not only did not try to join in the competitive individualism of the frontier, he held it, and its symbol, Andrew Jackson, in contempt. The doctor was critical of those who continually moved from place to place. He complained that western Indiana and Illinois were being "settled with a great deal of the sweepings of Indiana. . . ." While later writers would praise the pioneer as one of America's institutions, Dr. Hay pictured such men as lawless and irresponsible wanderers who never paid their debts. In the West, he wrote, "there is nobody so much dreaded as the constables and sherriffs."[16] He condescendingly described his fellow townsmen during an 1833 cholera epidemic as cowards "who fled and left the sick, the dead and the dying to be attended to by those chiefly who were in the same situation as the sick."[17]

In short, Charles Hay, having little faith in mankind, had less in democracy. The majority was "unprincipled" and voted for Andrew Jackson even though his "administration . . . has nothing to sustain it in its unbridled course but gen. Jackson's popularity." Yet, Dr. Hay lamented, in a democracy popularity "is a shield against any and every impression which truth ought to make against it."[18]

Hay was definitely not a Jackson man. One of his earliest letters from Salem mentions a Fourth of July oration which he delivered and which dismayed the local press because "there was nothing said about the 'hero of two wars,' (alias Jackson)."[19] Dr. Hay remained a good Whig and supporter of Henry Clay in a county where strong

majorities supported the Jacksonians.[20] All during the 1830s he was
active in Whig political campaigns on the local level. His attempts at
electing Whigs to office, however, proved even less successful than
his medical practice.[21]

For all that, Dr. Hay was apparently a more satisfied man than
most of those who sought to improve their position in the highly
competitive West during the 1830s. He was unhurried and unanx-
ious in a dynamically changing and anxiety-ridden frontier America.
While others sought prominence and wealth (few achieving either),
Charles Hay read the classics in Latin to his children. After seven
successively unprofitable years in Salem, the doctor was able,
nevertheless, to proclaim that "I have still a greater thirst after
knowledge than anything else and derive more pleasure from its
acquisition than from that of money. . . ."[22] He was no frontiersman,
no pioneer, and his children were not worse off because of it.

Some of Charles Hay's sanguine attitude in the face of bad fortune
may have resulted from the stability of his marriage. On October 12,
1831, he had married Helen Leonard in Salem.[23] Born February 7,
1804, in Assonet, Massachusetts, where her father, David Augustus
Leonard, was a Baptist minister, she too had reasons to resist moving. David Leonard, a 1792 graduate of Brown University, had
abandoned the Baptist ministry in favor of Unitarianism and, when
she was two, accepted a position as postmaster of Bristol, Rhode
Island. In 1818 he decided to move his family west to Vincennes,
Indiana, but died during the journey, leaving his forty-two-year-old
widow Mary alone with eleven children—eight girls and three
boys.[24]

Helen Leonard was fifteen years old when her father died. She
had, nevertheless, acquired some formal education, because she
had come to Salem in the fall of 1830 in order to take a position
teaching school.[25] She moved in with her older sister Evelyne
Leonard Farnham, who in 1821 had married John Hay Farnham, a
lawyer. Almost immediately Dr. Hay became enamored of Miss
Leonard—her education and refinement were her greatest assets,
he thought.[26] On November 2, 1830, the doctor wrote to his sister
that Miss Leonard was "far better educated" than any woman he
had met since coming to Salem and "besides, she is witty and a little
sarcastic withal, these latter qualities never made any lady popular
with her own sex."[27] Later Helen Leonard Hay would be remembered as "a strong minded woman" by those who knew her.[28]

Charles and Helen Hay presented their children with a commitment to educational and intellectual pursuits that was uncommon in frontier America of the 1830s and 1840s. When their fourth child, John Milton Hay, demonstrated unusual intellectual promise, his parents spared no effort to insure that his talents would be fulfilled.

John Milton Hay, born on October 8, 1838, was the fourth of six children born to his parents.[29] Aside from his own siblings, he grew up in a household that in the 1830s and 1840s contained at times as many as six other children, including two children of Mrs. Hay's sister Evelyne (Evelyne and John Farnham died of cholera in 1834), Mrs. Hay's younger brother, several young boarders, and one young black girl.[30]

In 1841, when John was almost three years old, he and his family left Indiana and settled on the Illinois side of the Mississippi River at a point where three states—Illinois, Iowa, and Missouri—meet. While young John Hay was growing up in his village, sixty miles downstream in Hannibal, Missouri, another young man, who was destined to become Hay's friend in later years, Samuel Clemens, had similar experiences. John's boyhood was a happy one. Later in life he looked back to that time of his life with nostalgia:

The years of my boyhood were passed on the banks of the Mississippi, and the great river was the scene of my early dreams. The boys of my day led an amphibious life in and near the waters in the summer time, and in the winter its dazzling ice bridge, of incomparable beauty and purity, was our favorite playground; while our imaginations were busy with the glamour and charm of the distant cities of the South. . . . We built snow forts and called them the Alamo; we sang rude songs of the cane-bake and the cornfield; and the happiest days of the year to those of us who dwelt on the northern bluffs of the river were those brought us, in the loud puffing and whistling steamers of olden time, to the Mecca of our rural fancies, the bright and busy metropolis of St. Louis.[31]

Such a picture could as easily have been given by Mark Twain of his own boyhood.[32]

Young John was by all accounts a very precocious child.[33] Physically smaller and weaker than his male siblings and friends, he outshone them all in his early learning skills. By the time he was twelve he had read six books of Virgil in Latin, had studied Greek, and had acquired a speaking knowledge of German.[34] His early academic success was highly rewarded, and he thrived on the praise he obtained.[35]

John and his older brother Augustus received their primary education under the direction of the local schoolmaster, Mr. Holmes. The boys were soon given over to the Reverend Stephen Childs, an Episcopal minister, who continued their instruction in Greek and Latin.[36] In 1849, eleven-year-old John was sent to live with his father's younger brother Milton, a lawyer in Pittsfield, Pike County. He spent the next two years attending the Pittsfield Private Academy, run by Mr. and Mrs. John D. Thompson, and once more John proved academically superior to his classmates and, often, to his teachers.[37]

Twenty-one years older than John, Milton Hay had read law in the firm of Stuart and Lincoln and had attained a local reputation for his writing. Ambitious, he appeared the opposite in all respects to his older brother Charles. Milton, whose own two children had died, quickly grew fond of John, and John reciprocated. For the next twelve years of John's life Milton Hay would take over part of the duties of a father and guide and support the young man through college and legal training. Milton's close connections with Abraham Lincoln would, in 1861, lead John Hay to a job as the President's assistant personal secretary.[38]

Education in the nineteenth-century West often meant leaving home. For Hay and his brothers it also meant living with, and being supported by, a network of relatives. Family letters make clear that no member of the Hay tribe had reason to feel alone; aid and concern were freely given and taken. Therefore, having exhausted the learning opportunities of Warsaw and Pittsfield at thirteen and a half, John and his brother Augustus were sent to attend Illinois State University in Springfield, and to live with their paternal grandfather. Uncle Milton contributed the tuition.[39]

The household included a bachelor uncle, Nathaniel, and four unmarried aunts; and it possessed a very different religious tone from either the boys' own home or that of Milton Hay. Grandfather Hay, who had retired from his profitable brickmaking factory in Lexington, Kentucky, and moved in 1830 to Springfield, was a devout Missionary Baptist. This rigid religious attitude was in total contrast to the almost agnostic beliefs of Charles and Helen Hay, neither of whom belonged to any church. Moral discussions in their home were far more likely to refer to classical authors than to the

Old Testament. However, John must have had the flexibility needed for an adolescent to live happily for the first time with elderly adults and a wrathful God, for he again excelled for the next three years at school.[40]

His letters from Springfield show many of the traits of later thoughts and conflicts. At fifteen he wrote home to his sister praising poetry as a career worth pursuing: "I think . . . that it is one of the noblest faculties of our nature and should be cultivated to the fullest extent." The poet's book, John proclaimed, was "not the counting house leger, or even the page of philosophic lore; but the great book of Nature. . . ." In apparent contradiction, however, another side of Hay's personality appeared in this letter to his sister. For he also argued that "all the sentimental talk we hear from the poet and the novelist, about the simplicity and quiet ease of village life, is all humbug. The city is the only place to gain a knowledge of the world, which will fit a man for entering the duties of life."[41] That was quite a statement for a youth who had never seen a town larger than Springfield, but it underscores the fact that, unlike his father, he was to seek out capitals—Paris, Vienna, Madrid, New York, Washington, and London. He would also crave the remote wild lands and there find respite; but he needed to live in the world's cities.

During the next year, as an entering student at Brown University in Providence, Rhode Island, John Hay was to view his first eastern city. If his letters from Providence are any indication, the city fulfilled his expectations.[42] Brown University was chosen because Grandfather Hay believed John would benefit from the environment of a Baptist institution. John's maternal grandfather had graduated from Brown in 1792, and that fact was an added reason for choosing the college. If Grandfather Hay thought that Brown would strengthen the youth's religious convictions, he must have forgotten that John's maternal grandfather left the Baptist ministry after his educational experience.[43]

Upon arrival at college John wrote his parents that "The life here suits me exactly." Informing them that his professors were "all men of the greatest ability and what is more, perfect gentlemen," he added that "any violation of the rules of the institution are strictly punished."[44] Nevertheless, he found the initial transition to eastern college life more difficult than expected. The best Illinois had to offer, its state university, proved to be little more than a good preparatory school. Planning to enter Brown as a junior, Hay soon decided that two years would not be sufficient time to "finish the course with justice." He told his parents that he thought he could "*graduate* in that time but will not stand high, or know as much about the studies as if I had been even more leisurely about them. Again, if I go through so hurriedly, I will have little or no time to avail myself of the literary treasures of the libraries."[45] Hay's parents were willing to indulge their son an extra year of college, and uncle Milton agreed to pay for it.[46]

The first two years at Brown proved very difficult. Hay's western speech and dress were made the subject of ridicule by many of his wealthier, eastern classmates. His lack of spending money added to his discomfort.[47] Moreover, he was passed over by the "best" fraternities. A classmate characterized him as "very young, very innocent, and affectionate in his manners."[48] An historian searching for neurosis might suggest that Hay's early unhappy experiences at college affected his health. During his first two years at Brown he suffered seventy-two days of illness; during his last year, which seemed to be his most satisfying, he was ill six days.[49] Other evidence, however, suggests that Hay's strong sense of himself protected him from the very beginning.

At Hay's first freshman dinner, the toastmaster told him to stand up and make a speech. John had been through several weeks of humiliation. As he stood up one of his classmates shouted, "We don't want anything dry!" The situation could have easily increased Hay's sense of shame and embarrassment; yet his sense of humor saved him. He retorted: "Hay that is green can never be dry." He had made his reputation.[50]

As always, he excelled in academic performance. In his first semester Hay placed in the "first class of honor" and remained at the top of his class until he graduated in 1858.[51] Professor James B. Angell (later president of the University of Michigan) who taught Hay literature, maintained that Hay was the best translator of French and German masterpieces he had ever had in his classes.[52] Hay had a reputation as a student who could excel with very little work. One of his classmates recalled that "it was the general opinion that Hay put his book under his pillow and had the contents thereof absorbed and digested by morning. He was never seen 'digging' or doing any other act or thing that could be construed into hard study. His quick perception, ready grasp of an idea and wonderfully retentive memory, made a mere pastime of study."[53] If not loved by all, at the very least most of his classmates acknowledged that John Hay had an outstanding intellect and John was well aware of that.[54]

Rather than a time of crisis, Hay's college days were among the happiest of his life. He enjoyed his fraternity, Theta Delta Chi, even if it was not the most prestigious at Brown. Not unlike many college students of a different era, he experimented with hashish.[55]

In his senior year, Hay was elected class poet and assigned the honor of writing the class poem, a task he performed with both relish and sentimentality. The message of the poem, to himself and to his classmates, was hardly an unambitious one:

> We may not stand sublime on history's pages,
> The bright ideals of the future's dream;
> Yet we may all strive for the goal assigned us,
> Glad if we win and happy if we fail;
> Work calmly on, nor care to leave behind us,
> The lurid glaring of the meteor's trail.[56]

Among the most pleasant of Hay's college experiences was his friendship with the Angell family. Professor James Angell made John a welcome visitor. Angell's sister Hannah, who was a year younger than John, lived in her brother's house while attending school in Providence. A romance soon blossomed between John and Hannah. While in 1858 Hannah returned to her parents' house in Scituate, twelve miles from Providence, she continued to visit her brother's house and John made frequent trips to Scituate.[57] By the time Hay departed Providence in July, 1858, the relationship had reached a serious level, and there is evidence that the two contemplated marriage.[58]

His final year in Providence also served as an introduction to the literary salons that he would lionize in later life. In the spring of 1858 John and Hannah were invited into a circle of writers which met at the home of Mrs. Sarah Helen Whitman, the former fiancée of Edgar Allan Poe and a well-known poet in her own right. At Mrs. Whitman's they also met Nora Perry, a young poet.[59] The experience at Mrs. Whitman's had a profound impact upon Hay. This was the type of refinement after which he apparently had hungered. Whenever he looked back to his college days he thought not of "The Professors . . . of the greatest ability," but of Providence, "where I used to eat Hasheesh and dream dreams."[60]

In July, 1858, John Hay left Providence. Part of him, like his
uncle Milton, wanted to "stand sublime on history's pages," while
another part, like his father, only desired "to dream dreams."

Hay's biographers see his return to Warsaw from Providence as
the beginning of a period of profound depression and melancholy.[61]
Dennett entitled his chapter on this period of Hay's life "Back to
Boeotia"; Thayer called his "The Poet in Exile," whereas Caroline
Ticknor's collection of Hay's letters during this period bears the title
A Poet in Exile. Hay's letters to his friends in Providence do provide
some evidence which supports the view that John was despondent
and felt trapped in the West by fate. On August 30, 1858 (within
days of his return to Warsaw), he wrote Miss Perry that he was
unhappy at being back in the West and turned "away from the
familiar faces that I meet in the streets of Warsaw and go to my room
to converse with the shadows."[62] On October 12, he wrote to Miss
Perry that he found his village and the West "a dreary waste of
heartless materialism, where great and heroic qualities . . . bully
their way up into the glare, but the flowers of existence inevitably
droop and wither." He predicted that such an atmosphere within "a
few years will find my eye not rolling in a fine frenzy, but steadily
fixed on the pole-star-of-humanity, $!"[63]

Hay, however, never fell into total despair. Even though he had
not been anxious to leave Providence, John wrote Hannah that it
would be "foolish" to try to live in the past. While he cherished his
years in Providence, he was prepared to return to Illinois. In a most
revealing statement he admitted that he had "always subjected my
affections to my will. My head has always ruled my heart." Having
written those sentences late at night, John read them over the following morning before sending them. He apologized to Hannah for
his "egotistic complainings," but decided to send her the note even
though he had written the letter late at night, when his defenses
were down. He admitted that "there is something strangely truth
compelling in the silence and solitude of midnight."[64]

Thus, if some of his letters to Nora Perry and Hannah Angell were
sentimental and even, at times, despairing, there were two reasons.
First, John had not yet gotten over his infatuation with Hannah,
and, secondly, his letters were aimed at his audience (Miss Perry
and Mrs. Whitman), sentimental poets who themselves wrote in
highly charged emotional prose.[65] In any case, John Hay could not
keep up the tone for long. His sense of humor and ability to laugh at

himself soon came through. On January 2, 1859, he wrote to Nora: "In the words of the poet Pigwiggen . . . 'I know I'm a genus [*sic*], 'cause I hate work worse'n thunder, and would like to cut my throat—only it hurts.' " Hay added that there was "as yet, no room in the west for a genius, I mean of course, of the Pigwiggen model." So as not to be misunderstood, he affirmed his decision to stay in the West: "I am a Westerner. I chose it, however, and my blood is on my own head."[66] Again, Hay's self-confidence and sense of humor, reinforced since early childhood, saved him from despair.

More than despondency, one finds emerging during this period of John Hay's life an elitist attitude toward Westerners similar to that which his father had expressed some twenty-five years earlier. Less than two months after returning to Warsaw Hay proclaimed that he had abandoned his dreams "of raising the mental standard of this place. The one cannot raise the many. Cannot the many drag down the one?"[67] By December, 1858, he had dismissed "the average Westerner" as one who "always spells badly and rides well" and who "has profound contempt for goodness and grammar. . . ." In short, John Hay saw his fellow Westerners as "barbarians."[68] Nevertheless, always the realist, John kept his contempt for his neighbors to himself and, safely, to his eastern friends. For, as he wrote to Hannah, "I may be a candidate for school-committeeman [schoolmaster] some day and continued abuse of my fatherland may damage my availability."[69]

While John embraced his father's view of the western pioneers, he clearly did not desire to spend a life, as his father had, in their midst. John explained to Miss Perry that his father, who has "more ambition and higher ideals than I has dwelt here a lifetime and even this winter does not despair of creating interest in things intellectual among the great unshorn of the prairies. I am not suited for a reformer. I do not like to meddle with moral ills. I love comfortable people. I prefer for my friends, men who can read."[70] Later, in his biography of his father, John would be proud that Dr. Hay "was destitute of that interior spur of restlessness which goads men into the race of competition."[71] To his credit, Dr. Hay understood his son's longings and instead of resenting John's decision to leave Salem, Charles Hay tried to help his son find a way out.

In the final analysis the thing that rescued young John Hay from despair was the continued support of his family. Once again, his kin encouraged John's own sense of individuality. Within a month of

John's return to Warsaw his parents and older brother Augustus recognized that John's mental state depended upon his removal, as quickly as possible, from Warsaw. Mrs. Hay and Augustus restrained Dr. Hay from submitting John's name for a position as schoolmaster in Warsaw.[72] Dr. Hay agreed with the other family members that such a position "would never suit his [John's] self esteem nor his pecuniary wants."[73] John's own desire was to return as a graduate student to Brown in order to "read extensively and write for eastern periodicals until a time and opening appeared for taking a high position *some where*."[74]

While Hay's family sympathized with his goals, they did not possess the funds to finance such a life-style. Instead Dr. Hay suggested that John find "some profession upon which he can fall back . . . while he is rising higher."[75] A legal career was decided upon as a stepping-stone to a literary one. All agreed, however, that John should not read law in Warsaw where his future prospects seemed both dim and dull. Charles Hay asked his brother Milton in Springfield if John could be made a clerk in Milton's firm. Dr. Hay agreed to pay the cost of John's board.[76]

Milton Hay quickly wrote to his favorite nephew.[77] John replied that, although he was in great demand as a lecturer, he had "been repeatedly told by lawyers here that I will never make a living by pettifogging." John knew that his uncle would not agree with the lawyers of Warsaw. John noted that, while he had been reading law on his own, he missed "the personal superintendence of a preceptor. . . ." If Milton thought his nephew could "engage in anything profitable . . . by coming to Springfield," John added, "I am ready to come."[78] Once more Milton Hay was prepared to aid his nephew in distress.

In the spring of 1859 Hay moved to Springfield in order to read law in his uncle's office. His most quoted letter about this period pictures him as "stranded at last, like a weather beaten hulk, on the dreary wastes of Springfield. . . ."[79] To Nora Perry, he proclaimed: "I have wandered in the valley of the shadow of death. All the universe, God, earth and heaven, have been to me but vague and gloomy phantasms."[80] To Hannah he wrote, "All the objects of my ambition . . . are changed. They are narrowing down to a respectable life and a cheap tombstone."[81]

This was fine rhetoric for eastern sensitivities and, again, Hay knew it.[82] In 1859 Springfield was the hub of western growth. Moreover, Hay's uncle's law firm was one of the most prestigious in the state. For fifteen years that Springfield law office had supplied Illinois with its most important leaders. Abraham Lincoln had been a partner. Two governors (John A. Palmer and Shelby M. Cullom) had moved directly from this firm to the governor's mansion. Cullom then went on to the United States Senate where he served for the next forty years. The town was filled with prominent men, all of whom Hay, through his uncle's prestige, could come into daily contact.[83] If one wanted to make it" in Illinois or the West, Springfield and Milton Hay's law firm were the places to be. Rather than a poet in exile, John Hay at age twenty-one should be seen as a young man on the make.[84]

Dennett saw Hay's twenty-first year as a time of personality crisis as John searched for some firm identity. The youth could find "no ready handle by which he could take hold of life. It is quite clear when one comes to understand the degree of emotional conflict which marked his later life, that he was already suffering from the multiplicity of his disjointed life. He did not know what to do with his life. His talents fought with one another."[85]

No doubt Hay's childhood and adolescence produced in him certain conflicts about his identity. But conflict is not evidence of illness. No more was Hay's ambivalence over whether to become a poet or lawyer proof of a serious disturbance. Hay's life choice was simple; he chose to be both a politician and a poet, and in middle life added businessman to his identities. The very fact that Hay, in later life, continued to pursue poetry and journalism as well as politics and business is not evidence of a personality split by indecision but rather of a human being who was able during his adult life to pursue varied careers so successfully that any one of them would have secured his reputation in history. Moreover, John Hay was able to play one off against the other. This ability to synthesize apparent disparities was to be a key mechanism in Hay's personality and in his ability to play many roles. Writing and politics, rather than being mutually exclusive, as Hay's biographers (including Henry Adams) seem to allege, were in Hay's case complementary. Furthermore, Hay's reputed melancholia was not extreme nor was it hidden by John in some secret diary; rather, it was the frank admission to some of his close friends that once in a while he was a little depressed.

Such an admission could be made by anyone who thinks, and, more important, Hay's ability to make such public confession demonstrates, once again, not illness, but therapy.

John Hay's later and well-known contempt for office seekers and politicians (though he was both) can be traced, in part, to his ambivalence toward ambitious people in general. Hay's father was a rather unambitious, if extremely intellectual man, who by all accounts was content with his life as a county physician. Dr. Hay's lack of ambition was in sharp contrast both to the many rising men in western Illinois in the 1840s and 1850s as well as to his own more famous and ambitious brother, Milton. John Hay had two models to choose from—his father and his uncle—and, instead of choosing either one, he chose both.

In other words, John Milton Hay's ego was strong enough to deal with the stresses that childhood and adolescence placed before it. His parents emphasized a very different set of values (including intellectual and academic excellence and agnosticism) from many of their contemporaries in western Illinois. Nevertheless, traditional western American values were offered to him at his grandfather's house in Springfield and by his uncle Milton. Moreover, he had received strong support from his family during this period of potential crisis. That support came in the form of advice as well as pecuniary support; and most important of all, he received understanding. Thus, John Hay's childhood presented him with excellent preparation for the society in which he would one day gain prominence. Springfield had been the first test of his adulthood; Washington in wartime would be the second.

CHAPTER 2

Lincoln's Secretary

JOHN HAY's relationship with Abraham Lincoln was a paramount influence over his life. For Hay, Lincoln proved to be a father figure who combined the values and personalities of both John's father and uncle. The familial connection between Hay and Lincoln did not develop all at once. The young man was initially skeptical about Lincoln's abilities and his values and referred to him as "The Tycoon." After two years of close contact with Lincoln, skepticism gave way to idealization. By August, 1863, Hay wrote of Lincoln: "There is no man in the country so wise, so gentle, and so firm. I believe the hand of God placed him where he is."[1] Lincoln reciprocated. He viewed Hay more as a son than as an employee. Hay lived in the White House and was treated as a member of the Lincoln family.[2] His experience with Abraham Lincoln made Hay's legacy—it was a calling card that established his credentials and reputation as an authentic Republican who had served that party's greatest leader during the nation's most serious crisis.

In February, 1861, John Hay left Springfield along with President-elect Lincoln, who had appointed the young attorney to be his assistant personal secretary. Hay, of course, had not come to Springfield because he knew that he would end up serving the next President of the United States. Luck, however, was among the minor reasons that he obtained this post from Lincoln; he earned the job.[3]

After Lincoln's nomination and especially following Lincoln's election Hay made himself a very useful voluntary aide. His boyhood friend John G. Nicolay, who had risen from editor of the Pike County *Free Press* to the clerkship of the Secretary of State of Illinois, had been an early and ardent Lincoln supporter. When Lincoln obtained the Republican presidential nomination, Nicolay became Lincoln's private secretary. Immediately Hay offered his services and together with Nicolay handled Lincoln's correspondence during and after the election campaign. Hay also made political speeches for Lincoln and wrote articles about Lincoln for eastern newspapers. Giving his full time to Lincoln for half a year, Hay got to know the nominee intimately. Hay was hardly naive about the facts of political reward—his duties included answering the hundreds of letters requesting positions in the upcoming Lincoln administration. Hay must have expected some compensation for his services. The story of Lincoln's offhanded appointment of Hay, while fitting neatly into Hay's later view of himself, fits poorly into the realities of Springfield politics of the 1860s.[4]

Hay's own position was somewhat irregular as there was no legal provision for an assistant secretary. Therefore, he was officially appointed a clerk in the Department of the Interior, detailed to special service in the White House, and paid at the rate of $1,600 a year. In 1862 he received a two hundred dollar raise—modest compensation indeed for a job which today would be titled Presidential Assistant.[5] If Lincoln's rein was light, the duties of the secretaries were demanding and often delicate. For in addition to routine office chores, the President used Hay as his personal representative to deal with disgruntled military and naval officers, to investigate secret societies and gauge their strength, to travel to Canada for ostensible peace negotiations, and to introduce his Reconstruction policy in the newly won Southern territory. The job exposed Hay to political intrigue and war as well as to basic training in public service.

Living in the White House, Hay and Nicolay were on duty twenty-four hours a day. Sometime that spring or early summer they requested and received permission to write Lincoln's biography—a task they were not to begin for fourteen years and not to complete until 1890. On April 18, 1861, the day after the President called up 75,000 volunteers to combat secession, Hay began a diary. It is a major source for understanding Lincoln, the Civil War, and John Hay. Written from the vantage point of a bedroom across from the executive offices, the diary is studded with vignettes of Lincoln's night wanderings, tastes, habits, and conversation. Its main impact is of war, a lonely leader, and a young man trying to make sense out of seeming chaos.[6]

During the first two years of war, Hay viewed the conflict primarily in personal rather than ideological terms. His reaction to the death of his friend Colonel E. Elmer Ellsworth offers one example among many of Hay's attitude.

Ellsworth was a likely candidate for Hay's enthusiasm; handsome, bright, and bold, he combined thought and action in a dashing way. The two had become friends in Springfield, where Ellsworth had read law in the office of Lincoln and Herndon and worked on Lincoln's campaign. Like Hay, Ellsworth had been part of the President-elect's suite; but when war broke out, Ellsworth had obtained a commission as lieutenant and gone to New York to organize a volunteer company of Zouave Cadets. Now a colonel, Ellsworth entered the Capital May 2, 1861, at the head of eleven hundred men. With much fanfare, he was welcomed by official Washington, including the President. A great deal was expected of Ellsworth and his Zouaves.

In increasingly loud voices the public and press had been calling for action after the fall of Fort Sumter; the Maryland imbroglio of halted trains, destroyed bridges, and cut telegraph; the secession of Virginia; and the abandonment of the arsenal at Harper's Ferry. An attack on Alexandria was planned, and on the night of May 23 the regiments were readied. By dawn of May 24 Colonel Ellsworth was dead.

After leading his regiment to the Virginia side of the Potomac and getting it into position, Ellsworth had spied a Confederate flag flying from an Alexandria hotel. Climbing to remove it, he was shot by the irate hotelkeeper. The murder quickly raised Ellsworth to the rank of martyr.[7]

Lincoln made much of Ellsworth's death. He praised him as a fallen hero and commanded that Ellsworth's funeral be held in the East Room of the White House. Hay quickly wrote an article on Ellsworth, which was published in the *Atlantic*.[8]

Hay's essay on Ellsworth tells us more about Hay than about Colonel Ellsworth. Hay hinted that the Ellsworth family was one of declining wealth—the nouveau poor. Ellsworth's story, however, was one of low social condition, poverty, and even starvation. In obvious identification with his own self-image, Hay pictured Ellsworth as a young dreamer who had not allowed "circumstances [to] . . . conquer his spirit." Paradoxically, and not unlike Hay, Ellsworth demonstrated "the eminent practicality of the man of affairs." In a paragraph that might as easily describe the views that

John Hay would one day assert as Secretary of State, Hay praised Ellsworth's plans for American expansion in Latin America: "His clear, bold, and thoroughly executive mind planned a magnificent scheme of commercial enterprise. . . . He dreamed of the influence of American arts and American energy penetrating into the twilight of that decaying nationality." Ellsworth's solution would later be Hay's (if it wasn't already): he "saw the natural cause of events leading on, first Emigration, then Protection, and at last Annexation. Yet there was no thought of conquest or rapine. The idea was essentially American and Northern."[9]

Hay's depiction of Ellsworth removed him entirely from the crowd. Ellsworth is shown "in gentlemanly exercise" fencing, sketching, reading from the poem which Hay claimed contained the "principles that guided his life." It was the "Flower of Kings." In his nobility, courtliness, chastity, and "high thoughts," Ellsworth becomes part of the Cavalier tradition. His American expansion dreams are set against those of the "ragged Condottieri" of the Spanish, and Ellsworth's practical commercial venture against those notions which are merely "Utopian." His ethical purity aroused the suspicions of the masses of impure office seekers in Washington; his clarity was defined by the muddle of army staff personnel. Even in death Ellsworth had no worthy opponent; he was killed by "a Virginia assassin," a "murderer." Thus Ellsworth was always alone, untouchable, unique.[10] John Hay had made Ellsworth a paragon—the aloofness and distinctness of the article's hero answered some need in Hay, not in Ellsworth. Hay's Ellsworth was distant from the crowd, beyond comparison, and, most important, utterly acceptable to proper eastern readers.[11]

Ellsworth's new program for militia training was based on rigid personal and group discipline and the absolute authority of the leader. As Hay viewed the turmoil about him, both discipline and authority were lacking. The result was the Union's poor military showing in the first year of war and the cause of needless deaths. General McClellan's repeated insolence toward his commander-in-chief especially disturbed Hay. After one outrageous snub, Hay complained to Lincoln. In response, the President quietly corrected his secretary, explaining that "it was better at this time not to be making points of etiquette & personal dignity."[12]

But Hay was convinced that the country needed a strong leader, and if Lincoln would do nothing about his dignity and public image,

Hay would. The death of Lincoln's close friend Colonel Edward
Dickenson Baker was the vehicle for Hay's image-building campaign. In December, 1861, Hay published an article in *Harper's
Magazine* on Baker's death.[13] It was another eulogy, and, although
in many ways different from the Ellsworth piece, it too tells us much
about young Hay's view of himself. The essay was a plea for recruit-
ment, a description of the talent and virtues of the statesmen of
Springfield, Illinois, and a new portrait of Lincoln to replace "Old
Abe" the rail-splitter, the gawky, the untried Westerner.

According to Hay, Colonel Baker's life was a capsule history of the
nation. It contained his birth in England, migration to the new
world, Mississippi Valley pioneering, an imperialistic excursion to
Panama, success in the gold fields of California, service in the Senate of the United States, and death on Virginia soil fighting slavery.
After successful establishment on the East coast, Baker's father "impelled by that spirit of restless adventure and enterprise that seems
the heritage of all the race, gathered up his household goods and
turned his face once more to the sunset," settling in Illinois, where
he set up a school. Baker's education, like Hay's, led him to law,
politics, and Springfield. Springfield was full of "men of industry
and learning," including Abraham Lincoln, Albert T. Bledsoe,
Judge Stephen T. Logan, Milton Hay, William H. Bissell, Governor
of Illinois, Congressman John J. Harden, Senator James Shields,
and Senator Stephen A. Douglas. This coterie embraced the "flower
of Western chivalry," leaders in the Black Hawk and Mexican wars,
leaders in the current war, orators, and statesmen. In Springfield
Baker received the training to carry him to success and wealth in
California and Oregon. Hay then produced the first strokes of his
new portrait of the President; Baker had known Lincoln "then as
afterwards, thoughtful, and honest, and brave, conscious of great
capabilities and quietly sure of the future, before all his peers in
broad humanity, and in that prophetic lift of spirit that saw triumph
of principles then dimly discovered in the contest that was to come."

Hay's picture of Lincoln was one of manifest dignity:

Lincoln stands, lonely in his power, a sadder, silenter, greater man than of
old, time beginning to sift its early snows upon the blackness of his hair, his
heart heavy with the sorrows of a nation; his mind and soul pledged to
solemn and self-abnegating effort to keep from detriment in his hands the
costly treasure of Constitutional Government.

Here were words to erase the popular image of a rail-splitting bumpkin and replace that image with a man of faith, competence, and "broad humanity."[14]

In his article on Baker, Hay insisted that Lincoln had changed in this crucial year which saw the peril of so many of the President's plans and the deaths of his friends. Clearly Hay's esteem for Lincoln had grown. Yet, he was still annoyed by Lincoln's undignified behavior, by the apparent need of the President to be open to everyone and at everyone's beck and call. Hay could appreciate that the conditions of war and the need for unifying the country required that Lincoln be responsible for, and responsive toward, his public, and he had placed these attributes of the President in the Baker article. But the overall impression of Lincoln derived from the article was remote and tragic. Hay refined the President for publication.

Sometime during the first war year, John Hay wrote a poem describing the consequences to culture of civil strife:

> At such a time Art sickens through the world,
> Song slumbers with lethargic pinions furled,
> Listless the painter at his easel stands,
> Drops the dulled chisel from the sculptor's hands.
> The harp hangs silent with untrembling chords
> For deeds are now more eloquent than words.[15]

The poem notwithstanding, Hay had demonstrated in his own publications the relationship between politics and art. His journals for 1861 and 1862 often read like an outline of a drama. The theatrical streak was strong in Hay. Abraham Lincoln too was a strong devotee of theater. The theme of Hay's scenario was Abraham Lincoln's victorious struggle for mastery over the chaos of events, conflicting goals and temperaments. For from these diversities his hero must shape a unity and maintain in war civilian control of the military as well as executive independence of the Congress.

Hay's diaries depict Lincoln as a striking figure of "indomitable will" and leadership. Lincoln, however, had failed so to impress two of his Cabinet. As Secretary of the Treasury Chase and Secretary of the Navy Welles viewed it, the President was a kindly man of good intentions who, through insufficient intelligence and strength of purpose, had bungled from one inadquate and indecisive course to the other. He had failed to provide the coherence of leadership needed and was gradually losing the respect of public, press, and party. In one volley of frustration, Chase accused Lincoln of being responsible for the defeat of Pope at Bull Run.[16] Whatever the astuteness of their judgment, Welles and Chase were correct in their estimate of the low point in administrative prestige by the fall of 1862. For in the off-year elections of November, Lincoln's men lost the key states of New York, Pennsylvania, Indiana, Illinois, and Ohio. The domestic disorder of the Lincoln regime continued. The secretaries were entirely unsuccessful in their attempts to protect the President from constant interruption. Despite the overwhelming work to be done, Lincoln insisted that the White House be an open house. Everybody and anybody brought forth his favorite military, social, economic, and political schemes.

Hay played an increasingly important role in the war. Lincoln used Hay as his personal representative for four major assignments and two minor ones. In each case, he desired not merely information, but the strategic advantage of being represented while not becoming personally engaged in controversy. The employment of Hay afforded the President both of these advantages. The first of these assignments may have occurred as a matter of convenience for both men. After two years, the routine of Hay's job was wearing; he badly needed a long vacation. The frequent illnesses and absences of Nicolay had not lightened Hay's load, nor had the increasingly hectic atmosphere of the White House. It was arranged that he take time off in March or early April of 1863, both to have a holiday and run a few errands for the President.

One of the most important points of interest to the President concerned the potential usefulness of the ironclads in the blockade as well as in attacks upon Rebel harbors, for the task of opening and holding the Mississippi River lay ahead. Despite all the public and official faith in the new ships, there remained many doubts about their usefulness. Admiral Samuel F. Du Pont, commanding a squadron of ironclads in Charleston Harbor, had pulled them out after less than an hour of offensive action. Hay was to determine whether the Admiral or the ironclads were "to blame for giving up so soon."[17] Hay "confidentially" reported to Nicolay and the President: "I do not think Du Pont is either a fool or a coward. I think there is a great deal of truth in his statement that while the fight in Charleston Harbor demonstrated the great defensive properties of the monitors it also proved that they could not be relied upon for aggressive operations."[18]

Hay then set forth on what he called "an inspection tour" of the Union seacoast installations. In his short stay in South Carolina Hay had accomplished a good deal. He had accepted General David Hunter's appointment to become a Volunteer Aid without rank, and he had handled the President's official affairs as well as his family's personal ones with dispatch.[19] On arriving he had found his brother Charles, Hunter's aide-de-camp, ill with pneumonia misdiagnosed as "a slight bilious attack."[20] A change of doctors, initiated by Hay, and the consequent care, enabled Charles to go with Hay on a vacation trip to Florida. They sailed April 24 and "skirted within sight of land, among the porpoises and pelicans."[21]

Much of what Hay was encountering was new. He had little or no knowledge of the people of the South, their land, or their way of life. Although he had traveled a little in and about Washington, he had never been in the deep South, and the whole of subtropical America was foreign to him. Endlessly he repeated its differences from the North: its alligators, its traces of Spanish settlement, its mixture of races.[22]

Hostility to the Southern war aims and to the slave system did not prevent Hay from admiring some aspects of plantation life. He could appreciate a "superb" avenue of pines and live oak trees, a "magnificent" garden. Of one estate he noted that the house was "ruinous," the whole bottom floor never apparently having been furnished, but that the view afforded from the top floors "was beautiful in the extreme." He had to add that he "was lost in wonder at the luxuriousness of nature & the evident shiftlessness & idleness that had characterized the owners."[23]

Hay's attitude toward blacks was ambivalent. Although he was strongly opposed to slavery, he feared that immediate abolition might cause as many problems as it resolved. Nevertheless, he favored both Lincoln's limited Emancipation Proclamation of September, 1862, and Lincoln's 1863 Proclamation. Of course, neither of these executive orders freed any slaves in pro-Union slaveholding states. However, it did legalize the *de facto* emancipation which had accompanied the army's advances and hastened the end of slavery. Lincoln's long-term solution for former slaves was colonization outside the United States, preferably in Africa. Hay, however, had serious objections to colonization on both moral and practical grounds.[24]

During his Southern trip Hay noted the unsuccessful attempt of his old Illinois friend General David Hunter to create a company of black troops.[25] Hay made a point of carefully noting each differentiation among blacks that he found.[26] The dialect interested him, and he tried to capture the rhythms and words of the "strange & wild" spirituals.[27] On an inspection tour of St. Helena and Lady's Islands (on which the former slaves were tenanted), he noted: "The plantations neat and well tilled, people apparently contented and happy. . . . They work better on their own grain crops than on Govt. cotton crops."[28] But Hay did not take the next logical step and call for land redistribution.

Despite his semiofficial status this had been a vacation for Hay, and one which he thoroughly enjoyed—perhaps the more so for its hint of presidential representation. He liked wearing "the blue and gold" uniform and receiving the confidences of generals and commanders. He also liked collecting prose sketches of the scenes about him, attending garden parties, and wearing his white suit.[29]

After Hay's return from his Southern tour, the notion of beginning a political career of his own began to appeal to him. There were several reasons for this growing desire. Hay had come to Washington suspicious of republican institutions as well as the manners and morals of the average man. Like his father, Hay considered Andrew Jackson to have been a "brawler, good for nothing but courage," and his election an example of the poor taste prevalent in the politics of republics. Hay asserted that he would choose King Victor Emmanuel's cause in Italy over that of the republican Garibaldi's, because "the right man was rarely seen in the right place in a Republic."[30] Hay seemed sure that he could recognize the "right man," and that, in general, the citizens of a republic would not. Given these convictions, it did not disturb Hay that the President he served was a minority leader—that the press, the politicians, and the people were loudly berating him. To remain President, however, political realities required that a sizable number vote for Lincoln, and to be an effective President, that a sizable number of the right men be chosen to support his programs. John Hay had become politically conscious and now concerned himself with the problem of making a minority President into the choice of the majority, for by the summer of 1863 Hay was convinced that only Lincoln could preserve the Union.

Writing to Nicolay August 7, Hay reported:

The Tycoon is in fine whack. I have rarely seen him more serene and busy. He is managing this war, the draft, foreign relations, and planning reconstruction of the Union, all at once. I never knew with what tyrannous authority he rules the Cabinet, till now. The most important things he decides and there is no cavil. I am growing more and more firmly convinced that the good of the country absolutely demands that he should be kept where he is till this thing is over. There is no man in the country, so wise, so gentle and so firm. I believe the hand of God placed him where he is.[31]

With Nicolay away in the Rocky Mountains, Hay worked more closely with the President. Together they burrowed through piles of courtmartial decisions, swapped poems and jokes, rode horseback, practiced with the new repeating rifles, attended parties and church services.[32] They talked philosophy and read Shakespeare together; and they also discussed the future of the freedmen. Hay was pleased to learn that the President was no longer thinking primarily of foreign colonization for former slaves.[33] "It deeply interests him now," Hay wrote of the problem of the freedmen. "He considers it the greatest question ever presented to practical statesmanship. While the rest are grinding their little private organs for their own glorification the old man is working with the strength of a giant and the purity of an angel to do this great work."[34]

Hay also applauded the calm and continued assertion of the primacy of the central government by Lincoln that summer. For in Hay's view, the whole issue of the war would be lost if the evil of states' rights was allowed to gain power during the crisis. And he noted with care that days of Thanksgiving were proclaimed after victories by the President for the whole country rather than by governors for their states alone, and that governors were consistently and sometimes sharply brought into line with national policy on many issues.[35] To Hay, "That infernal heresy of State sovereignty—was in the minds of every good man 'the little speck within the garnered fruit, that rotting inward slowly ruined all.' "[36] He even welcomed the New York draft riot "if as one of its results we set a great authoritative precedent of the absolute supremacy of the National power, military and civil, over the State. Every nail that enters the coffin of that dead-and-gone humbug of States Rights is a promise of future and enduring peace and power."[37] In this instance his fear of military encroachment upon civilian authority was subordinated to his growing belief in the necessity of centralized power and obedience to Lincoln's leadership.

Lincoln's plan for Reconstruction centered around his desire to readmit Rebel states as quickly as possible.[38] With the Union army in control of much of Florida by December, 1863, Lincoln hoped that it would become the first state readmitted under his Reconstruction program. Moreover, if Florida could be readmitted under a pro-Lincoln government, it could participate in the 1864 election and add crucial electoral votes for Lincoln.[39] In December, Hay received an offer from pro-Union Floridians he had met during his spring trip asking him to return to Florida and run for Congress as soon as the state was readmitted.[40] This provided Hay with an opportunity to take a more active role in politics, and Lincoln supported the plan. In order to give Hay a reason to return to Florida Lincoln sent him as his official representative to oversee the state's readmission.[41] By January 1, 1864, Hay was en route South with a presidential commission as a major, and the oath books for Southerners' return to citizenship.[42]

Election to Congress required evidence of settlement in a district. Therefore, Hay openly viewed the possibilities of business and real estate and invested in Florida citrus lands. He renewed old friendships and courted new contacts. After establishing his offices in the District Attorney's office in St. Augustine, he began to look about at the local real estate, noting that orange culture was "just now especially interesting to me."[43] It was interesting enough to him to make at least an $1,850 investment, and by January 17 he had made arrangements for the care of "our property here" at the rate of twenty-five dollars a month and a quarter of the crop.[44] Just two days after setting up the President's program in St. Augustine, he decided to delegate it to others, while he returned to Jacksonville.[45]

Hay had for some time been sanguine as to the outcome of the war, and it is fairly certain that he would not have invested so heavily in property had he expected the reverses which were to come on his heels. Not only was the army severely repulsed and defeated seven miles from St. Augustine, but the day after he left, accounts of the New York press's attack on the Lincoln Reconstruction program and Hay's part in it reached him.[46] With "headache &

misery" the young man debated what he should do and conferred with others. The program was pictured by the newspapers as a million dollar trick by which to gain votes for Lincoln in the coming election.

The *New York Herald* accused Lincoln of seeking Florida's electoral vote and Hay of seeking a seat in Congress.[47] While the accusations were true, the tone disturbed Hay. Yet, he was somewhat philosophical, noting that "at my age, the more abuse I get in the newspapers the better for me. I shall run for constable some day on the strength of my gory exploits in Florida."[48] The newspaper assault brought Hay back to Washington sooner than he might otherwise have come. Certainly it had ended his immediate prospects for a seat in Congress. But Hay was correct—the attacks had not harmed his career.

Late on the night of June 9, 1864, Lincoln came to Hay's room with another delicate diplomatic errand.[49] General William S. Rosecrans had uncovered evidence of a conspiracy to overthrow the government. He requested permission from Lincoln to send Colonel J. P. Sanderson directly to Washington with full information and the request was seconded by the Governor of Missouri. It was a difficult situation. Rosecrans' request should have gone to Secretary of War Stanton; however, a feud had developed between the General and the Secretary, and Stanton had recently court-martialed one of Rosecrans' officers sent to Washington without the permission of the War Department. Lincoln told Hay that he doubted Rosecrans' report. What the general really wanted, Lincoln concluded, was conflict between the President and the Secretary of War.[50] If Lincoln agreed to Rosecrans' request, he would, in effect, be overruling Stanton's order that the general not send men to Washington without prior approval by the Secretary of War. By sending Hay as his personal emissary, the President could get the information, demonstrate his confidence in the general by the intimacy of his response, and avoid offense to Stanton.

Hay arrived at Rosecrans' headquarters in St. Louis, Missouri, on June 13. He dined with the general and interviewed him that evening, spent an hour reading the evidence, and departed the next day for a short visit with his family.[51] From his own observations, Hay believed Lincoln was underestimating the threat involved in the conspiracy. Concentrated in the states of Illinois, Indiana, and Ohio with smaller but formidable groups in Missouri and Kentucky, an estimated four hundred thousand men were plotting to overthrow the government, end the war, and halt further emancipation. The current of the conspiracy was channeled through hundreds of secret societies.[52] The experience was to leave Hay with a lifelong hatred of secret groups. Try as he might he could not convince the President of their danger. Yet Hay had to agree with Lincoln's initial suspicions of Rosecrans' intentions—executive embarrassment had been their end. By sending his secretary to interview Rosecrans, Lincoln neatly avoided being in the middle of a confrontation between one of his generals and his Secretary of War.[53]

Fed by continued Union defeats, the movement for peace had gained strength during the early spring and summer of 1864. On July 8, Lincoln received an impassioned letter from Horace Greeley asking him to meet with, and offer terms to, a commission of three men allegedly empowered by the Confederacy to negotiate peace. The men were now in Canada awaiting the President's pleasure. Greeley suggested minimal terms beginning with the restoration of the Union and the abandonment of slavery.[54]

Although the validity of the commission was dubious, Lincoln had to give attention to it. Greeley as editor of the *New York Tribune* was a most influential man. As Lincoln put it, "While Mr. Greeley means right, he makes me almost as much trouble as the whole Southern Confederacy."[55] The Greeley proposal came hard upon the resignation of Secretary of the Treasury Chase and the stalemate of Grant at Richmond, and it was followed immediately by Rebel invasion of the North and threatened siege of Washington. Under the circumstances, Greeley at least offered Lincoln a way to answer the accusations that the President persisted in war despite opportunities for peace.[56]

Lincoln was not eager for a compromise peace and in a clever move Lincoln turned the tables on Greeley. He insisted that Greeley act as his representative and meet with the Confederate commissioners at Niagara Falls. Greeley's charge was to escort the commissioners to Washington to meet with Lincoln. The President realized that the Confederates would not agree to such a proposal and Greeley would be blamed for the mission's failure. Being no fool, Greeley balked at Lincoln's proposal. Lincoln quickly sent Hay to New York to meet with Greeley. Hay, acting for Lincoln, insisted

that Greeley accompany him to Niagara Falls or admit in the press
that the Confederate peace move was a fraud. Greeley agreed to
travel to Niagara Falls with Hay.[57]

Greeley and Hay met with the Confederates on the Canadian side
of the Falls on July 21, 1864. Almost immediately it was clear that
the commissioners had no authority to make peace. Hay remained
in Niagara Falls for several days awaiting some further communication from the envoys, while Greeley quietly returned to New York
City. Finally the commissioners issued a statement accusing Lincoln
of bad faith and the negotiations were over. Hay had done his job
well.[58]

Amidst a barrage of recrimination over peace, war, emancipation,
inflation, and the elections, Hay was called home in August to attend to family affairs. As he traveled about Illinois and Missouri
inspecting schools for his sister's education and lands for his family's
investment, he also gauged the political temper of the people.[59] The
rural folk struck Hay as soundly behind the President and the war,
but in the towns he found "the Copperheads are exultant and our
own people either growling & despondent or sneakingly apolege-
tic."[60] His disgust was greatest in Illinois. Asked to speak before the
Springfield Union League, he refused, as he explained to Nicolay,
because "the snakes would rattle about it a little & it wd. do no
good. I lose my temper sometimes talking with growling Republicans. There is a restlessness about men in these times that unfits
them for the steady support of an administration."[61]

From Washington, Nicolay corroborated Hay's fears. Prominent
Republicans wanted Lincoln to resign as their candidate. "Hell is to
pay," gloomily reported Nicolay. "The N.Y. politicians have got a
stampede on that is about to swamp everything. . . . Everything is
darkness and doubt and discouragement. Our men see giants in the
airy and unsubstantial shadows of the opposition and are about to
surrender without a fight."[62] Hay believed that the opposition was
quite substantial and that Lincoln's defeat by the peace party was
very likely. Fearful that a victorious Democratic party would re-
pudiate the wartime currency, many were getting rid of their
greenbacks and buying land as fast as they could. Hay and his father
joined the stampede.[63] "If the dumb cattle are not worthy of another
term of Lincoln," Hay angrily concluded, "then let the will of God
be done & the murrain of McClellan fall on them."[64]

Returned to his post in Washington, Hay watched Lincoln's control over the party grow daily and the campaign gain strength. The publicity of his Florida and Niagara Falls missions also had resulted in an increased political prestige for Hay. In August he had carefully interviewed and checked the loyalty of prospective appointees in the West and was now the recipient of letters petitioning for posts and giving information on various candidates.[65] His political influence on Lincoln was growing. On October 2, he suggested that Lincoln appoint Judge Advocate General Joseph Holt of Kentucky to the vacant position of Attorney General. Lincoln agreed and offered to appoint Holt, somewhat to Hay's surprise.[66]

Manner was becoming increasingly important to Hay. He would have defined the perfect statesman's attitude as one of calmness and candor in public demeanor. He had turned down an opportunity to speak for Lincoln and the war effort while in Springfield expressly on the grounds that he might lose his temper.[67] Believing that despite all inner dislike one should maintain an amiable countenance, he took the urbanity of Lincoln and Seward as models.[68] Hay valued manner as a means of achievement and as a product of achievement. He admired the times when the President had been "graceful" in speech or action, when he had faced obstreperous and rancorous enemies with candor and logic and won them with the calm flow of his argument.[69] Hay respected Lincoln even more because, as an intimate, he knew well the degree of Lincoln's grief, the passion of his anger, and his fight for self-control. Control counted with Hay, especially when duty directed its use.

Hay himself had been deeply moved by the events of the war and his position next to Lincoln. Nevertheless, he counted it a compliment when the editor of the *National Intelligencer* publicly commented that, unlike any of the intense and partisan presidential secretaries he had ever known, Hay had "laughed through his term" of office.[70] Hay had come to see an open and amiable manner as a political asset; it was a form of neutrality in conflict—attractive to opposing sides.

The young man had grown greatly under Lincoln's tutelage. He had managed the conflicts of his youth by maintaining both the diffidence of his father and the ambition of his uncle. But on coming to Washington, the complexities of both Lincoln and wartime had initially proved to be too foreign. Stretch and strain as he might, he had not been able to make sense of them and had retreated to forming impressions by the primitive means of simply excluding what did not fit his preconceptions. Thus he had misrepresented the truth about his friend Ellsworth and had constructed dramatic pictures of Lincoln for the press and in his journals which were untrue to the evidence before him.

Although he had immediately seen the evil of states' rights as the "snake" poisoning the vitals of union, he had been slow to the point of backwardness in grasping the importance of politics in maintaining the Union or the war effort. He had failed to appreciate the necessity of Lincoln's point that the Cabinet be representative of differences—including different political parties—and that the government protect and retain differences, including slaveholding border states. Yet in serving one of the century's ablest politicians, Hay had been introduced to the give-and-take of practical politics and by 1863 had been converted to the cause of the Republic, at last fully appreciating the basic issue which Lincoln underlined in the first week of conflict when he defined for Hay what the war was about: "the necessity . . . of proving that popular government is not an absurdity." The Republic, a system granting representation to differences, was the ultimate unity. It was premised on inclusion not on exclusion. With increasing perception Hay served that unity with his person and his pen. Finally he was ready to serve it with his life.

Although intrigued and stimulated by the 1864 election campaign's intensity, and very much enjoying his own part in it, Hay wanted to go to war. He made plans to join the ill-fated campaign against Wilmington, North Carolina.[71] As usual his hopes depended upon a sufficient improvement in Nicolay's health to allow him to assume the full burden of White House duties. In addition to his absences for illness and often in conjunction with them, Nicolay too had been used by the President on several occasions as a peace envoy.[72] Despite his hopes, on November 12 Hay got as close as he was to get that fall to war; he was sent on his last mission for Lincoln, this time to General Grant.[73] Lincoln was concerned with Grant's views on the condition of the army, the enemy, the use of Negro troops, and the relationship between military and civilian authority. Most important, Lincoln was anxious to learn Grant's position on the forthcoming election. Hay was pleased to report that Grant was for Lincoln's reelection.[74]

After Lincoln's second inauguration, Nicolay and Hay looked forward to release from their assignments at the White House. About the outcome of the war, neither had any worries; Hay had been predicting Confederate collapse since the spring of 1863, and Nicolay set the date for July 4, 1865.[75]

In February Nicolay wrote to his faithful fiancée of over ten years, Therena Bates, that the President was aware of his hopes of leaving, and that in two or three weeks his plans would be more definite.[76] By March 12 he was writing to confirm the newspaper reports that his appointment as Consul at Paris at a salary of five thousand dollars had been approved and that he and Therena would be married.[77] Ten days later, John Hay accepted the appointment to Paris as Secretary of Legation. The Paris assignments were meant as rewards for Nicolay's and Hay's services.

In the last days of March, Hay wrote to explain to his brother Charles that he would miss his wedding, because he was overwhelmed with preparations for leaving Washington.[78] Nicolay had already departed on a Caribbean cruise in pursuit of better health, and he was not to return until April 18.[79] John Hay was in the White House on Good Friday, April 14, 1865, when the President was assassinated. Lincoln's death was for Hay a personal loss, like the loss of a father—the center of his world for four turbulent years.[80] Now there was nothing to keep him in Washington.

He collected the dead President's papers—papers he and Nicolay knew they would be using for a planned biography. But, as he left Washington, John Hay must have known that his position of intimacy with Abraham Lincoln, nineteenth-century America's greatest martyr, had assured him of a high place in his nation's future.

Lincoln's assassination erased any remaining doubts Hay had about Lincoln's greatness. Lincoln's personality, programs, and policies now inseparably merged in Hay's mind. The Lincoln Administration would, as Hay looked back on it in the years to come, serve as both a personal and national standard. Hay was convinced that Lincoln had saved the nation by altering it. Thus, John Hay increasingly viewed the Civil War as a revolution which had redirected the course of American history. Hay would spend a good deal of his life protecting and affirming both the results of that revolution and the image of its greatest hero, Abraham Lincoln. He also would use his relation to both to advance his own career.

CHAPTER 3

The Ideology of John Hay

A CENTRAL argument of this book is that John Hay's political career was not at war with his literary career. Certainly Hay's literary associations were as impressive as his political ones. He counted among his correspondents most of the important literary figures of post–Civil War America. His personal friendships included Walt Whitman, William Dean Howells, Mark Twain, Bret Harte, Richard Watson Gilder, Edmund Clarence Stedman, Henry James, and Henry Adams. What is more, all these men were convinced that Hay had impressive literary talents.[1] By contemporary standards Hay's literary efforts were as successful as his political ones. Until 1898 he was as well known to his fellow Americans as an author and lecturer as he was as a political figure and diplomat. When the American Academy of Arts was organized in 1904, John Hay was selected to be one of its seven charter members. Hay was chosen, whereas Henry James and Henry Adams were not.[2]

Hay's reputation as a man of letters was not as undeserved as some of his biographers hint.[3] He was, after all, a poet, essayist, novelist, journalist, and historian. In each of these fields, except as a novelist, it is arguable that Hay's work was of the highest quality. More important, his work reflected the values of the dominant culture it served.

Perhaps Hay's literary reputation has been underrated by current historians because of his diplomatic and political successes. An assumption—a *dictum* in recent times—is that the man of letters is at odds with the man of action.[4] Such notions received their fullest statement in works as diverse as Henry Adams' *The Education of Henry Adams* (1918) and Robert Sherwood's play *The Petrified Forest* (1937). However, the nineteenth-century careers of Washington Irving, George Bancroft, Nathaniel Hawthorne, Herman Melville, and others suggest another tradition. For Hay, one symbol of that tradition was John Bigelow, the Minister to France under whom Hay served as Secretary of the Legation.[5]

As we have seen, Hay's poetry and writings moved from the very personal concerns of his childhood and college days to the more ideological problems of the Civil War and his association with Lincoln. His post–Civil War writings invariably are presented as moving from a radical, almost revolutionary, stance in the late 1860s and early 1870s to a reformist view in the seventies, and finally, to a conservative, even reactionary position by 1883, when he anonymously published *The Bread-winners*.[6] While this model neatly fits the expected life stages of rebellious youth and conservative old age, such notions are generally simplistic and, almost always, misleading. If examined carefully, we will discover that Hay's calls for social change, even social revolution, were never made for American society—which to him was the model for the rest of the world. Hay's calls for revolution were always aimed outside of the United States. Even his demands for revolutionary change in the South during the Civil War fit this pattern, since the Confederacy was literally outside the Union. Revolution was required, Hay argued, in the slave South, Napoleonic France, Spain, Cuba, the Philippines, or China, precisely because these nations did not conform to free republican institutions which he believed were the model for the modern world and the key to individual success and freedom. So, while Hay, as an editor of the *New York Tribune*, called for political reform at home (adjustments to make the American system work as altered by the Civil War), he would never support revolution inside the United States. Any domestic revolution would overthrow the basis of the Union's victory. While social evils may have been endemic outside the United States, he was certain that they could never be systemic within. Therefore, Hay consistently viewed post–Civil War revolutionary movements in the nation as coming from the outside, and he was convinced that such movements resulted, by and large, from a misapplication of European class structure and inequality to the American case. Hay believed he *was* a revolutionary, for he had participated in the American Civil War and built his career on that association. It would have been strange indeed if John Hay had become a domestic revolutionary against what was, at least in part, his own creation.

In another sense, Hay reflected the mentality of America's founding fathers, since, for him, the causes of evil were always external.[7]

As Leslie Fiedler argues, this projection of evil was also a key element of American fiction in the nineteenth century.[8] Certainly, Hay's literary works fit Fiedler's pattern. His regularity in literature and in politics was a key to his success.

Hay believed that the results of the American Civil War were revolutionary in that they altered the Southern way of life and reestablished the basic principles of the Revolution of 1776 and the Constitution of 1789.[9] He argued that it was the legitimate task of the American people to overthrow despotic slavery. In that case, as with the Girondins of France, "the destiny of the people" was "accomplished through their fervor and their struggles."[10] With the American Civil War ended, so, too, were all questions of legitimacy. Arms had decided that, while "Everyman should do what he thinks is right . . . he should know also that what the Republic does is right—in the largest sense."[11] In short, American society could be reformed, but not overthrown. Hay thus saw himself as a spokesman for a successful revolution. With the revolution at home secured, he perceived it his duty to extend that revolution to the less fortunate and more traditional nations of the world. His writings reflected this concern.

Shortly after he arrived in France in 1865 to begin his service as Secretary of the American Legation, Hay wrote "Sunrise in the Place de la Concorde," a poem attacking the reimposition of despotism by Louis Napoleon. The poet had been critical of some of the excesses of the French Revolution, especially the execution of the King and Queen. Now, he argued that the people's debt to royalty had been repaid as the result of the Bourbon "usurpation" which "washed the stains from . . . tortured hands." He defended the 1848 revolution as a valid attempt by the people to overthrow aristocracy and feudalism. "Sunrise at the Place de la Concorde" attacks the reinstitution of monarchy by Louis Napoleon:

> When she [Liberty] gave him her child to keep;
> Did she know he would strangle the child
> As it lay in his arms asleep?

The solution would only come when the people "again shall rise" and "wither this robber-power."[12]

France under Louis Napoleon seemed to Hay similar to the United States before the Civil War—a nation whose goals had been perverted by a usurping aristocracy. That government must be removed (even if violently) in order to restore and enshrine popular power. Discovering that Louis Napoleon had been nicknamed "the Sphinx of the Tuileries," Hay wrote a poem about Louis with that title: "The Charlatan whom the Frenchmen loathe/ And the Cockneys all admire." He described the "Sphinx with breast of woman/ And face so debonair," which from behind had only the "ignoble form of a craven cur." The Emperor, Hay insisted, was a "bastard sphinx" leading the "same base life" as the legendary monster. Like her, Louis would "perish in pain and shame," when the "Oedipus-People" realized the truth and came "to their own at last."[13]

In a poem entitled "A Triumph of Order," Hay described the final days of the Paris Commune of 1848. Order had been "saved" by Louis' soldiers as they lined up "desperate men, wild women," and a small boy against a wall and shot them. As would be the case in Hay's later *Pike County Ballads*, the victims of traditional society's prejudice were his heroes if they performed noble deeds.[14]

In his attacks on aristocracy Hay included the Roman Church as well.[15] In "The Monks of Basle," published in the fall of 1865, he pictured the monks as a useless feudal holdover. "They hammered and slashed about,—/ Dry husks of logic,— old scraps of creed,—/ And the cold gray dreams of doubt,—."[16]

On his way to his second diplomatic post, as Chargé d'Affaires in Vienna, Hay stopped in London. He was then, as he remained later, much less critical of the British than of other European governments. However restricted the franchise, the English were ruled by representation, even if they retained the veneer of aristocratic social hierarchy. Values such as individual freedom and suffrage were as central to British politics as they were to post–Civil War America. Hay visited the Commons and listened to Disraeli, whose Reform Bill would extend the suffrage to the laboring classes. England, the young diplomat was convinced, required only such reforms, not revolution.[17]

In Vienna, and later in Spain, where he served as Secretary of the Legation, Hay found the aristocracy pernicious and fatalistic. In both instances it was wed irrevocably to the tyranny of a parasitic Church and the ineptness of a stagnant monarchy.[18] Hay thought that he understood something about Europeans before he visited Europe. He had spent years studying their languages and literature

and the war years had brought large numbers of Europeans to
Washington as military volunteers as well as observers. Many
Americans like Nicolay and Carl Schurz were recent immigrants.[19]
Close association with these immigrants had convinced Hay that
German-speaking people were independent and industrious. His
experience in Austria, however, forced Hay to revise his opinions.
He was surprised to discover easygoing, dependent, and idle Germans.[20] His opinion of Jews was "revolutionized": "In America we
always say Rich as a Jew, because even if a Jew is poor he is so brisk
so sharp and enterprising that he is sure to make money eventu-
ally." In the Jewish section of Vienna, however, Hay discovered
only apathy, indolence, and the rankest poverty.[21]

At first he tried to ascribe southern and central European indolence to evolutionary factors.[22] The Jew and the Hungarian seemed
to carry "a king's deep curse of treason and wars." But, Hay concluded, "the slow light withers a despot's powers,/ And a mad king's
curse is not forever."[23] Indeed, the success of these people in the
United States indicated the remedy, republican revolution. Hay
was confident that a comprehensive revolution was coming to central and southern Europe. In Austria he saw evidence that "new
forms of intellectual vigor and activity are preparing among the
people, to rebuild and save the nation, after the storm of the coming
revolution has destroyed the useless forms of the past and swept the
field clean for the future."[24]

For Hay change was inevitable because the American model was
the wave of the future. He saw in Vienna the "people starting off in
the awkward walk of political babyhood. They know what they want
& I believe they will get it." The last days of feudalism were coming.
"The Aristocracy are furious and the Kaiser a little bewildered at
every triumph of the Democratic & Liberal principle." Hay was
delighted by what he saw: "Two years ago—, it was another Europe.
England has come abreast of Bright. Austria is governed by Forty-
Eighters. Bismarck is beoming appalled by the spirit of freedom that
he suckled with the blood of Sadowa. France still lies in her com-
atose slumber—but she talks in her sleep & murmurs the 'Marseill-
aise.' "[25]

Strengthening his analysis were his experiences while Secretary
of the Legation in Spain in 1869 and 1870. He published his views
on Spain first in serial form and then as a book entitled *Castilian
Days*.[26] Again it was the feudal holdovers—the Catholic Church and

the Spanish monarchy—which stood in the path of modernization. Hay formed a close relationship with the liberal Emilio Castelar and pictured him as a Spanish Lincoln leading his people to "see that God is greater than the Church and that the law is above the King." Hay was not calling for reform when he added that for the Spanish "the final day of deliverance is at hand."[27]

In his poems, journal, and publications concerning Europe, Hay demonstrated much the same set of assumptions as those found in his undelivered Florida address of 1864. The base of the state, the populace, he assumed to be sound; what was unsound was its ruling class.[28] Self-interested monarchy and aristocracy, using the twin tyrannies of Church and Army, robbed the people of their freedom. But an awakening was coming—controversy was straining to be heard, and with free discussion would come revolution and the overthrow of all evil restrictions. In his speech to the Floridians, Hay had asserted that free discussion had been what really killed slavery in the border states.[29] In Austria he had heralded as a most significant sight a meeting of schoolteachers: "the first of its kind," which "spoke out freely and boldly upon the question that underlies all education—freedom from religious or political trammels."[30] In Spain he cheered the efforts to secularize education and noted that from the opposition there was "coiling and hissing, but the fangs of the serpent are much less prompt and effective than of old."[31]

Hay's famous *Pike County Ballads* illustrate a major argument of this chapter. The *Ballads*, written in dialect and published as a book in 1871, often are pictured as shocking to genteel Americans.[32] While the poems glorify the common man, they are not a call for revolution but an argument for reform and increased liberty. These democratic poems are not critical of the basic political structure, only of its failure to live up to its announced goals. Whereas the ruling classes in France, Austria, Spain, and Italy had to be overthrown for the people to enjoy freedom and liberty, in the United States the basic values, laws, and institutions protecting freedom and liberty were intact. Although the American institutional structure was sound, Hay feared that it often could be abused by individuals. His *Pike County Ballads* and other works on America expressed this concern.

Hay's target was the hypocrisy of the pious. His Pike County heroes were common men whose life and manners served as an affront to the upright of society. Jim Bludso, a steamboat engineer,

spoke ungrammatically and was a bigamist. Yet, Bludso sacrificed
his life for others when the steamboat caught fire:

> He weren't no saint,—but at jedgment
> I'd run my chance with Jim,
> 'Longside of some pious gentlemen
> That wouldn't shook hands with him.
> He seen his duty, a dead-sure thing,—
> And went for it thar and then;[33]

The poet argued that performance should replace posture as a
goal for America. It came down to this: Hard, honest work was
morality. Of this, Hay even reminded the angels in his poem "Little
Breeches":

> And I think that Saving a little child,
> And fotching him to his own,
> Is a derned sight better business
> Than loafing around the Throne.[34]

In his poem "Banty Tim" Hay demanded that the sacrifices of the
Civil War should not be ignored. Tim, a black former Union soldier,
was ordered to leave Spunky Point, Illinois, by the White Man's
Committee. Tilmon Joy, a former Union sergeant—symbol of the
common man facing hypocrisy—proclaimed that he would not allow
the White Man's Committee to expel Tim. Banty Tim had saved
Joy's life during the war. Now Joy would not turn his back on his
savior:

> You may rezoloot till the cows come home,
> But if one of you tetches the boy,
> He'll wrestle his hash to-night in hell,
> Or my name's not Tilmon Joy.[35]

While in poems like "Banty Tim" Hay worried about the tyranny
of the majority, his greatest fear concerned the misuse of power by
those in leadership positions. In the "Pledge of Spunky Point" all
the men cheated each other, but the Deacon's gambling cheated the
whole community.[36] With good leaders the many could change and
"The ever-mutable multitude at last/ Will hail the power they did
not comprehend."[37] The system was basically sound, and if it occa-

sionally seemed to fail, better leaders could set the nation back on course.

Hay believed in a natural aristocracy of talent rather than of birth. In "Esse Quam Videri" he praised those practical leaders who acted rather than preached.[38] Like his friend Henry Adams, Hay feared apathy as democracy's most dread disease—a disease which could only be kept from spreading by the employment of good leadership. And, with many others of their generation, they both attempted to lead the masses by using the press.[39] Hay's preparation, however, differed from that of Adams. Hay's teachers were his father Charles, his uncle Milton, and his mentor, Lincoln. His schoolrooms had been in Warsaw, Pittsfield, Springfield, Providence, and Washington. Adams' teacher had been his father Charles Francis, and his schoolrooms were Harvard and the Court of St. James. While Adams spent the Civil War in London, Hay spent it in Washington, the eye of the storm. Thus, as close as they were as friends, Hay and Adams inevitably viewed the world quite differently. For Adams the past was a judge; for Hay the past was a springboard for future progress. Adams' birth and experience set him apart from the times, whereas Hay's brought him closer to the people he hoped to awaken. He did not, in fact, expect to change the masses' direction very much.[40] Like Jefferson, Hay was beginning to think that democracy was more often right than wrong. Hay was convinced that the United States was the land of opportunity, as it proved to be for him.[41] Adams saw America, like his family's power, in decline.[42]

If Hay believed that America's basic institutions were sound, he doubted its leaders' capacities. On that point Hay and Adams agreed. The lack of leadership in America was a constant theme in Hay's life. As early as 1869 he wrote to John Bigelow, "I am not a hero worshipper any more & if I were, where is the Hero?"[43] The job of the reformer was to help discover and retain the proper heroes. Of course, Lincoln was the model of the proper hero-leader. Hay wrote to Lincoln's son Robert Todd that "Year after year of study has shown me more clearly than ever how infinitely greater your father was than anybody about him. . . . He is the unapproachably great figure of a great epoch."[44]

In the 1870s and 1880s Hay's writings as assistant managing editor of the *New York Tribune* were reformist. He called for the removal of bad leaders such as Ulysses S. Grant and the election of reformers like Samuel J. Tilden. His editorials, lectures, and books constantly urged fidelity to the principles of Lincoln and to the victory of Union. [45]

Hay had not yet fully analyzed the relationship between political and socioeconomic forces that had resulted from the Union's victory. He did not foresee the immense rise of corporate power during the Civil War. Returning from Europe in 1867, he was surprised and "shuddered in horror" at the kind of men running the economy and their methods. [46] Yet in his thinking he had much in common with them.

Hay assumed that republican institutions included free labor, open [though not free] commerce, and universal male suffrage. As soon as Northern forces had retaken Southern ports, he had strongly urged Lincoln to open them to world trade as proof of what the Union stood for. [47] Introducing Lincoln's Reconstruction policy in Florida in 1864, he had seen the chance to sell their cotton as a powerful attraction for encouraging Floridians to overcome their fears of reprisal, to sign the oaths of allegiance, return to the Union, and to vote. [48] The ballot was the base of all other freedoms to Hay. Although despising secessionists, he approved the President's plan for speedy reinstitution of self-government in Southern states and later decried Southern Democrats' barriers against black voters. [49] Equally he opposed the radical Republican proposals for punishment or postponement of Southern voting rights and cheered John Bright and Richard Cobden's crusade extending the franchise to England's laboring classes. [50]

As he championed increased trade, free labor, and the ballot, so did he champion free status. The open society was the only natural environment for republics. How else could men of talent and virtue come to power? Contrary to allegations of his abandonment of this principle in the face of the strikes of 1877 and 1883, his later works, his speeches, and his 1896 revival of Ellsworth's story—this time including his humble origins—all support the notion of a fluid society. Even the major source for the allegations, his anonymously published novel, *The Bread-winners*, depicts the hero, Arthur Farnham, striving to marry the daughter of a successful machinist and trying to get another young woman the library job she sought in order to "better" herself.

What Hay did not see and did not ask questions about was the power of Gilded Age capitalism to negate the open society, the power of the ballot, and the principle of free labor.[51] This is not easy to explain. Two of his friends, Charles Francis Adams, Jr. and Henry Adams, had painstakingly detailed the corruption and its effects on the entire American system. Evidence abounded of the suffering and degradation at the bottom of the economic ladder partially due to unprincipled behavior at the top. Rediscovering his own diaries from the Civil War in 1878 while working on the Lincoln biography, Hay repeatedly and carefully crossed out the nickname "Tycoon" for Lincoln. Like so much else in his world, the word had changed meaning. It now referred to a magnate of industry and was inappropriate for his hero, Lincoln.

Hay admitted the unscrupulousness of business leaders, but he never admitted the appalling conditions of the laboring classes nor the correctness of any but individual political means for reform. Trade unions, the right to strike, and government regulation of business he condemned. To Hay the American system was the best devised. Corruption was due to individually evil persons and the refusal of talented and virtuous people to operate within the system, for by the 1870s when he began his own business career, corporate capitalism and the strength of the American republic had become inseparable in his mind. When his friend Henry Adams opposed big government and big business, Hay thought him simply impractical. "You . . . are known throughout the country," he told Adams, "as a Democrat, and an Anarchist, and an unemployed."[52]

In his 1883 novel, *The Bread-winners*, John Hay's views were consistent with those he had espoused during and since the Civil War.[53] The novel is only antirevolutionary or reactionary if seen in a present-day context. Viewed from his own position in 1883, Hay was convinced that he was defending his own revolutionary cause—a cause that was only two decades old, after all. In the novel it was appropriate to him that the mob be quelled by a former Union officer leading a picked group of veterans. Clearly, the dangers posed by a working-class revolution seemed to undercut the basis of national power and the Union's victory.[54] Had Hay realized how neatly the labor movement could be contained within modern capitalism, he might have rested more easily.

The origins of the plot for *The Bread-winners* go back to the summer of 1877. Amasa Stone, Hay's father-in-law, was in Europe, and Hay was left in charge of Stone's interests when several railroad strikes followed by riots shook Cleveland and Pittsburgh. Hay wrote to Stone telling him of the strikes:

The prospect of labor and capital both seem gloomy enough. The very devil seems to have entered into the lower classes of working men, and there are plenty of scoundrels to encourage them to all lengths. . . . I am thankful you did not *see* and *hear* what took place during the strikes. You were saved a very painful experience of human folly and weakness, as well as crime. . . .[55]

Again in 1883 the Brotherhood of Telegraphers struck Western Union of which Hay was a director.

In *The Bread-winners* John Hay applied his ideology to strikes in general and these two in particular. This was among the first American novels avowedly in defense of property and capitalism.[56] The novel attempted to picture the everyday lives of the American working class and to expose the way in which this class, due to its ignorance, fell prey to the villainies of false social reformers such as Hay's antagonist, Andrew Jackson Offit. Hay desired to show how strikes began and spread; how corrupt and evil rogues took advantage of honest workers and persuaded them to violate their own best interests. His position in telling the story is undisguisedly partisan, while the struggle reduces itself to a battle between good and evil.[57] Arthur Farnham, who doubles as a strikebreaker and a dispenser of justice *par excellence,* is clearly speaking for the author. Farnham is Hay's image of the proper leader for American society.

Hay's fear of domestic revolution is apparent in the characterization of Andrew Jackson Offit, outside agitator. Offit, of course, is a caricature of Andrew Jackson. John Hay was truly his father's son in his dislike of Jackson.[58] In part, Offit and his Brotherhood of Bread-winners are pictured as counterrevolutionaries who want to return to the false values of Jacksonian America, which Hay believed supported not only corrupt party politics but also rested upon Southern slavery. If Hay had had the benefit of modern scholarship, his hatred of Andrew Jackson as anticapitalist might have diminished.[59] In any case, the author of *The Bread-winners* was as frightened of a return to past values as he was of the dangers of socialism. Hay presented the union members as "the laziest and most incapable workmen in town."[60] This description fits Herbert

Gutman's argument that resistance to factory work came as much from preindustrial values of the workers as it did from the rhetoric of union leaders.[61] The novel also pictures the ideas of the Brotherhood of Bread-winners as foreign in origin. Offit is a stereotype of the outside agitator, who has no redeeming features and who makes his living by misusing union funds. Hay's description of Offit reads remarkably like his diary characterizations of the Southern peace commissioners as well as the Polish refugees in Vienna.[62]

Hay thus fully accepted Herbert Spencer's arguments in *The Principles of Sociology* that individual progress was only possible in free individual competition. All restrictions on man's pursuit of his own self-interest, such as labor unions, were an impediment to the natural evolution of man.[63] John Hay, in *The Bread-winners*, argued for progress.

Criticism of the novel came swiftly. A letter published in the *Century* magazine argued that the novel was "a piece of snobbishness imported from England. . . . It is simply untruthful and worthy only of the more ignorant class of journalists to continue the assertion that trade unions are mainly controlled and strikes inaugurated by agitators, interested only for what they make out of them."[64] The novelist answered the criticism anonymously:

Mr. Shriver makes the familiar claim of the harmless and rational process of trades-unions; yet he knows that no important strike has ever been carried through without violence, and that no long strike has ever been ended without murder. He insists on the right of the workman to sell his labor at the best price; yet he knows that trades-unionism is the very negation of that right. . . . It is only a few years since we saw the streets of Pittsburg [*sic*] devastated by murder, arson, and rapine, through a rising which agitators could originate, but not control. . . .[65]

Violence was only acceptable against kings and plantation owners because they denied the will of the people. In America the vote made that will law. There existed for Hay no barrier to its powers and therefore no excuse for violence.

The Bread-winners is often pictured as the key to Hay's mentality.[66] Such a conclusion has neatly fit the thesis that the older Hay grew, the more reactionary he became, and the more this was reflected in his writings.[67] One problem with such an argument is that *The Bread-winners* was not his last word on the subject of revolution. The capstone of Hay's literary career was his and Nicolay's ten-volume work *Abraham Lincoln: A History*. This work, published in book form in 1890, appeared first in serial form in the *Century* magazine beginning in 1886 and won for the authors over one million readers. Hay had found the hero he sought in 1869, and *Lincoln: A History* is a restatement of what he believed to be Lincoln's and his own ideology.[68] The work is 4,700 pages long, almost one and a half million words, and it took the authors thirteen years to write.[69] A production of such proportions should not be ignored in searching for Hay's world view.[70]

Abraham Lincoln is pictured as the epitome of republican talent and virtue, the perfect leader for, and the "founder" of, the new American state. As an example of success in the open society, Lincoln typified "the variety and solidity" of the Republic, which even in war "showed a prodigious advance in prosperity and population." Even his death became a model for other leaders to follow:[71] "The quick instant by which the world recognized him even at the moment of his death, as one of the greatest men, was not deceived."[72] The martyred President became a moral force, a symbol of American culture. Nicolay and Hay quoted a prediction that Lincoln would "stand out in the tradition of his country and the world as the incarnation of the people and of modern Democracy itself."[73] No wonder that Hay could never approve of domestic revolution against Lincoln's successes. What could justify a revolution against "the incarnation of . . . modern democracy itself"?

Hay's clearest statement of his attitude toward revolution appeared in his poem "Liberty," published a month after his death in July, 1905. Since this poem is a call for revolution, many of Hay's biographers assume that it must have been written during the 1860s. Actually it was written in 1880.[74] Given his view that revolution to create a liberal society from an aristocratic one was always legitimate, there was no reason to assume that the poem was written by a younger John Hay.

In this poem Hay argues that "freedom" and "liberty" have their "own eternal law." The enemies of liberty are, not factory owners or the new capitalist elite, but the aristocracy. The poet calls for the "crimson axe" to fall upon "the knell of shuddering kings." Only then will liberty shine as a "light whereby the world is saved." Legitimate revolution will replace the old aristocracy with the new liberalism.[75]

John Hay's religious ideas were closely tied to his views on liberty. In contrast with his earlier silence on the subject, a good deal of his poetry written after 1865 dealt directly with religion, and it is equally clear that in Europe Hay for the first time met a religious institution as a dominant factor in human affairs. His reaction to the Roman Catholic Church was understandably Protestant and quite in keeping with his affirmed republicanism. He called for individual inspection of the life of Jesus and the gospels; he avowed a basic faith in the laity. But Hay went further; in accord with his times, but significantly in accord with a dominant European mood of the period which was shared by his friend John Bigelow, Hay became rampantly anticlerical.[76]

The negative aspects of his religious thinking are not, however, the most salient developments which appear to have occurred during his European years. Of particular importance to his increasingly clearer interpretation of his world, was the relationship he sought and found between religion and heroism. In one of his earliest writings, the eulogy of Ellsworth, he had drawn a parallel between Christ and Ellsworth in the purity of their lives and the circumstances of their deaths. Colonel Baker, too, had been depicted as heroic in terms of self-sacrifice, but there had been little direct biblical allusion, nor do any of the extant works written between 1862 and 1865 contain any. But in *Pike County Ballads*, Hay's correlation between the hero and the figure of Christ is quite clear.

Hay had used dialect for pungent emphasis in his earliest extant letters from Indiana and Illinois to eastern college friends in the 1850s. The tendency toward dialect had been strengthened through the Lincoln experience by his quotation of Lincoln's stories about Westerners, Lincoln's readings from the *Nasby Papers*, and Hay's interest in the speech and songs of black people. The first instance of his use of it in his own composition is in the two poems in his travel diary of 1864, written on the Rosecrans mission, and in both poems unrepentant sinners are speaking.[77] In the *Pike County Ballads* Hay used dialect to depict saints. It is tempting to think that, when reading of Tilmon Joy, Jim Bludso, and Golyer Ben, Hay had reread his diary account of Southern travels in 1863 and had found his transcription of the slave song, "J.C. was no respectable person."[78] For like the Christ of the slave song, the saints of Pike are pillars of impropriety.

In describing his own "American," Henry James wrote: "If he was

a muscular Christian, it was quite without doctrine."[79] James' friend
Hay was both a muscular Christian and a man of doctrine, but he
detested the doctrinaire and the institutional element of orthodox
Christianity. Although his family had produced ministers and devout members of the Baptist and Presbyterian congregations, Hay
himself gave little sign of the sectarian in either his immediate
family's religious life or in his own behavior.[80] In the letters of his
college days, chapel is mentioned only when it is skipped, and he
impolitely declined the vocation of the ministry. In his poetry of the
late 1860s and early 1870s, a prime target became the standard
church and church-goer, and Hay was sharply criticized for his "ir-
religious" attitudes.[81]

Adulterous Jim Bludso's ghost went straight to heaven, although
his one good act was his last—saving the lives of his passengers.
According to Hay: "Christ ain't a-going to be too hard/ On a man
that died for men."[82] From his college letters and wartime diaries,
one might find ample support for the general theory that Hay, like
the father of Little Breeches, would have said, "I don't go much on
religion/ I never ain't had no show."[83] Yet an inspection of his
poetry and prose reveals religious concepts as among the most constant and unifying aspects of Hay's intellectual development.

Among many other pursuits, his mother's father had been a Baptist minister, but John and his brother Augustus were sent to Dr.
John D. Thompson's Anglican Academy, where the younger brother
spent three years preparing for Illinois State University. Hay resisted the strong religious atmosphere of Brown University by not
attending prayers and by seeking out for friendship such unorthodox
persons as Mrs. Sarah Helen Whitman. Her writings about Keats
and Shelley had brought her the stern disapprobation of proper
Providence residents, who "regarded Shelley as an atheist and any
defender of his work as one who had fallen from grace."[84]

Both English Romantic strains and those of Transcendentalism
are visible in John Hay's poetry and may have been intensified by
the Whitman circle; but he did not succumb to the Emersonian
tendency to transcend evil in human affairs. He retained a sense of
original sin; the "savage world," as he wrote in "Mount Tabor,"
must move "Upward through law and faith to love."[85] The way was
clear, but, like the pharisees, some moved only as far as law, and
others moved through law to faith, but not to love. In the "Monks of

Basle," Hay showed the old monks "bickering about doctrine" on a
beautiful day and ignoring the "lures of summer and sense."

> And one by one from the face of earth
> They pined and vanished away
> . . . .
> He has no ears for Nature's voice
> Whose soul is the slave of creed.
> Not all in vain with beauty and love
> Has God the world adorned;
> And he who Nature scorns and mocks
> By Nature is mocked and scorned.[86]

The monks carried faith to enslavement; their scorn of nature
became scorn of the nature of man. They ignored the love of God
visible in nature, and Hay banished them for adoring false gods
rather than the God in man and nature. In a way significant to an era
which produced Mark Twain's *Innocent Abroad,* equating Catholi-
cism and hypocrisy, Hay sentenced the monks on the basis of their
own doctrines. Their hangman is a perverse being who, when speaking through the bird's song, arouses their once-free passions and
then identifies himself to the doctrinaires as the Devil. This confrontation frightens the holy men into extinction, for they believe the
Devil would thus tempt them from holy thoughts through the song
of a bird. But Hay was gentle; he let them "vanish away." They are
useless items in his world of social responsibility.

His moralism was not altogether traditional, but it was no less
staunch because of its lack of orthodoxy. Through Hay's poetry run
the themes of righteousness and retribution—sometimes merely
suggesting but more often blantantly threatening. In the "Prayer of
the Romans," autocracy in the guises of both Church and State is
chastised by the republican poet as "polluters," "pampered swine"
who "devour the fruit" of Italy. Hay called the Lord to "Let the
people come to their birthright,/ And Crosier and Crown pass
away"; and he ended the poem with a prayer for "One freedom, one
faith without fetters,/ One republic in Italy free!"[87] Prayer was useful, but insufficient. In "God's Vengeance," Hay cried out to men
who "sit and wait" for the Lord to begin their work against the
"bruised serpent of sin"; "Strike! God is waiting for us!"[88]

Hay's Pike County heroes were people whose salvation was guaranteed by their actions. The same justification by works is obvious in "Religion and Doctrine." Before the scowling rabbis of the Sanhedrin, the beggar told them in defense of Christ, "I know not what this man may be,/ Sinner or saint; but as for me,/ One thing I know, —that I am he/ Who once was blind, and now I see."[89] His sight gave the poor man strength to stand unperturbed before the doctrine and the threats of the massed rabbis.

Christ's example, that of the lordly individual ready to give his life for his beliefs, was a recurrent theme of Hay's religious and political work. The beggar in "Religion and Doctrine" gazes with his miraculous new sight to the "Open heaven" above the "hate-clouded face of men"—the one against the many. The same is true of Tilmon Joy, who challenged popular bigotry.[90] Tyranny, whether of an autocratic church, a government, or the populace, Hay attacked. But, in his poetry, the tyranny of the populace remained subject to reason and to proof, and he portrayed it as less venal than that of men in places of power.

Lincoln was the logical conclusion to Hay's thinking about heroism, the republic, and religion. The ten volumes of *Abraham Lincoln: A History* became the Lincoln gospel according to St. John and St. Nico, who, like "two everlasting Angels," would transmit to their fellows the truth about their hero and the message by which the republic could be saved.[91] Hay's Christianity was "muscular"—his idea of justification was action, service, sacrifice. But the sacrifice must be, like Lincoln's, for a socially useful goal, the measure of which Hay believed was its practical application. These criteria of leadership left no room for the mystic, the asocial, the exclusive, or the alienated. Holding such an ideal of service, he shunned idleness.

John Hay's search for the proper leader for a modern progressive America was reflected in his writing and then in his life. Finding few leaders in whom he could believe in the 1880s, he created Arthur Farnham, the hero of his novel *The Bread-winners*. And then he recreated Lincoln of the 1860s in *Abraham Lincoln: A History*. Finding even fewer heroes in the 1890s, Hay offered himself. By 1898 John Hay became the leader he had created in his literature. The following chapter will explore how he used politics to insure a victory for his world view.

CHAPTER 4

The Political Career of John Hay

I N 1904 a young man wrote to Secretary of State John Hay for advice as to how to plan a diplomatic career. The Secretary of State.replied that while it was true that he had "held a good many diplomatic positions, . . . they were all the result of accident, and no one had any relation to the other."[1] All of his life John Hay maintained that he had never sought a public office. True to his family's classical tradition, he relentlessly attributed all his successes in obtaining political appointments to fortune. To all he presented his life as a series of happenstances, and in *Una*, a poem written in 1870, Hay articulated what he wanted posterity to say of his career: "for soon unhorsed I lay / At the feet of the strong god circumstance."[2]

His closest friend in later years, Henry Adams, in his autobiographical *Education of Henry Adams*, publicized this view of Hay's life as well.[3] William R. Thayer in his two-volume biography argued that Hay was never a "professed office seeker. . . . An innate refinement, coupled with shyness, and an abiding personal dignity, kept him from the suppliant's posture."[4] Though at times contradictory, Tyler Dennett's 1933 Pulitzer-Prize-winning biography concluded that Hay's political success was the result of a "chain of accidents."[5] A recent article has let Hay's 1904 assertion stand.[6]

John Hay's political career, however, was no accident. He held successively positions as Lincoln's assistant personal secretary (1861–1865), Secretary of the American Legation in Paris (1865–1867), Chargé d'Affaires in Vienna (1867–1868), Secretary to the American Legation in Madrid (1869–1870), Assistant Secretary of State (1879–1881), Ambassador to England (1897–1898), and Secretary of State (1898–1905). For twenty-one years of his adult life John Hay held appointive office. This in itself was quite a feat for any man in the second half of the nineteenth century, let alone for one who claimed "I never asked for an office, and never shall while I live."[7]

After serving as Lincoln's assistant secretary and sometimes private emissary for four years, Hay accepted appointment as Secretary to the United States Legation at Paris on March 22, 1865. Appomatox was two weeks away, and Lincoln had a month to live. Hay described the position to his brother Charles, explaining that he was ready "to go back to Warsaw and try to give the vineyard experiment a fair trial, when the Secretary of State sent for me and offered me this position abroad." The appointment, he added, "was entirely unsolicited and unexpected. I had no more idea of it than you have."[8]

This modest stance was in keeping with classical convention, but it was not true to the facts. From the very beginning of Hay's tenure in Washington he had formed a close relationship with Secretary of State William H. Seward which lasted until Seward's death in 1872. The Secretary of State took young Hay under his protective wing, freely discussing both personal and governmental matters with him.[9] Hay's close relationship with Seward was so well known that some office seekers wrote to the President's assistant secretary in order to gain favor with the Secretary of State.[10] In late 1864 Hay and Nicolay let it become known that they were growing weary of their positions and desired to change jobs.[11] Being a presidential secretary was in many ways a limiting career. Seward through Hay, no doubt, was well aware of the secretaries' desires. Lincoln, of course, gave his blessing. On March 11, 1865, John G. Nicolay was appointed Consul at Paris and ten days later John Hay was appointed Secretary of the Paris Legation. Yet on March 31 Hay wrote his brother Charles that the appointment "was entirely unsolicited and unexpected."[12]

When John Bigelow resigned as Minister to France, Hay, as custom required, submitted his resignation as well.[13] Asked to remain in Paris until Bigelow's successor was installed and settled in January, 1867, Hay complied. By February he was back in Washington requesting Seward to find a place for him, for he told the Secretary of State that he would "like anything worth having." Neither his orange groves in Florida nor his vineyards in Illinois was paying, and a brief stop in New York had convinced him that business was too uncertain to afford him "an available counter."[14] On February 3 Hay dined with Seward, Thurlow Weed, and Senator James R. Doolittle of Wisconsin. The Secretary of State urged Weed and Doolittle to use their influence to get Hay a job.[15]

Seward told Hay that if General Dix were not confirmed by the Senate as Minister to France,[16] Hay could be sent to Paris as Chargé d'Affaires. For the next three weeks John Hay embarked on a campaign to obtain an office for himself. On February 4 he paid a call on Seward's rival, Senate Foreign Relations Chairman Charles Sumner. Hay sought and soon obtained a promise from the Senator that, should he be nominated for any office, the Massachusetts Senator would work for Hay's confirmation. They discussed Dix's case as well as the rejection by the Senate of the nomination of George F. McGinnis as Minister to Sweden.[17]

On February 6 Hay was back at Seward's. The Secretary of State informed him that his name had been proposed to President Johnson for the Swedish mission. "The President," lamented Seward, "said he had another man for it." The Secretary of State then offered to appoint Hay a temporary employee of the State Department. For the present he could act as Seward's private secretary. Holding out for a better position, Hay declined.[18]

Seward suggested that a visit to Lincoln's old confidant, Secretary of the Interior O. H. Browning, might help Hay in his quest for an office. On February 8 he called on Browning who promised him his full support.[19]

For the next several days Hay talked and dined with congressmen, senators, and other influential Washington figures including Congressman Samuel Hooper of Massachusetts, Secretary of the Navy Gideon Welles, General Phillip H. Sheridan, Senator Reverdy Johnson of Maryland, Congressman Shelby Cullom of Illinois, and Chief Justice Salmon P. Chase.[20] On February 10 he again visited Sumner and discussed Seward's promise of a position.[21]

After another week or so of cementing his relations in Washington, Hay traveled to New York, to make sure that, if his hopes for an office were dashed, he would have something to fall back on.[22] He then went home to Warsaw to await the call from Washington. In the midst of all his office seeking Hay wrote to Nicolay that Seward had "offered me any mission that was falling in;—proposed my name to the President for the reversion of Sweden. . . . But the President wanted the place for a deadbeat copperhead. . . . Seward says the Senate will reject him. . . . I am inclined to decline a nomination in that state of affairs."[23]

On March 3 Hay learned that Dix had at last been confirmed for

the Paris mission. Hay at once wrote Seward a long letter of thanks
for his efforts, adding that when an appointment became available,
he could be reached in Warsaw.[24] There was nothing to do but wait.
In May, 1867, the call came. John L. Motley had resigned his post
as Minister at Vienna and Seward offered Hay the post of Chargé
d'Affaires. Without hesitation Hay accepted the $6,000 a year posi-
tion, and on June 29 he sailed for Europe.[25]

In October, 1868, Hay returned to the United States, having
been replaced by a full Minister.[26] "Neither then, nor later," proclaimed Thayer in his two-volume biography, "was Hay a professed
office-seeker."[27] Nevertheless, when Hay returned to the United
States in 1868 he went straight to Washington, not to Warsaw. For
the next two months the former Chargé d'Affaires spared little effort
in search of political appointment. "I . . . came to Washington," he
wrote Nicolay on December 8, 1868, "in the peaceful pursuit of a fat
office. But there is nothing now available."[28] By the end of December John Hay returned to Warsaw unemployed while the outgo-
ing Secretary of State promised to "keep his weather eye open" for a
job for the ex-presidential secretary.[29]

As soon as the new Grant administration was inaugurated Hay
reopened his campaign for a government position. On March 13,
1869, he wrote to Sumner that he was "an applicant for the mission
to Portugal. . . . Mr. Seward twice presented my name to Mr.
Johnson for a mission—but the President preferred someone who
made personal court to him."[30]

Finding that by remaining in Warsaw he could not successfully
press his claims for an office, Hay journeyed to Washington in May,
1869. Success, however, eluded him. Writing an apologetic letter to
Nicolay on May 14, he implied that he really did not want a position:
"I am sure that by hanging around and eating dirt, I could get some
office. But my stomach revolts. It is almost too great a strain of a
man's self-respect to ask for an office; still worse to beg for it."[31]
Almost too great a strain, but he proved up to it.

By June, 1869, convinced that he would have to seek a source of
income outside of the government payroll, Hay took a job as editor
of the *Illinois State Journal* in Springfield. Within the month the
Grant administration, at the intercession of Hay's friends, offered
him the post of Secretary of the Legation in Madrid. Even though
the position meant a cut in pay compared to his salary at the *Journal*,

he literally jumped at the offer,[32] and, before the end of July, took up his duties in Spain.

But he did not stay long. In May, 1870, he resigned his post in Spain citing "pecuniary circumstances,"[33] though he remained until September, 1870, when he returned to the United States.[34] This time he apparently made no attempt to secure appointive office. The reason for this may have been, as Dennett suggests, that Hay had no standing or influence within the Grant administration.[35] More likely, he was just tired of positions abroad. In any case, he had spent the first ten years of his adult life as a public officeholder.

Before leaving Spain, Hay was offered a position as assistant editor of the *New York Tribune*. Both Horace Greeley, the *Tribune* editor, and Whitelaw Reid, the managing editor, were eager to obtain Hay's services.[36] Taking a job with the *New York Tribune* in October, 1870, was not in any sense a withdrawal from politics. In fact the paper was the leading reform journal in New York, and within a year and a half both the Liberal Republicans and the Democrats nominated Greeley for President. One of Hay's major responsibilities as assistant editor was to compose essays calling for national political reform.[37]

Hay was a firm advocate of the dump-Grant movement of the early 1870s even before Greeley received the nomination.[38] All during the campaign of 1872 Hay wrote strong editorials calling for the defeat of Grant and for a return to political honesty. Hay even personally campaigned for Greeley.[39] In 1874 Hay and the *Tribune* strongly urged the election of Democrat Samuel Tilden as governor of New York.[40]

It was during this period John Hay came to enjoy national renown as a poet, lecturer, and author. His famous poems "Little Breeches" and "Jim Bludso" appeared in the *Tribune* during the winter of 1870–1871.[41] Soon after, these poems and others were issued as the *Pike County Ballads*. His *Castillian Days*, a combined travelogue and call for the institution of republican government, appeared in installments in the *Atlantic* from January to July, 1871.[42] By the end of that year Hay was already as well known as he was to be in 1899 when he issued his Open Door Notes.[43]

Like his *Tribune* editorials in the early 1870s calling for an end to political corruption, Hay's essays, lectures, and poems of the same period were truly reformist. He remained on the *Tribune* staff for five years. With Horace Greeley's death in 1872 the paper had abandoned neither its independence nor its national stature as "The Great Moral Organ." Hay's power of invective had been visible from his first articles on Ellsworth and Baker as well as in his Civil War diary entries and letters, but it had sharpened during his years in Europe and was admirably suited to the cut and slash of journalistic crusading in the 1870s and 1880s. It was later said that, when Whitelaw Reid was managing the *Tribune*, "the rule of the paper . . . was that of whips, while with Hay it was that of scorpions."[44]

The reform spirit was carried into all facets of the paper's coverage, from diplomacy to literary reviews. Some of Hay's sting can be felt in his long article on Alexander Dumas: "In romance he was not poetical; in the historical novel he was conspicuous for a bold and sublime ignorance; in essays and travel he showed neither keenness of observation nor comprehension of the human heart; but in the hazy glories of the French literary paradise which lies between the borders of the poetical, the grotesque, the witty, and the sensuous, Alexander Dumas was without a rival."[45] Similarly he criticized the State Department: "In one of the oriental cosmogenies the world rests on a serpent, which rests on an elephant, which rests on a tortoise, which rests on nothing. If you can believe the first three propositions your faith becomes sufficiently robust not to give way at the last. Those who loyally trust the present Administration are expected to believe something like this."[46]

Hay spent five years as assistant managing editor of the *New York Tribune*, working closely with its editor, Whitelaw Reid. His duties included helping direct the paper's financial affairs, and by 1875 he had become Reid's most trusted lieutenant. Hay wrote editorials and columns on domestic and European politics; he translated essays written by foreign correspondents, reviewed books, and recruited staff members.[47]

As his salary rose—Hay was earning one hundred dollars a week by the end of 1872—so did his attempts to increase his fortune through speculations. If his investments in Florida lands during the Civil War had proved disappointing, his purchase of diamond mine stock in 1872 was a near disaster. But the assistant editor was not easily deterred; he assured his father that he had got his money back and that future investments would prove less dangerous, for he was "embarking, with powerful friends, in another enterprise, where the loss, if any, will be small, and the profit, if it comes, will be large."[48]

All the while Hay enjoyed the social world of New York. He was elected to membership in the Century Club and asked to join the newly formed Knickerbocker Club.[49] He met financial leaders like William Astor, Cornelius Vanderbilt, Jay Gould, and Thomas Eckert, and in later years he worked closely with all of them. A frequent and sought-after guest at dinner parties, the young bachelor was a favorite among the city's matchmakers.[50] By his own testimony, as well as that of others, Hay continued actively seeking the company of women.

That aspect of his life changed in 1873 when he met and courted Clara L. Stone. By then he was sufficiently well known and well-off to propose to Clara, daughter of the wealthy Cleveland bridge builder and railroad financier, Amasa Stone.[51] She was, Hay wrote Nicolay, "a very estimable young person, large, handsome and good. I never found life worth while before."[52] On February 4, 1874, they were married, and within a year Hay wrote Reid that Helen, the Hays' first child, had been born.[53] "It is painful, but I must tell you. My wife says, when you come to the house, that you have got to hold the baby."

The *Tribune*, a morning paper, required long night hours of its editorial staff. Reid's health was even more precarious than Hay's, and when the editor was ill or out of town Hay took over Reid's duties as well as his own. Journalism, his family, and the social life of a cosmopolitan city now occupied too much of his time to continue his lecturing. Even without lectures, the toll of four laborious years began to tell, and in early 1875, moved by the constant invitations of Clara's family, and by Hay's illness, the couple went to live in Cleveland.[54]

Hay thus gave up his formal career in journalism, but he did not end either his contributions to the *Tribune* or his interest in reform politics. A steady flow of articles, reviews, editorials, criticism, and encouragement to Reid continued to stream from Hay, running from inside information on the Ohio campaigns to suggestions concerning staff and the hiring of budding young writers like Henry James.[55]

While Hay had been fairly prosperous as a result of his salary, lectures, and writings before his marriage, his wife made him financially independent. The prevailing economic order thus afforded Hay the chance to pursue a life of increasing leisure, and neither the *Tribune* nor Hay attacked industrialism as destructive of traditional American values.[56] Politics did not become a lesser concern for him as he entered into his association with Amasa Stone. If anything, his interest in politics grew more intense and more urgent as he grew more successful and more wealthy.

Nevertheless, it would be an error to ignore Hay's career as a businessman, for in large measure his success in that sphere served as a bridge between his poetry and his politics. His interest in the world of finance was not in contradiction to his other concerns. Often pictured as a dabbler who married into industrial wealth, Hay had been a successful money manager long before he met Amasa Stone's daughter. Indeed, it was his previous financial experience, as well as his proven managerial skills, that convinced Stone that his daughter had made a fine match and that he had gained a son-in-law capable of managing the family's substantial holdings. For over a year Stone tried to convince his son-in-law and daughter to move to Cleveland, and he did not do so merely because he desired Clara's presence.

Stone, whose health was failing, and whose only son, Adelbert Barnes, had drowned while a student at Yale in the 1860s, needed someone he could trust to watch over his investments. By the time John Hay arrived in Cleveland, Stone had transferred most of his assets from railroads to banking, though he continued to hold a large share of the Lake Shore Railroad Company along with Cornelius Vanderbilt. Stone's banking interests included directorships in five Cleveland banks: The Merchants Bank of Ohio, the Bank of Commerce, The Second National Bank, The Commercial National Bank, and The Cleveland Banking Company. He also owned controlling interest in the Mercer Iron and Coal Company and was on the board of directors of the Western Union Company. Having begun his career as a self-educated carpenter, Stone had risen to the top of the American corporate structure in a manner that must have reinforced Hay's belief in the American Dream. Hay admired the older man and Stone demonstrated his satisfaction with his son-in-law by presenting him with substantial gifts, including a luxurious home on Cleveland's fashionable Euclid Avenue.[57]

Politics, however, continued to fascinate Hay, even if it simultaneously seemed to attract and to repel him. At least until 1878

Hay remained a political reformer and a political independent. He wrote to Whitelaw Reid in September, 1875, that the upcoming contest between Republicans and Democrats in Ohio centered on the "issue whether the nation shall be run by a liar and a thief or not." The Republicans of Ohio, he told Reid, were "bellowing, howling hounds" and the Democrats were worse.[58] Distrusting his fellow Ohioan Rutherford B. Hayes, he opposed his bid for the presidential nomination in 1875–1876.[59] As Hay explained to Reid, he was anxious only "to have a man on one ticket or the other for whom I can vote without nausea."[60] By April, 1876, Hay saw the best two candidates as Tilden and Blaine: "If anybody wants a better pair of candidates," he wrote to Reid, "he must wait till he gets to heaven. . . ."[61]

With Hayes' victory in 1876, John Hay was clearly an outsider. By opposing the President, Hay had defied the Ohio Republican machine. This was the wrong approach for any man who desired a future in politics, and John Hay most assuredly did. In the next three years, in search of political office, he would abandon his political independence, which had failed as a vehicle to gain him political power, and once again follow the party line.

Along with his political troubles Hay had developed physical disorders which continued to plague him until his death. In the spring of 1876 Hay experienced his worst episode of diplopia (double vision), an illness that had periodically recurred since his days on the *Tribune*. A physician's prescription of corrective lenses failed to alleviate the condition, and in 1878 Hay complained also of a buzzing in his ears. Since no physiological origin could be located for either disorder, Hay decided to travel to Paris to seek the opinion of Dr. Jean Charcot, considered at the time to be the world's leading neurologist.[62]

From May until September, 1878, along with his brother Leonard, John traveled in Europe, meeting with Charcot and taking the mineral baths at Schleingenbad and Schwalbach (Prussia). Although no record remains of Charcot's diagnosis, several factors about the neurologist's work in the 1870s and Hay's continued symptoms are suggestive. Charcot had achieved his reputation by identifying and treating cases of hysteria—disorders where no apparent physical cause could be located. In 1878, when the Hay brothers visited Paris, Charcot had just begun to employ posthypnotic suggestion as a method of alleviating hysterical symptoms.

Whether the doctor used hypnosis on Hay remains speculative, and, in any case, Hay continued to experience the buzzing in his ears after seeing Charcot.[63] While his diplopic condition frequently reappeared during the next twenty-five years, he apparently felt well enough in the fall of 1878 to hope for a diplomatic appointment.

Hay's chance came in December, 1878, with the death of Bayard Taylor, the American Minister at Berlin. The position was offered to Whitelaw Reid, who declined it. Instead Reid suggested to President Hayes and Secretary of State William M. Evarts that they sound out John Hay. Rejecting the idea, Evarts informed Reid that Hay "had not been active enough in political efforts. . . ."[64] Angrily, Hay told Reid that Hayes had wanted the place "for his friends." But Hay was sorry that he had been turned down since he would have liked "a second-class mission uncommonly well."[65]

For the next seven months Hay tried to prove that he was both an attractive political figure and a man of national stature. Moreover, he demonstrated to the regular Republicans that he could be more regular than most. He set out on a barnstorming and speech-making routine which, with the gracious aid of Reid's *Tribune*, soon attracted national prominence. On August 20, he sent Reid a copy of a speech he "made . . . last night in the strongest Democratic ward of Cleveland" and asked Reid to publish it, which the editor did.[66]

On August 25 Hay forwarded another oration he was about to deliver: "I am invited to make four speeches this week," he wrote Reid. By the beginning of October Hay was "making a speech nearly every night" and sending copies to Reid for publication in the *Tribune*.[67] On October 7, in case no one had noticed, the newspaper reported on page one that "All Tribune readers will . . . be glad to learn that Colonel John Hay has come out of . . . retirement to take part in the Republican canvass. Few men," added the *Tribune*, "are as well equipped as Colonel Hay for a successful political career."[68] On October 9 the *Tribune* reported a speech which must have convinced the most skeptical that Hay was now an orthodox Republican: The Democrats, he proclaimed, "reeking with the contact of repudiators and thieves . . . dare to accuse their betters of malversation in office." The Republican party, on the other hand, had a "spotless shield . . . which has reduced the debt a thousand millions, and given us, through honest resumption, a credit unparalleled in history."[69] Strange words from a man who only two years before had referred to the Hayes administration as "that herd of wild asses' colts in Washington. . . ."[70]

On October 15 the *Tribune* reported another all-out attack by John Hay on the Democrats. The Civil War, he said, was caused by the Democratic party. If the Democrats were returned to power, the result would be continued "riot and murder" in the South by "hired bands of ruffians." The Democrats have "trample[d] under their brutish hoofs the last sacred things we have saved from their lust, the free ballot-box. . . it is time to call a halt."[71] This was the same man who four years before told Reid that "There is really no Democratic or Republican Party left, and a man can with perfect consistency favor one in one state and the other in another."[72]

By October, 1879, Hay's conversion was complete. Symbolically, President and Mrs. Hayes attended a reception for Hay's friend William Dean Howells at Hay's Euclid Avenue home in Cleveland.[73] Later that same month Frederick Seward resigned his position as Assistant Secretary of State and Hay was offered the job.[74]

At first Hay resisted the offer, telling Evarts that he could not accept the post because "interests which I cannot disregard, make it impossible for me to be away from Cleveland this winter."[75] But he was more explicit in explaining to Reid just what those interests were: "Mr. Evarts has written me a most urgent and kind letter— but I have declined the place. It now looks as if I could get the nomination for Congress. . . ."[76]

While Hay went on to say that he really did not want the nomination, although his later letters suggest he did, clearly an acceptance of the Assistant Secretary of Stateship would severely damage his congressional hopes. In fact, President Hayes, an Ohio politician himself, may have had just that fact in mind when he offered him the State Department position. Hay had been making quite a political name for himself following the Hayes' administration's refusal to offer him the Berlin post in March, 1879. His campaigning in the next six months was aimed at gaining a national reputation. Surely he was seeking office. By late October, 1879, he constituted a clear threat to Hayes in Ohio and perhaps even as a choice for higher office. The offer of the position as Assistant Secretary of State may have resulted more from an attempt to keep Hay out of the political spotlight (and a possible congressional seat) than from a desire to reward him.

Ultimately Hay decided to accept the Hayes' offer.[77] After a quick trip to New York on November 7 to discuss the matter at Reid's office, Hay decided that his chances to obtain the congressional nomination were slim and would require more effort than he was willing to employ. On October 21, 1878, he had written Reid: "This Congress matter is not so simple as my high-toned friends think. All Euclid Avenue says with one accord that I am the man, but, E[u-clid] A[venue], with all its millions and its tone, does not influence a single primary, and there are four or five other candidates, who are all more or less strong with the 'boys.' I have not yet made up my mind whether to try for it or not."

Hay's biographers have insisted that his vacillation over the Assistant Secretaryship is just another example of Hay's reluctance to assume public office. Often cited is his November 5, 1879, letter to William Dean Howells in which he presented himself as "chivied and worritted" about accepting the position. "I stand," he dramatically told Howells, "like a hydrophobiac on the edge of a bath tub."[78] Talk like this, however, Hay reserved for his literary friends like Edmund C. Stedman, Howells, and later, Henry Adams. Hay never wanted these people to view him as the office seeker he was. His indecision in October and November, 1879, was whether to seek a congressional office or an appointive one.[79]

There were, as is often the case, private and public reasons, both for Hay's candor to Howells and for his reticence in accepting the post. Hay's description of Cleveland in *The Bread-winners* should leave no surprises. After Washington, Paris, Vienna, Madrid, and New York, Cleveland left much to be desired as a residence for Hay. There was the additional factor urging removal from "Buffland": Hay had married, had children, but found himself living not only in the house his father-in-law had built but also in the shadow of his wife's parents. These factors supported his hopes of finding appropriate reasons and chances to leave Cleveland. Others held him back. Hay was very much in love with his wife and attached to his children. Mrs. Hay was now pregnant for the third time and would not be able to accompany him to Washington. Howells' own happy marriage made him a likely person to understand Hay's agitation.

Hay remained at the State Department until March 31, 1881, when President James A. Garfield was inaugurated. Apparently Reid and Evarts had convinced him that he could assume the position of Assistant Secretary of State and still run for Congress in 1880 if he decided to. By the end of March, requesting Reid to stop

putting his name forward in the *Tribune* as a candidate for Congress
from Ohio, Hay told him that he "did not want to run for Congress"
even though "I think I can be nominated."[80] While there is no way
to determine if Hay was correct—and all evidence seems to point
the other way—no doubt he had decided that an appointive position
was more attractive and more secure than elective office.[81] He
wrote to Howells on May 24, 1880, "I have positively and definitely
given up Congress, and I shall hold no more office after next March.
I think there is no such apples-of-sodom fruit in the world, and I am
out, finally, as soon as I can get away. I would give a pot of money to
get out today,—nothing but my personal regard for Mr. Evarts
keeps me through the administration."[82]

The actual office may not have been appealing to Hay, but
Washington society certainly had its charms. A steady stream of
letters to Clara Hay who remained in Cleveland described his
bachelor life with Clarence King and the gaiety of dinners at the
homes of Marian and Henry Adams and Elizabeth and Senator Don
Cameron.[83] After their child Alice's birth, Mrs. Hay came for a visit.
The friendships begun that winter were to last the rest of their lives,
and they constituted another magnet drawing Hay to Washington.

No matter what Hay wrote to his literary friends, he had no
intention in 1880 and 1881 of withdrawing from political life. He
campaigned strongly in 1880 for the election of James A. Garfield.
On July 31, 1880, Hay delivered a speech entitled the "Balance
Sheet of the Two Parties" to an overflow crowd at Mark Hanna's
Cleveland Opera House.[84] The speech was quickly reprinted by the
Republican party and used as a major piece of campaign prop-
aganda.[85] In it Hay argued that the Republican party held "the
greater portion of the virtue and intelligence of the land . . . its past
is luminous with the story of beneficent achievements . . . ," while
the Democrats had a "discredited and soiled record." The Republicans had given the nation Lincoln, and the Democrats "vilified and
killed him." The Republicans had freed the slaves, built the Pacific
Railroad, and "saved the Union and the honor of the flag." The
Democrats, concluded Hay, were "not fit fellowship for brave and
magnanimous youth."[86] For a man who allegedly saw politics as
repulsive, one wonders just what he saw as repulsive.[87]

All during the campaign and after the election Hay maintained
close contact with Garfield.[88] Garfield asked Hay's advice about
appointments, and Hay freely gave it.[89] Even Henry Adams implied

that Hay expected to be rewarded with a cabinet post.[90] Hay had
hinted as much in an October 18 letter to Garfield: "It will pay you
to keep a cheap friend to drone continually in your ear, 'It was *you*
who were nominated at Chicago and elected by the people.' "[91] The
best Garfield offered was the position of presidential secretary, a
post which Hay had held under Lincoln twenty years before. Hay
was hurt and turned down the offer on December 25, broadly hint-
ing that he might be inclined to accept another post: "I shall have a
good deal of leisure and shall always be at your service for
anything—'except these bonds.' "[92] The President-elect chose to
ignore the hint and asked Hay to reconsider, this time implying that
as secretary Hay could exercise almost cabinet powers.[93] Garfield's
response again angered Hay. He told Reid that he had grown "disgusted with the small intrigue of office seeking here," while to
Garfield he replied that he would not accept the post: "There are
many things which you must traverse absolutely alone [and] . . . I
wish I could save you one moment of annoyance or perplexity, but it
is hardly possible that anyone could do that."[94]

Hay retired from public life on March 31, 1881, and did not
return to a public position until March, 1897, when he assumed the
important position of Ambassador to England under President William McKinley. But he did not withdraw from political activity for
the next sixteen years. No doubt after his 1880 attempt to secure a
congressional seat, he abandoned all hope of electoral politics for
himself, but he never gave up his preoccupation with politics.[95]
Directly upon leaving the State Department in March, 1881, he
took over the editorship of the *New York Tribune* for seven months
while Whitelaw Reid left for an extended honeymoon.[96] Concentrating the *Tribune*'s attention on New York State political boss
Roscoe Conkling, Hay temporarily reestablished his own image as a
Liberal Republican.[97]

Garfield's death in September and Reid's return in October left
Hay, once more, outside the center of Republican political power.
Nevertheless, Hay continued to expend much of his interest and his
energy on Republican politics.[98] In 1884 he plunged into the presidential campaign with vigor. Infuriated by the "mugwumps" support of the Democratic nominee, Grover Cleveland, he angrily
wrote to Richard W. Gilder, editor of the *Century*, "Yes, I mean
Hurrah for Blaine! I have never been able to appreciate the logic
that induces some excellent people every four years because they

cannot nominate the candidate they prefer to vote for the party they don't prefer."[99]

Hay actively campaigned for Blaine and generously contributed to his campaign chest.[100] He grew increasingly chagrined with his "mugwump" friends. Warning Gilder that Cleveland, if elected, would turn out of office two hundred thousand experienced and efficient Republican officeholders, he did not mention the corollary effect that the defeat of his friend Blaine would have: John Hay would not be appointed to high public office.[101]

While Blaine's defeat did not diminish Hay's interest in national politics, it certainly lessened his potential influence in Washington.[102] He spent the next two years working on the history of Lincoln which he and Nicolay finally completed in 1886.[103] There was, he believed, an immediate need for Lincoln's unifying capacity by both the Republicans and the nation. Hay saw party rifts widening steadily while the Democrats capitalized upon divisive economic and social issues. The year 1886 was critical. Labor unrest, developing since the Panic of 1883, erupted into riots as mobs battled militia, and it culminated in the Haymarket disaster in Chicago. In the November elections internal disorders in the Republican party made easier the Democratic victories at the polls. The monthly serialization of the Lincoln *History* in the *Century* magazine also began in November. The partisan intent of the work was recognized at the time as well as in later years. "After reading your volumes," Theodore Roosevelt wrote Hay, "I do congratulate myself that my father was a Republican and that I am a Republican . . . [and] it would be a dreadful thing to have to live down being descended from Vallandingham; and I would mortally hate to have had men like Seymour or McClellan for ancestors."[104]

The year 1886 was also a turning point in the personal life of the Hays. In January the family with its four children moved to Washington into an imposing home on Lafayette Square facing the White House.[105] This was a curious location for one who professed no interest in obtaining political power. In a sense, since 1869, Hay had never taken his eyes off the White House. Now only a statue of Andrew Jackson interfered with his view.

Over the past eleven years, Hay had proven an apt pupil in the art of money making and had been handling his own affairs as well as those of his father-in-law, since 1880. At Stone's death in 1883, Hay and his wife had inherited three and a half million dollars, and Hay, thanks to Jay Gould's influence, was appointed a director of Western Union.[106] Substantially increasing his holdings in Western Union, Hay worked vigorously along with Gould to insure minimal congressional interference in the company's affairs. He won Senator John Sherman's assurance that he would not support "confiscation or any other injustice" as a result of the Senate hearings on the telegraph.[107] Hay continued to maintain a close personal watch over his financial holdings. Deciding that investing in securities was a superior way to protect their fortune, he assured his wife that he would avoid putting their funds out for interest only.[108] When the Western Union Company began to lose money, Hay sold off much of that stock and purchased large amounts of the Northern Pacific Company. He handled his inheritance well, and he left his wife a larger and even more secure fortune than her father had.[109]

The move to Washington and the elegant new house put the Hays in the center of a most exclusive social circle, which included the artists John La Farge and Augustus Saint-Gaudens; the geologist, writer, and explorer Clarence King; the novelists William Dean Howells and Henry James; the diplomats Sir Cecil Spring Rice, Joseph Chamberlain, Arthur Balfour, and Alvey A. Adee; and the politicians Henry Cabot Lodge, Theodore Roosevelt, and James Donald Cameron. If this group composed an elite, it was a working elite.[110] The intimate friendship of the Hays and the Adamses had begun during Hay's residence in Washington from 1879 to 1881, although they had known one another since 1861, and in the early 1870s had a growing group of mutual friends, the most important of whom was Clarence King.[111] With King, the two couples made up the "Five of Hearts"—a mutual appreciation society, exclusively devoted to gaiety and gossip. Marian Hooper Adams' suicide in 1885 and King's increasingly erratic behavior drew the remaining three members of the group closer together. They accompanied one another to Europe, visited the same people together, and, when apart, carried on a constant correspondence. Through Adams, Hay was introduced to an important group of English statesmen, whose friendship and hospitality he warmly accepted.[112]

But friends and wealth are not enough if your party is out of power. By November, 1887, Hay was writing "I told you so" letters to his "mugwump" friends who had crossed party lines and supported Cleveland.[113] The President's annual message of December, 1887, particularly enraged him because of its low tariff stand. When

Blaine responded to the message with an angry protectionist letter to the *New York Tribune,* Hay was elated both by Blaine's strong hand and by the possibility that the "Plumed Knight" had sounded the signal for a new campaign for the presidency.[114] Hay wrote to Blaine that Cleveland's message had disgusted him, but that Blaine had blown a "clean blast of the trumpet declaring battle and bringing the fighting men well into ordered ranks. You have already given," Hay hopefully predicted, "your platform for the next year."[115] Hay's hopes were soon dashed when Blaine reiterated his decision to retire from politics.

Managing to recover from his dismay, by March, 1888, he was busy kingmaking with his old political confidant Whitelaw Reid. Hay suggested that John Sherman of Ohio would make the best candidate: "If Blaine is irrevocably out, what is the matter with Sherman?" Answering his own question he concluded, "It seems to me Sherman is the best possible man . . . ," and Hay then set out to obtain the nomination for his candidate.[116]

But the effort was unsuccessful, for the Republican convention nominated Benjamin Harrison of Indiana. Disappointed, Hay at first proclaimed that, although he would vote for Harrison, he would do so reluctantly and only out of party loyalty.[117] Quickly overcoming his skittishness, in the early fall he had the Harrisons to dinner. And by October he was writing to Harrison that his election would "save the country, not only from present shame and disgrace, but from the most serious evils and disasters."[118] He donated a thousand dollars to the campaign. When Harrison triumphed at the polls, Hay announced a "glorious victory."[119]

Hay could hardly condemn President Harrison's appointments. The President made Hay's political idol James G. Blaine Secretary of State; his friend Robert Lincoln, Minister to England; and his longtime friend and political ally Whitelaw Reid, Minister to France. Privately, however, he was chagrined that the new President had not called upon him to serve the administration.[120]

Hay would not receive the call for eight more years. Anyone reading over his published correspondence, Thayer's volumes, or Dennett's biography would be forced to conclude that Hay spent the first six years of the 1890s doing very little but writing letters to Henry Adams. For instance, almost every letter in Hay's *Diary and Letters* from May, 1889, to November, 1892, is to Henry Adams, who was out touring the South Pacific. In most of these letters Hay, half joking, half serious, implored his friend Henry to return to Washington where life was "dull as chelsea . . . because you are away."[121] This was not surprising. Henry Adams edited these three volumes of Hay's letters, and as always, Adams presented Hay as Adams wished him to be.

During this period Hay never lost his enthusiasm for politics and, at the slightest excuse, he joined in the fray. Even Adams could not entirely edit Hay's political mania from these letters. By April, 1890, working for a midterm Republican election victory, he returned to the hustings.[122] In October, he delivered a campaign speech to ten thousand people in New York City, but his efforts were in vain. The Republican party went down to smashing defeat in November.[123]

Thayer argued that Hay was unenthusiastic about Harrison's campaign for reelection in 1892.[124] Hay did in fact write to Adams on August 26, 1892, that while "there is, I am told, a good deal of politics about, . . . I know nothing about it."[125] Adams, however, neglected to include in Hay's edited correspondence a letter of June 16, 1892, in which Hay informed Adams that he had contributed a substantial amount to Harrison's reelection campaign fund.[126] Moreover, since the Republican nominee for Vice-President was his old friend and colleague, Whitelaw Reid, he was eager to see a Republican victory and campaigned vigorously, proclaiming to Reid, "How can any honest or rational man be against us this year?" Of course, he confided to his old friend, "If the ticket were turned end for end we should do better."[127] When Harrison and Reid lost to Cleveland and Stevenson, Hay was disappointed.[128]

By the middle of 1893 Hay determined that he must return to public life. If he had subtly sought office for twenty years, his quest would now be more direct. Aside from his long-term desire to hold an appointive position, the depression of 1893 as well convinced him that men like himself must return to public power before the nation was ruined.[129] In believing that this crisis, like many others in America's history, had a single cause: poor leaders and selfish men in power, he had been quite consistent. In his 1861 poem "Esse Quam Videri" he claimed that "the ever-mutable multitude" could avoid deception only if moral leaders held power.[130] In the 1870s he saw evil men as the root of America's corruption.[131] In his 1883 novel, The Bread-winners, he argued that good men, like his hero Arthur Farnham, were all that was needed to save America from either counterrevolution or socialism.[132] Now, in the 1890s he had an obligation to wrest power from the Democrats and their evil allies, who were the real cause of America's economic and political ills.

The Democrats' policies, he wrote to Reid, not only had led to the depression, but also would ultimately bring about "a revolution so complete [that it] will throw us into confusion for years."[133] Cleveland had only one talent according to John Hay, that of "being an ass!"[134] In May, 1894, Hay proclaimed to Henry Adams: "I must take office again" as soon as Cleveland and the Democrats were driven out.[135] Realizing, however, that if he really intended to pick the next President, and in turn, be picked by the next President, he could no longer play the role of reluctant politico, he admitted to Reid, "The men who play politics 365 days in the year have an awful advantage over the gentlemen who play *at* the same game. . . ."[136]

Hay was done playing at politics; now he was deadly serious. He had always desired political power and office, but now, added to his longtime desires was the belief that once again he must take a part in saving the nation from imminent disaster. His attitude was best summed up in an undated memorandum, perhaps written during this period:

It is absurd for the sentimental reformer in politics who scorns political methods to say 'office should go to the best man—one who fights for a nomination is unworthy of it'—as it would be to say 'money should go to the wise, the gentle, the liberal—the men who would use it best.' It might be lovely to have it so, but in this workaday world, honors and wealth alike go to the men who seize them, who love and desire them in a practical and aggressive way. If they were less desirable the gentle and good might perhaps have a monopoly of them.[137]

By the end of 1894 Hay became deeply involved in Mark Hanna's plans to obtain the 1896 presidential nomination for William McKinley of Ohio. A firm supporter of McKinley's presidential aspirations as early as 1891, he gave ardent support to McKinley's campaign for the governorship of Ohio.[138] In 1893 Governor McKinley almost was forced to declare bankruptcy. He had endorsed a friend's note for over one hundred thousand dollars. Unfortunately, the friend forfeited on the note, and McKinley was left to pay.[139] If Governor McKinley went into bankruptcy his chances for the presidency as a hard money man would have been severely, if not irreparably, damaged. Hay along with prominent McKinley backers came to his aid.[140] The Governor was grateful. "How can I ever repay you . . . ?" he asked Hay.[141]

With that problem out of the way, the path was open to launch McKinley's campaign for the White House. Hay, who had been associated with McKinley's political manager Mark Hanna since the late 1870s, served as a key fund raiser for McKinley's organization. Hay's major duty was to obtain financial support from Republican contributors who were not yet committed to McKinley's cause.[142] In pursuit of this goal, Hay traveled widely.[143] He was also assigned the task of trying to obtain the backing of the Pennsylvania delegation for McKinley before the convention.[144]

Hay might have been tempted to retire from public life in the summer of 1895. He was fifty-seven, very ill, often depressed, and the world seemed to be crumbling about him. If he had hope of action from the next generation, it was lost as he watched and listened to the "clamor" of his own son and daughters and their college friends. "The world is still young," he wrote Reid, "but I am sure that you and I were never so young as the boys today. The riddle of the painful world suggested itself to us earlier and more imperatively. The fellows who came of age in the Lincoln years were forced to look at life in wider aspects than the sophomores of today."[145] Both domestic and foreign events had combined to move Hay to action. The depression deepened to the cries of Free Silver, Free Trade, and war with England, as Cleveland tried in vain to stop the drainage of gold from the treasury. Kaiser Wilhelm added his contribution to the instability in the form of a telegram to the Boer President Krueger in January of 1896 supporting the Boer stand against England and encouraging Transvaal independence. In May, Hay went to Europe to view affairs for himself.[146]

As he traveled that spring and early summer in England and on the continent with Adams and "the Bicyclones"—his daughter Helen and a schoolfriend—Hay's fears of dissolution increased, and he became convinced of two things: McKinley must be elected in November, and American representation in England must be corrected and strengthened. He found English public men grossly misinformed about the sentiment in the United States, especially concerning Venezuela. In July, 1895, Secretary of State Richard Olney announced that the United States refused to recognize Great Britain's claim that 108,000 square miles of Venezuela was part of the British Guiana. That December President Grover Cleveland reiterated Olney's warning, noting that the proposed British action violated the Monroe Doctrine. It was "the duty of the United States," Cleveland added, "to resist by every means in its power, as a willful aggression upon its rights and interests, the appropriation by Great Britain of any lands . . . we have determined by right belong to Venezuela."[147]

A Republican, Hay strongly supported the Democratic administration in this dispute and even wrote a letter explaining his view to the London *Times*. Reporting to Secretary of State Olney, Hay noted that Sir William Harcourt (the leader of the opposition) had asked him if McKinley's impending election would have any effect on the negotiations over Venezuela because ". . . Lord Salisbury desired delay in the hope that the next Administration [in the U.S.] may be less exacting than the present." "I told him," Hay wrote Olney, "I thought any such calculation would be a great mistake; that the public sentiment of the United States was virtually unanimous in support of the administration [and] . . . that no steps backward would be taken by McKinley."[148]

In his letters to Olney summarizing his activities Hay told the Secretary of State that his negotiations had support from Harcourt, which had not been made public for fear of embarrassing the government; and Hay also pointed out why the English had evaded and continued to "dread" arbitration. Arbitration had cost them dearly in the past, and, Hay explained, "Chamberlain [Colonial Secretary] seems afraid of making a precedent which may be injurious hereafter in Canada."[149] Olney would have a better chance of getting a quick agreement on arbitration of the Venezuelan dispute, Hay hinted, if it were made clear that the United States was not desirous of setting a precedent from which it would insist on arbitration as the method of settling all the thorny difficulties between the United States and Canada.

Three days after sending his letter to Olney, Hay wrote to McKinley enclosing a check with which the candidate could meet personal election demands, and he promised another each month until November. To this pledge he added:

I want to make one matter perfectly clear. I do not know whether or not I shall ask you for any public employment. It will depend on various

considerations,—health, domestic or business affairs, &c. But whether I do
or not, I want it understood that anything I may have done, or shall do,
between now and next March, shall have no bearing on the case whatever, I
shall feel as free to make known my wishes, and you must feel as free to
grant or refuse them, as if we had never met. You are to be under no
obligation whatever to me, and I am to consider myself under no disability
in regard to you or to the public services.

With that understanding I propose to do everything in my power to
support you and the Republican party in this canvass.[150]

The letter then detailed his English visit. When he arrived in London in the spring, Hay reported to McKinley, he had found English
public men misinformed, and "decidedly hostile" toward the Republicans and favoring the Democrats in the coming election. Hay
spread the word that the Democrats would champion Free Silver,
and when he returned to England from the Continent in July he
found "a wonderful change." "They were all scared out of their wits
for fear Bryan would be elected, and very polite in their references
to you," he told McKinley. Hay outlined his conversations with
English officials, in which, while disclaiming special knowledge or
representation of any kind, he had sought to disabuse the British of
their erroneous idea that the "incoming administration would fall
behind the present one in the firm and resolute upholding of the
Monroe Doctrine."[151]

Not the least of the impressions McKinley would have derived
from the letter was the fact that Hay's advice was trusted and sought
by English leaders, and that Hay did not consider fawning to be the
proper attitude toward England. A clear and unmistakable stand
upon traditional United States policy stressing the control of American affairs by Americans was implicit. He had also made it clear that
he thought there were considerable areas in which cooperation between the two powers would be beneficial to both, economics being
one.

For economic considerations must have been uppermost in Hay's
mind as he threw time and money into the support of "the Majah,"
as Hay called McKinley. Should William Jennings Bryan and the
silver standard win the election, Hay stood to lose a fortune. In
addition to the shock that free silver would cause to the business
community and America's international credit, Hay, like all inves-
tors, believed he would be repaid in coin of far less value than that of

his original investment. Worse, yet, the campaign threatened to divide Americans along class lines, as Hay angrily wrote his Democratic and pro-silver friend Henry Adams in September:

> The boy-orator makes only one speech,—but he makes it twice a day. . . . he simple reiterates the unquestioned truths that every man who has a clean shirt is a thief and ought to be hanged:—That there is no goodness or wisdom except among the illiterate and criminal classes:—That gold is vile:—That silver is lovely and holy,—in short, very much such speeches as you would make if you were here. He has succeeded in scaring the goldbugs out of their five wits;—if he had scared them a little, they would have come down handsome to Hanna. But he has scared them so blue that they think they had better keep what they have got left in their pockets against the evil day.[152]

Returning to the United States, Hay assumed the role of a key Republican speechmaker for the fall campaign. His most important speech, "The Platform of Anarchy," was carried in full by the *Tribune* and other newspapers. It was reprinted as an election pamphlet and widely distributed.[153]

Hay also had proved a very generous contributor to the Republican fund. In October, 1895, he sent Hanna five hundred dollars for the Ohio Republican campaign.[154] The following March he sent McKinley two thousand dollars. Hanna thanked him, adding that he hoped more would be forthcoming.[155] And more was forthcoming. In August Hay had sent McKinley another thousand dollars and promised similar amounts monthly until November. [156] As Henry Adams later wrote, "I would give six-pence to know how much Hay paid for McKinley. His politics must have cost."[157]

Indeed, they had, but they paid off in 1897 when Hay was appointed Ambassador to England. While he clearly desired this post, nevertheless, he actively supported Whitelaw Reid's bid for the spot, so much so that Hay offered to have his name excluded from consideration for a position if it meant that Reid would be appointed. McKinley, however, did not want Reid as a cabinet member or as Ambassador to Great Britain. Instead, the President-elect prevailed upon Hay to aid him in gently excluding the editor. At Hay's suggestion McKinley issued a statement declaring that while he desired Reid's services, he could not in good conscience place the editor's ill health in further jeopardy.[158] Subsequently, when Hay's selection as Ambassador was announced,

Reid was certain that he had been wronged by his old friend. The incident so embittered the editor that their twenty-six-year association almost ended. "Like you," he wrote Hay, "I hate to lose a friend—above all, to lose him because I trusted him and found it a mistake."[159]

Hay's activities during and after the election had persuaded McKinley to choose Hay whom he preferred over Reid. John Hay had secured the second most important diplomatic post that the United States had to offer in 1897. Within eighteen months he would be appointed Secretary of State where he remained until his death in July, 1905. His association with Lincoln, party regularity, and industrial wealth proved the keys to Hay's upward mobility and political success. The "strong god circumstance" played only a minor role.

CHAPTER 5

A Partnership in Beneficence: Hay as Ambassador to England

THEODORE Roosevelt testified that John Hay was so pro-British that he "could not be trusted where England was concerned."[1] Roosevelt, however, missed the point. Hay did admire the British immensely, but that admiration was due to the fact that Great Britain seemed to have the most successful representative and free enterprise government in the world.[2] While Britain retained the veneer of rule by aristocracy, it was possible, Hay believed, for a man of merit to rise to the top of British society and government. Hay admired Britain, not for its aristocracy of birth, but rather because in England, as in the United States, the natural aristocracy of talent was not held back by false feudal values. In short, in Britain the acquisition of power and manners was not limited by birth. Such values were important to Hay, a man who intended to achieve both power and fame. During his first trip to England in 1867 Hay was impressed by men such as Disraeli, Gladstone, and Forster; men of common birth whose success made them symbols of British values and manners.[3]

Hay did object to blatant American prejudice against Britain. He protested the treatment that his friend Henry James received from the American press for his alleged preference for England over the United States. "The worst thing in our time about American taste," Hay wrote Howells, "is the way it treats James. . . . If he lived in Cleveland he could write what he likes, but because he finds London more agreeable, he is the prey of all patriotisms. Of all vices I hold patriotism the worst when it meddles with matter of taste."[4]

Yet Hay's sympathetic stance toward Britain did not make him less vigilant in his support of American interests. He could hardly forget the British Government's pro-Southern behavior in the Civil War.[5] During the 1895–1896 clash between the United States and

Britain over Venezuela, Hay had strongly supported the Cleveland administration's position.[6]

In his Thanksgiving Day speech before the American Society in London in November, 1897, Hay clearly expressed his views on the nature of Anglo-American relations: "The great body of people in England and the United States are friends . . . —any other relation would be madness." The two nations, added Hay, based their mutual relationship on "that intense respect and reverence for order, liberty, and law which is so profound a sentiment in both countries."[7] In many respects, Hay would argue, American and British vital interests were identical. In such cases, cooperation was essential for America's success as a world power. Hay's April, 1898, Easter address drove that point home. He welcomed Britain's successes in "trade and commerce" because he believed that "all the nations in the world will profit . . . from every extension of British commerce and the enterprise and enlightenment that go with it." For his part Hay believed that the United States had nothing to fear from England because the leaders of both nations shared the same world view and thus "all of us who think cannot but see that there is a sanction like that of religion which binds us to a sort of partnership in the beneficent work of the world."[8]

Nevertheless, as Ambassador to Great Britain and later as Secretary of State, Hay was firm in dealing with the British. In 1900, in a fit of exasperation over the constant accusations about his alleged Anglophilia, he wrote: "All I have ever done with England is to have wrung great concession out of her with no compensation, and yet these idiots say I am not an American because I don't say 'to hell with the Queen' at every breath."[9]

John Hay reacted to his selection as Ambassador to Great Britain with gratitude, humility, and triumph. "In spite of all the approval your appointment of me has received here and in England," he wrote President McKinley, "I know the place is far beyond my merits, and that I owe it entirely to your kindly favor and good will." While promising not to "discredit" the President, Hay added that "Even Grover Cleveland says 'your selections for office are all admirable.' "[10] He could hardly be blamed for a feeling of satisfaction, for the post was one which Hay and others prized as a great distinction as well as a potential delight. As one of the unsuccessful candidates for the appointment, Whitelaw Reid had congratulated Hay two weeks before, "You are going to London at the most interesting season, socially, politically, and diplomatically in a quarter of a century; and you are better fitted for all the various duties than anybody we have had there in that time."[11] The German Ambassador, Hermann von Eckardstein, fondly remembered his own ten years at the Court of St. James between 1895 and 1905: "Of all the capitols [*sic*] of Europe," he wrote, "there was never, except ancient Rome, a metropolis where the pulse of the whole world beat so distinctly as in London."[12] A distinction and a delight sought by many had been given by McKinley to Hay and Hay was grateful.

The note of triumph in his letter to McKinley was also genuine; Hay had worked hard for the prize, and he was proud of it. Nations sent their best men to represent them in London; to work successfully with such peers, intellectual and social weight were needed as well as affluence, for the post cost far more than it paid. When he was younger, he had shrunk from the thought of "coining life in dollars," but he had proved most successful in that endeavor. Political importance was also required; and for twenty years, he had been striving to obtain the political weight which Secretary of State William Evarts once accused him of lacking. There were many men, however, of equal political, financial, or social eminence whom McKinley might have sent: Joseph Hodges Choate, Whitelaw Reid, Horace Porter, Chauncey DePew, and Levi P. Morton had all been suggested for the post. What Hay had that others lacked were practical qualifications: twelve years of experience in executive representation, no powerful enemies, an harmonic aura of western and eastern acceptability by virtue of *Pike County Ballads*, Lincoln, and Lafayette Square, and evidence of important contacts in England. Last, and most practical of all, during the past four months McKinley had discovered ample evidence of Hay's talents for grasping and expressing the President's wishes.

Many years later, in something less than a generous spirit, Henry Adams described the diplomatic events of the winter and spring of 1896–97 as the culmination of a process toward which the Adamses had been bringing to bear argument, remonstrance, and war for a hundred and fifty years—"the object of bringing England into an American system." Then, Adams summarized, suddenly, "by pure chance, the blessing fell on Hay." Hay, "understanding nothing of the process," but accepting as natural the growing British belief that her best interests lay in cooperation with the United States, put the "arcade" on the Adams family structure. His family pride assuaged at the expense of evidence he certainly possessed, Adams ended the passage gracefully: "In the long list of famous American Ministers in London, none could have given the work quite the completeness, the harmony, the perfect ease of Hay."[13]

John Hay arrived in London on April 21, 1897, to begin his term as Ambassador. Hay was particularly pleased to have his old friend Henry White as First Secretary. White had long experience at the American Embassy and was quite knowledgeable about British affairs.[14] The Ambassador had opposed the State Department's suggestion that he be a member of the Jubilee Committee sent to congratulate Queen Victoria in the spring of 1897.[15] Instead, he suggested Whitelaw Reid.[16] Ever the manipulator, Hay could both assuage Reid's hurt feelings over not having been chosen Ambassador and avoid too lavish praise for the crown.

Hay believed that among the reasons why Anglo-American relations had broken down so badly in the Venezuela crisis were the complete lack of respect of English public men for Americans, as well as their total ignorance of America.[17] Part of the cause for this attitude was the patriotic extremism of American and British newspaper correspondents. Part was due to the fawning behavior of Ambassadors like his predecessor Thomas F. Bayard.[18] Since all that Englishmen had ever heard from Bayard was endless praise, they were considerably unsettled by the outright hate emanating from Americans during the dispute over Venezuela.[19]

While part of the problem may have been Bayard, a good deal of the difficulty was built into the job. Hay proposed that as Ambassador he should accept as few public speaking engagements as possible, as they were traps for the true representative.[20] No courteous man, asked to speak after a gracious dinner, could avoid complimenting his hosts. Such a course proved difficult. Immediately upon arrival, Hay was obliged to attend a banquet given by the American Society in honor of Bayard. Hay's report to McKinley was succinct: "Mr. Bayard spoke an hour . . . I spoke five minutes. . . . The *Times* printed four lines of his speech and printed my remarks *verbatim*. . . . The fact is, they are sick to death of him, and of his vapid flattery."[21] With heavier irony he wrote to Reid of Bayard: "His last day was pathetic. He wept at the station,—made two long speeches at Southampton and started a third as the ship moved off."[22]

If blubbering would not do, neither would bullying. Yet Hay was almost immediately put in a position which made him appear to be taking a very hard line against the British. The British government had agreed to consider an American proposal for an international conference to discuss American claims that Canadians who hunted Alaskan seals on the high seas (called pelagic sealing) were illegally seizing American property.[23] Much to Hay's chagrin, McKinley appointed former Secretary of State John W. Foster to negotiate the sealing issue with England. From the very beginning Foster alienated Hay by drafting a strong note accusing the British government of rejecting a conference on fur seals for "unsubstantial and inadequate reasons." The note continued for ten pages, charging the British with "indifference amounting to disrespect" for international tribunals, negligence in performance of commitments, and misuse of scientific information for political purposes. Foster concluded by labeling the British Government's policy as "suicidal," "unneighborly," and unapproved by the British people.[24] Appalled, Hay held back the note and wired for wording of a more moderate tone.[25] The State Department, however, ordered him by telegram to submit it as written.[26]

To make matters worse, Foster's entire note was published in the *New York Tribune.*[27] The British press, in turn, reacted strongly against the now public note.[28] Hay privately wrote McKinley that "success was in sight," but thanks to Foster's note "the British Lion is standing on his head and lashing his tail all around the lot." Hay separated the President from what he saw as the unnecessary "severity" of the State Department: "It is certainly not your style—you have the rare gift of being strong and courteous at the same time."[29] These were, of course, qualities which Hay found in Lincoln, and Hay believed he exemplified himself. In frustration over this matter Hay wrote to Adams. "I wish you were here, I need some discreet person to listen to about an hour's steady cussing."[30]

As it turned out, Hay's fears were exaggerated. At the end of July, 1897, Salisbury, who was then serving in the dual capacity of Foreign Secretary and Prime Minister, agreed to send a delegation to a conference on the sealing dispute to be held the following October.[31] Hay replied that in addition to the Canadian, British, and United States delegations, he was going to invite representatives from Russia and Japan.[32]

Hay and his secretary, Henry White, were in a self-congratulatory mood. They believed that Hay's more moderate assurances had placated the British into ignoring the tone of Foster's note.[33] The celebration was short-lived. In September, 1897, the British gave notice that they would not attend the forthcoming conference because the Russians and Japanese had been invited. The British claimed that Russia and Japan had no sealing experts.[34] So the October conference was held in Washington without the British or the Canadians. The delegates from the United States, Japan, and Russia unanimously agreed that sealing on the high seas would be outlawed.[35] Of course, such an agreement was useless without the British.

Hay placed the blame for failure on Foster's shoulders.[36] However, Hay must not have been able to ignore the fact that the British explained that they had refused to attend the conference because Hay had invited the Japanese and Russians. The British never mentioned Foster's May 10 note. Any mention of it would have laid them open to charges of allowing pettiness to interfere with national policy. The Ambassador may well have rued his own provision of an alternate excuse for England's avoidance of a conference which she did not desire under any circumstances.

Seals were not the only controversy between England and America; the silver issue provided another. Contrary to general impression, the 1896 Republican Party Platform was not unconditionally opposed to the free coinage of silver. In fact, the platform supported the free coinage of silver by gaining "international agreement with the leading commercial nations of the world."[37] President McKinley favored international bimetallism, establishing a ratio of silver to gold within which the unlimited coinage of silver would be allowed.[38] Such an agreement would help stimulate the domestic economy of the United States by increasing the money supply as well as by boosting foreign trade. In any case, growing farm surpluses and continued labor unrest required that the Administration redouble its efforts to increase exports.[39] British agreement was essential if international bimetallism was to have a chance for success. Hay thus left for England with instructions from McKinley to set up negotiations for an international conference on bimetallism.[40]

Hay's own views on the subject had changed since 1895 when he had thought that international bimetallism was a useful device by which the Republican party could hold on to its lower-class membership, but "impractical" and meaning "nothing more than the present state of things."[41] He was now convinced that the plan had merit. With international bimetallism, the silver issues would be removed from the passions of politics into that of "science and administration." More important, with the stabilization of silver prices, both outrageous speculation and dangerous inflation would be curbed, lessening the chances for economic and social upheavals.[42]

British policymakers seemed more willing than their public utterances indicated to support bimetallism.[43] Hay's investigation tended to sustain the hope that a conference could be called by the fall of 1897. An important factor in the apparent change of heart by the British was the fact that the flow of gold had changed its direction during the spring and summer and was now favoring the United States.[44]

Britain's support for the conference depended upon two factors. France must agree to be part of such a conference, and the Indian Colonial Government must support it. India had gone off the silver standard in 1893; to return to it now would mean a major reversal in policy and would risk inflation. French policy was to some extent tied to her new ally Russia, who had just adopted the gold standard. If Russia proved opposed to the conference, the French might decline to attend.[45]

The first of these hurdles was nicely cleared by the end of June; the second proved a barrier. The American envoys appointed by McKinley and working with the Ambassador to France, Horace Porter, had "come to an understanding" with the French government and left for England the first of July.[46] By the middle of the month, with the support of the Secretary of the Exchequer and leader of the House of Commons, Arthur Balfour, and the personal and public aid of the French Ambassador, the Baron de Courcel, Hay thought considerable progress had been made.[47] In addition to the official contacts, he had insisted that the commissioners be presented to the Queen, to give them "dignity and standing in the public mind," and had set about bringing them into contact with London court society and London financiers who were notoriously opposed to bimetallism. Two invitations to parties at Buckingham Palace and a luncheon given by the Lord Mayor of London were the results. "They all made friends," Hay reported to McKinley. Of the group, Hay thought Colorado's Senator Edward O. Wolcott the most impressive, for "his whole heart is in the work, but his manner is refined and conciliatory."[48] As Hay gradually built up popular

support, and the commissioners worked, only Charles Francis
Adams presented a problem, "roaring about that neither McKinley
nor Wolcott, nor I want the Commission to succeed."[49] Despite the
delays of diplomatic methods, however, and the blasting of Americans in the British press, Wolcott reported to McKinley in August,
"If trouble comes, I do not think it will come from here, where I
think there is a real desire that our efforts shall prove successful."[50]

Through that summer and fall, however, prosperity relaxed
American pressures for bimetallism, the French became alarmed at
the new United States tariff legislation, and the British position in
the Far East was threatened by Russia and Germany.[51] These
events, over which neither Hay nor the commissioners had the
slightest control, caused the failure of two conferences on questions
besetting Anglo-American relations—bimetallism and the Bering
Straits.[52] Remorsefully, Hay answered Henry Adams' excited demands for *more* evidence supporting his thesis that the world was
disintegrating into financial anarchy, that England would agree to
no conference: "I have been wrestling with England and getting a
disgust with human nature that will last me long. We have not yet
received our answer on *silver*, but I know what it is to contain—
some sinuosity of words, but the substance a categorical negative.
With that we go back to France; she shrugs her shoulders, and backs
out. We go home."[53] Henry White, keeping a close watch over the
meetings of bank directors in London in mid-September, had sent
discouraging word that "at best they had not denied the possibility of bi-metallism" in any of their public statements.[54] By the end of
the month, White's forecast was gloomier; Arthur Balfour had told
him that the Indian Government's decision was made and was "un-
satisfactory, silly," and "stupid," but adamantly opposed to reopen-
ing of the mints at the alleged expense of their export trade.[55] By
October 11, Hay could no longer delay the "bad news" to McKinley.
He had had a long unofficial talk that afternoon with the Chancellor
of the Exchequer, Sir Michael Hicks-Beach, and "in the face of the
unanimous opposition of the business world and of the Indian Government," the Cabinet must refuse a conference.[56]

Hay laid the defeat to several additional causes: the slump in the
price of silver and the improved domestic financial condition had
changed the views of men in the British government and in Commons, and Hay had been faced by the Chancellor with names of
prominent American bankers who had "been talking bi-metallism

for two years, and who now, thinking they can make a little money on the present tide, are working vigorously against us under-hand."[57] The unkindest cut of all had been the information from Henry White that documents had reached the English Cabinet through American bankers indicating that the United States Secretary of the Treasury, Lyman G. Gage, was "going in for a gold monometalism standard in his proposed currency reform."[58]

In his private message to McKinley, Hay did not mention Gage's behavior, for the President should have been aware of it; instead, Hay suggested that, until the English rejection of the conference was made public, *only* Gage be informed. And he carefully tried to make clear to the President that failure was no fault of the Commission. The commissioners had been well chosen to augment British sympathy for further Anglo-American negotiations by a method particularly dear to McKinley and Hay for the settlement of disputes—arbitration. "Wolcott," Hay specified, "has been untiring in energy, tactful and persuasive in argument; has made a most favorable impression on friend and foe. I have done what I could. But circumstances have worked against us more powerfully than any argument."[59] The uses of commissions were an important device by which Hay had hoped to make the Ambassador's position more neutral and thereby more useful to American interests.

By October, 1897, Ambassador Hay could not point to much success. His two assignments—to obtain agreements with the British government on pelagic sealing and bimetallism—had ended in failure. Even in these two matters his authority was diminished by special envoys. The retelling of these incidents seems to lend further credence to the tale that, as a diplomat, John Hay was a dilettante, whose major function as Ambassador was to serve as a figurehead.[60] In sustaining such a view, many of the published accounts of Anglo-American relations during Hay's Ambassadorship neglect his role in attempting to secure Anglo-American cooperation in keeping the Far East open to commerce.[61] Yet, it was in this matter that John Hay was most active; for he not only had to convince the British, who were already inclined to act, but also to persuade his own government that events in China were serious enough to require joint action.

Hay had been concerned about American interests in the Far East at least since the 1870s. As assistant managing editor of the *New York Tribune*, he had written editorials critical of the Grant

administration's Far Eastern policy.[62] In 1880 when the United
States had negotiated a treaty with China reasserting the ban on
discrimination against American trade there, Hay had been Assistant Secretary of State.[63] Extensive information about the Far East
had been provided to him by friends traveling or working there—Sir
Cecil Spring-Rice, Henry Adams, John LaFarge, William S.
Bigelow, and James B. Angell. A growing concern over Far Eastern
markets had surfaced in Hay's novel, *The Bread-winners*. After a
romantic disappointment, the hero, Arthur Farnham, decided to
seek a new frontier as an escape valve for his emotions. "He made
up his mind . . . that he would sail by an early steamer for Japan."
Farnham was not too upset to note that the journey might also yield
some financial return: "I want to get there before the end comes. At
the present rate of progress there is not more than a year's purchase
. . . left in the Empire. I must hurry over and get my share."[64]

In the months prior to his departure for England Hay urged
McKinley to take a firmer stand than that of the previous administration in protecting and extending American interests in the Far
East. Hay warned of an impending crisis in China, [65] events supported his alarm.[66] On November 18, 1897, Germany seized the
important port of Kiaochou in Shantung Province. About the same
time a Russian fleet threateningly dropped anchor at Port Arthur.
Within British government circles there was talk of war with Germany and Russia if China were closed to British trade and investment.[67]

Unofficially the British government sounded out Hay about what
response his government was going to make to the German seizure
of Kiaochou.[68] Reporting this to the State Department, Hay added
that Great Britain favored joint action against the Russian and German threats.[69] Quickly the department replied that the Ambassador
was to make it clear that the United States had no interest in the
territorial expansion taking place in China and no plans to land on
any coast. The McKinley administration, he was to inform the
British, would only guard established American interests in
China.[70]

The *New York Times* and the *New York Tribune*, in identical
stories, reported that the McKinley Cabinet's decision to refuse the
British suggestion of joint response to the recent events in China
"put an end to any possibility of an Anglo-American Japanese alliance such as foreign cables have suggested."[71] Since the British

suggestion for joint action was an unofficial sounding, Hay, unlike the New York press, did not see the administration's response as unconditional. He believed that if the British could be persuaded to make a formal offer to joint action in China, McKinley would consider the matter more seriously. To that end Hay continued to encourage the British to make a formal proposal, while simultaneously attempting to persuade the administration in Washington of the seriousness of the situation in China. Thus Hay in reporting to Secretary of State Sherman stepped up his accounts of British fears of the closing of China. On January 11, 1898, he wrote Sherman at length about First Lord of the Treasury Arthur Balfour's speech on events in China, a speech with which Hay agreed. Balfour saw British interests as commercial and not territorial. "Britain," reported Hay, "asks no exclusive trading privileges and . . . will do their best to see that that [*sic*] equality of opportunity . . . shall not be destroyed."[72]

Even though he had been instructed to the contrary, Hay informed Salisbury that the United States was still receptive to a British initiative offering cooperation in maintaining equality of opportunity in China. He told Salisbury that "if the commercial or other rights of the treaty powers were at all infringed . . . the United States would be the first country with which her Majesty's Government would desire to communicate."[73]

Hay had Henry White send copies of speeches to the State Department demonstrating the gravity with which the British regarded recent events in China. One such speech was by the Chancellor of the Exchequer, Sir Michael Hicks-Beach. Sir Michael made it quite clear how intent his government was about keeping China open. We "are absolutely determined at whatever cost, even . . . if necessary at the cost of war, that the door should not be shut."[74] White reported that Hicks-Beach's views were strongly supported by Joseph Chamberlain, Secretary for the Colonies. Chamberlain, however, went one step further. If there was no way to avoid everyone's taking a piece of China, he warned, Britain would take her sphere as well: "if the acquisition of new territories be indispensible to the maintenance of such free markets Her Majesty's Government would not be adverse thereto."[75] The problem seemed clear to Hay and White: if the United States refused to join with Britain in maintaining an open China, the British would, by taking territory there, join the other continental powers in exclusivity. The great loser in such an event would be the United States, with no territory and no support, and more important, with no access to China's markets.

Hay was serving notice on Washington that if the United States did not move to cooperate with Great Britain in China, Britain would act in such a manner as to exclude further American participation in the China market. Hay believed that the business community in the United States was well ahead of the administration in understanding the importance of what was going on in China. As White reported to Sherman, the government of Great Britain was under the impression that "with regard to the maintenance of free markets, [England] will have the sympathy and support of the people of the United States and not improbably of the Government also."[76] The British government had received that impression, no doubt, from Ambassador Hay.[77]

However, Secretary of State Sherman thought that his Embassy in Britain was unduly alarmed. Sherman had received assurances from the American Minister in Germany, Andrew D. White, that "the harbor of Kiaochau will be open to vessels and commerce of all nations upon equal terms and conditions."[78] In February White again assured Sherman that the Germans had "no intention to close any port to foreign trade and commerce."[79] Hay, however, did not accept the German promises at face value. If the State Department offered no encouragement, there were others in Washington who did. Senator Henry Cabot Lodge wrote to Henry White in February that, "If I had my way, I should be glad to have the United States say to England that we would stand by her in her declaration that the ports of China must be opened to all nations equally or to none."[80]

In March of 1898 an exhausted John Hay left London to tour Egypt and the Holy Lands with his wife and Henry Adams. Efforts to persuade the British to make a formal offer for joint action in China seemed lost. Just as Hay was to set sail up the Nile a cable arrived from Henry White informing him that the British government had decided to make an official proposal to the United States for joint action in China.[81] White reported that, unlike Sherman, the British government "does not believe the promises of Germany and Russia with regard to their ports would hold good any longer than it suited the convenience of those powers."[82] What apparently had confirmed the British fears was the German government's refusal to allow the construction of a British and American financed railway in Shantung province. The Germans had vetoed the project on the ground that if such a railroad were to be built in their sphere it must "be of German material and built by German engineers."[83]

Pleased by the British offer, Hay was eager to return to London and to "the fuller information I shall get there."[84] The case of the German veto of the railroad had proved Hay correct. While the State Department saw the open door to China safeguarded so long as American goods could be unloaded in Chinese ports, Hay and the British government argued that if transportation and investment were controlled exclusively by other powers, the right to land in the port cities would be worthless.

If anything, however, by March, 1898, the administration in Washington had grown more reluctant to join any plan committing itself to action in China. The problem of Cuba had reached the crisis stage. Whether he believed it or not, President McKinley in rejecting the British note alleged that "advices up to the present time indicate no foreign occupation which interferes with that trade or aims at exclusive commercial privileges."[85] In any case, the Russian government also had assured the United States that while they intended to keep Port Arthur closed for military and strategic purposes, they had no desire to occupy Chinese territory other than Port Arthur and would not interfere with the trade of other nations.[86]

Charles Denby, the American Minister to China, argued that events in China were much more serious than the administration supposed. Denby, writing on the same day that the Russian assurances arrived, insisted that the Russians must not be trusted, and urged his government to cooperate with the British for "with our moral support Great Britain might, even now call Russia to give an account of her plans . . . and save our treaty rights." If the United States did not join with the British, Denby warned, England may also take an exclusive sphere.[87]

The administration, if not perfectly satisfied by the Russian guarantees, had Cuba and Spain to worry about, and the added pressure that Hay now exerted did not bend the State Department. On March 25, Hay warned that there was "an understanding between Russia, Germany, and France to exclude as far as possible the trade of England and America from the Far East and reduce China to a system of tributary provinces."[88] Four days later Denby confirmed Hay's estimate of the urgency of the situation: "The action of Russia renders it almost certain that England will follow the example set by Germany, Russia, and France, and will in turn demand the cession of territory." Denby argued that German and Russian promises to allow American trade in their ports would not guarantee the open door for United States commerce. "If Germany, France, and Russia proposed simply to open new ports to the trade of the world nobody could object; but," Denby warned, "they claim . . . jurisdiction exactly as if they owned ceded territory. They will construct all the railroads, and work all the mines."[89]

On April 11, 1898, the probable war with Spain over Cuba became unavoidable. Hay spent much of April attempting and succeeding in securing British sympathy for the American position in Cuba.[90] All during the war with Spain he continued in his efforts to bring about an Anglo-American agreement on the Far East. He still did not accept the administration's decision on the British offer for cooperation as final, especially given the high stake he believed his country had in China.[91] His doubts were leaked to the British press and on April 15 an article in the *London Daily Chronicle* noted the great concern of unnamed American "officials" about the future of China. The *Chronicle* argued that American and British interests were identical and it urged an understanding between the two nations on China.[92] The next week, at the Annual Easter Banquet given by the Lord Mayor, the Ambassador delivered an address urging Anglo-American cooperation.[93]

Admiral Dewey's victory at Manila Bay made Hay "very happy." With the Philippines in American hands he saw added incentive, as well as an important power base, for the United States to act with Great Britain in China.[94] Setting out to gain British acceptance of American occupation and annexation of the Philippines, Hay knew that he would have little trouble. The British, seeing American possession of the archipelago as assurance of further American commitment to the Far East, as well as a safeguard against German expansion in the Pacific, had told him that they would not oppose the American course.[95]

Throughout May Hay continued in his efforts to convince the British government that the United States ultimately would cooperate to maintain an open China and to persuade his own government of the urgent need for action to avoid a breakup of China. On May 13 Chamberlain made an extremely pro-American speech in which he urged Anglo-American cooperation in the Far East. The Colonial

Secretary admitted that joint action in the Far East might lead to war, but he asserted that "terrible as a war may be, even a war itself would be cheaply purchased if, in a great and noble cause, the Stars and Stripes and the Union Jack should wave together over an Anglo-Saxon Alliance."[96] Admitting to Henry Cabot Lodge that "Chamberlain's startling speech was . . . due to a conversation I had with him," Hay urged Lodge that action must be taken in the Far East as soon as possible for "It is a moment of immense importance not only for the present but for all the future. It is hardly too much to say the interests of Civilization are bound up in the direction the relations of England and America are to take in the next few months."[97]

On May 29, McKinley writing to Hay "the longest [letter] I have sent to anyone" recently, urged Hay to keep him personally informed about the British position.[98] In his response on June 3, Hay seized the opportunity to appeal personally to McKinley to reconsider the subject of the British proposal of March 8 for Anglo-American joint action in China.[99] But the President saw his priorities differently. Sherman had resigned as Secretary of State and was replaced by Assistant Secretary of State William R. Day. McKinley directed Day to inform Hay that the suggestion was still inopportune, but that "the outcome of our struggle with Spain may develop the need of extending and strengthening our interests in the Asiatic continent."[100] When John Hay was appointed Secretary of State in August, 1898, the time seemed more opportune than ever for the United States to act in China. President McKinley knew full well what Hay's attitudes were toward American commercial interests in China, and these strong views may well have been a significant factor in McKinley's choice of John Hay for Secretary of State.[101]

John Hay departed from England without achieving satisfactory solutions to the three main problems he set out to solve: pelagic sealing, bimetallism, and cooperation with Britain in China. While he had been successful in maintaining British neutrality in the war with Spain and British acquiescence to America's retention of the Philippines, there had been no significant opposition on either of these matters. Yet he regarded his tenure as a great success and, it is fair to say, so did British policymakers. The reason, in part, was that John Hay was the first in a line of American ambassadors whose job was to discover ways in which Britain and the United States could cooperate on issues involving third parties rather than on ways they could avoid conflict with each other. The American Revolution was finally over, and John Hay proved to be a fine representative for what would become, in effect, a new alliance.

CHAPTER 6

The Open Door Notes

A S Secretary of State for William McKinley, John Hay was able to bring together and to test many of the strands of his world view. Hay's belief in the need for strong executive leadership was exemplified by McKinley.[1] Such leadership could unify the nation and reaffirm its commitment to republican principles. As Secretary of State, Hay was in a special position to insure that domestic unrest could be avoided. For, so long as the agricultural and industrial structure continued to produce, it would require of its government both protection for its output and markets for its surpluses.[2] He believed that the social fabric of America rested upon its industrial growth, which, in turn, required that its government (especially its executive branch) lead the way in creating conditions which promoted individual competition, thus insuring national prosperity and a society open to talent.

Therefore, Hay's policy in the Alaskan boundary dispute or in relation to the need for a transoceanic canal reflected the requirements of the modern industrial nation that the United States had become. More important were the Secretary's famous Open Door Notes. The Notes are symbolic not only as a key to Hay's foreign and domestic ideology but also as a logical capstone for much of the foreign policy of post–Civil War America and as a foundation for United States foreign policy in the twentieth century.[3]

Certainly Hay's views on the direction that American foreign policy should take were not unique. Indeed, had they been, McKinley would never have appointed him. In fact, Hay was, as we have seen, the perfect representative of the post–Civil War America. What was unique was his opportunity to cement, through foreign policy, so much of what Lincoln and the Civil War had made possible.

Born in preindustrial America, Hay now lived in an industrializing modern state, and sought to make the machinery of the State Department more efficient. The department virtually had been

101

without a head for well over a year, as the aged and infirm John Sherman proved unable to handle the task. His replacement that April by Assistant Secretary William R. Day had been a temporary appointment made necessary by the exigencies of the Spanish American War.[4]

Even under ordinary conditions, refitting the department's organization and reviving its morale were formidable tasks. For the war had projected America from the quieter waters of insular concerns into the storms of competing empires. Hay's friend and neighbor, Henry Adams, took one look and confided to an English correspondent that the administration's task was impossible— "converting an old Mississippi-raft of a confederate government into a brand-new ten-thousand-ton, triple screw, armoured, line of battleship is the work of a hundred years."[5] The Secretary dismayed Adams by undertaking it.

The first of the duties before the new Secretary of State, the building of a department capable of carrying out the complexities of policy besetting a world power, was, Hay believed, hamstrung by an old enemy—the Senate. No amount of compromise, reasoning, or patriotic urging could curb the Senate's greed for control of diplomatic offices, and no amount of patronage could satiate it.[6] For the Achilles' heel of the Executive in the area of foreign affairs, he concluded, was and always had been "the advice and consent of the Senate." Thirty men could undo the labors of nations and the policy of years.[7]

Nevertheless, Hay had his way with several major diplomatic appointments. Despite his assertions that he had no hand in choosing diplomats, the Secretary managed to bring his friend, the Far Eastern expert William Woodville Rockhill, into the department, to retain the valuable services of Henry White in London, and to urge McKinley's appointment of Joseph Hodges Choate as Ambassador to Great Britain.[8] With Rockhill's knowledge of the Far East, the irreplaceable contacts of Henry White in England, and the adroit legal mind of Choate as Ambassador, he had three trusted friends in key positions implementing his policy. His old colleague of Madrid days Alvey A. Adee would be his Assistant Secretary, and with Adee on the job, Hay proclaimed, "The country is safe!"[9]

When McKinley appointed Hay to office, he was already identified with the closer cooperation of Great Britain and America in the troublesome areas of the Pacific and the Caribbean.[10] It had been Hay who informed the President that Britain would support the United States in a quick annexation of Hawaii before the war with Spain got underway. The British feared that Germany would demand Hawaii after the war, just as she had claimed territories from the victors after the Greco-Turkish and Sino-Japanese wars.[11] It had also been through Hay that McKinley learned of Britain's action warning Germany not to oppose the United States during the Spanish American War.[12]

Despite the hostility of continental powers evidenced during and after the war, Hay and McKinley were aware that America's serious threats even in wartime were not all external. They had seen America through the Civil War, and that was not an easily forgotten experience. Unlike McKinley, Hay had been reexposed to that experience during his writing of the Lincoln *History*, and his rediscovery in 1878 of his own diaries of the period. He had considered as facts and had used as such the materials in those diaries which repeatedly noted the urgency of maintaining national unity, the dangers of military subversion of civilian authority, and the congressional challenge to Executive leadership.

Hay had applauded the use of force against Spain, but he well remembered the threat which military men like McClellan and Frémont represented. As he told a British audience during the war, it was "a lamentable necessity of the present condition of the world, that if a nation would have peace it must be capable of war."[13] Warriors were necessary—they were the force behind sound policy—but they were inherently dangerous to republican institutions.[14] Moving to avoid this danger after the Spanish American war, he urged the appointment of Elihu Root, a noted New York lawyer, as Secretary of War rather than a military man.[15] And when the President sought his advice about going to New York to meet Admiral Dewey, victor at Manila Bay, Hay bluntly told McKinley that the Admiral should come to the President: "For you to travel all the way to New York to take part in a municipal demonstration in honor of a naval officer returning home from a tour of duty would be a compliment never before paid, I believe in the world's history."[16] McKinley received Dewey in Washington.

In this and other matters McKinley trusted Hay and relied on his advice beyond foreign policy matters. The President also shared Hay's distrust of the Senate. It had been the fear of a Senate veto which caused McKinley to annex Hawaii by joint resolution of both

Houses.[17] Some Senators were so outraged at the President's ma-
neuver that they held up implementation of a Joint High Commission to settle Canadian-American disputes from March, 1898, until
August.[18] Such action only reinforced McKinley's views. Nevertheless, Hay and the President accomplished much of what they set out
to do, albeit with the Secretary complaining loudly about "that un-
speakable Senate."[19]

As Secretary of State, Hay continued to deal with the issues that
concerned him when he was Ambassador to Great Britain. Only
now, he was fully in charge. In the following chapter we shall discuss many of these issues, especially Canadian-American relations
and the trans-Isthmian canal.

A month after entering upon his duties as Secretary of State, a
dispute arose which may have provided a precedent for Hay's tactics
regarding China and the Open Door Notes. In the fall of 1898,
reports of French and German coercion of Liberia (a nation founded
by United States citizens and populated with many former American slaves) aroused Hay to determine if Salisbury would be interested in "concurrent" but separate Anglo-American moves toward "moderating the appetite" of the European powers.[20] Hay's
actions in trying to bring pressure to preserve the governmental,
commercial, and territorial integrity of Liberia were not entirely
disinterested. That African state was one of the few nations which
attempted to follow the American model of republican government.
In addition, the Navy had expressed interest in the Liberian coast as
a possible naval base or coaling station, and there was the American
desire to keep Liberia open for future trading and investment opportunities. The Liberian government had even suggested trade
and investment concessions in return for American guarantees of
Liberia's territorial integrity. Added to all of this were the pressures
of American Methodist missionaries who urged Hay to protect
Liberia from foreign encroachments.[21]

As a result, Hay directed his Ministers in Berlin and Paris to
protest any moves by Germany and France which endangered the
commercial or territorial integrity of Liberia.[22] Under Hay's and
Henry White's urging the British government sent similar but separate notes.[23] The Secretary's notes to the Germans and French were
an attempt to obtain an agreement on the principle of the open door
in Africa without resort to treaty or to the threat of military force.
Responding to the messages, Germany and France accepted the

principle of Liberian political independence and freedom of competition for all powers in Liberia.[24] Hay had gone through a successful rehearsal for his China policy.

By the end of December, 1898, the diplomatic outlook matched the weather: harsh, destructive, and cold. The Joint High Commission was in virtual collapse; tentative canal negotiations were in abeyance; Anglo-American cooperation in the Far East appeared less than hopeful; the House rejected Hay's request for increased funds for the consular service; and the President hesitated to present the treaty with Spain to the Senate.[25]

The treaty with Spain was finally ratified on February 6, 1898, by the narrow margin of fifty-seven to twenty-seven.[26] The major obstacle to ratification was the annexation of the Philippines, which were not intended to become states and were on the verge of revolting against their American occupiers. The islands contained a potential market of seven and a half million customers. That market was just five hundred miles from the four hundred million potential buyers of China. McKinley had made the connection between the retention of the Philippines and the China market explicit in his instructions to the American peace negotiators in 1898. Retaining the Philippines, McKinley argued, was necessary as a "legitimate means for the enlargement of American trade." The President noted, as his Secretary of State would soon reiterate, "we seek no advantage in the Orient which are not common to all. Asking only the open door for ourselves, we are ready to accord the open door to others." As McKinley viewed the matter, American commercial expansion "depends less on large territorial possession than upon an adequate commercial basis and upon broad and equal privileges."[27] In his Annual Address of December 5, 1898, he enlarged upon this theme, noting that "The United States has not been an indifferent spectator of the extraordinary events transpiring in the Chinese Empire." The threat of the exclusion of America's "vast commerce" by the European powers in China and the resulting "revival" of Chinese restrictions requires "the fullest measure of protection . . . for any menaced American interests."[28]

It was precisely because Hay shared these views among others that the President decided to appoint him Secretary of State. After all, Hay had been urging McKinley to take action in China since early 1897.[29] On the Secretary's first official day in office riots broke out in Peking. Acting quickly, he dispatched two gunboats from

Manila and telegraphed American Minister Edwin Conger to "act vigorously for the protection of Americans" and their property.[30] As a result of this prompt action, the New York Chamber of Commerce adopted a resolution expressing its "high appreciation" to the Secretary of State for protecting American commercial interests in China.[31] Petitions and letters flooded the State Department during his first year in office demanding firm American action in China aimed at protecting and extending American trading and business enterprises.[32]

New troubles broke out in the Far East in December of 1898 when reports began to filter back to the State Department that France was pressing for larger concessions in Shanghai. Hay instructed Conger to warn the Chinese not to yield.[33] Within this context the British government made a final attempt to obtain American cooperation in keeping the door open in China. On January 8, 1899, Salisbury cabled his Ambassador to the United States, Sir Julian Pauncefote, that the British government planned to protest against the French extensions in Shanghai. Salisbury knew that the United States was making similar objections and suggested that "if these protests were made conjointly their force would thereby be much increased."[34] As much as Hay may have desired to join with the British, both he and McKinley realized that such a move would have serious domestic political repercussions.[35] Instead, as in the Liberian situation, the Secretary sent a separate note to the French which paralleled the British position. Hay presented Sir Julian copies of his correspondence with the American Minister in China, Conger, and kept the British up-to-date on all information he had and Pauncefote did the same.[36]

The inability of Hay and McKinley to cooperate openly with the British in issuing a joint protest played into the hands of those in the British government who had been urging that Britain take her own sphere.[37] Thus in April, 1899, Great Britain concluded a treaty with the Empire of China extending to the British exclusive rights in the coast city of Weihaiwei. The British also obtained an exclusive railroad concession connecting Nanking with Shanghai and strengthened their position in Yunnan and Kwantung province.[38] The United States remained the only major world power without a sphere of influence in China.

Lord Charles Beresford, a member of Parliament, had been sent to China by the British Associated Chambers of Commerce in the fall of 1898. A strong advocate of maintaining an open door in China, Beresford's trip confirmed his fears that equality of commercial opportunity was in serious danger.[39] Before leaving for the Far East he had discussed his views with Hay, who was then serving as Ambassador to Great Britain.[40] When he became Secretary of State, Hay instructed all diplomatic and consular officials in China to cooperate in providing Beresford with any information or aid he might require.[41] On his part, the British agent kept Hay informed of his findings in China beginning in November, 1898, until he landed in San Francisco in February, 1899.[42] For two weeks Beresford, urging support in pressuring the European powers and Japan to cease their dismemberment of China, at Hay's suggestion, traveled from the Pacific to the Atlantic coast. The British emissary spoke to influential groups in San Francisco, Chicago, Buffalo, New York City, and Washington, D.C.[43] After arranging a meeting between McKinley and Beresford, Hay gave a luncheon honoring Lord Charles, an affair to which he invited those Senators upon whom he wanted to impress the urgency of the situation in the Far East.[44]

Events seemed to confirm the most pessimistic assessments. The Italian government hinted that it intended to establish its own sphere at Sun Mun Bay, near Shanghai. By late February rumors abounded that the Italian fleet had set sail for just such a purpose. On March 1, Conger cabled Hay that "This action of the Italian Government is only additional evidence . . . that China is going to pieces." The American Minister suggested taking a sphere since "a strong foothold here by the United States . . . might compel them [the other nations] to keep open the door for our commerce."[45] Hay, however, opposed taking territory in China, as he wrote Paul Dana, editor of the *New York Sun:* "We do not think that the public opinion of the United States would justify this government in taking part in the great game of spoilation now going on." Nevertheless, the Secretary assured Dana that the State Department was "keenly alive to the importance of safeguarding our great commercial interests in that Empire."[46]

When Hay assumed control of the State Department he had requested McKinley to transfer William W. Rockhill to Washington from his position as Minister to Greece.[47] Rockhill was an expert on the Far East whose judgment the Secretary trusted and whose advice on China he desired during this critical period.[48] Returning to the United States in June, 1899, Rockhill was immediately assigned the task of reviewing the Shanghai cession.[49]

That same month Alfred E. Hippisley, a British citizen and former member of the Chinese Maritime Customs Union, arrived in Washington. Rockhill knew Hippisley rather well and the two spent long hours discussing the impending breakup of China. They agreed that immediate action was essential for the open door's preservation.[50] Rockhill, who kept Hay informed about his conversations with Hippisley, took the latter to meet with the Secretary of State in the middle of July.[51] Hay, of course, agreed that something ought to be done regarding the situation in China; however, he disagreed with them on several issues—especially on timing. Rockhill and Hippisley urged immediate action,[52] but the Secretary was less impulsive, explaining that he would not act until he was certain of success, for while he was "fully awake to the great importance of what you say . . . the senseless prejudices in certain sections of the 'Senate and people' compel us to move with great caution."[53]

In early August Hay toyed with the idea of trying to get a treaty signed by all the powers involved in China and pledging adherence to an open door.[54] However, he feared that the Senate might not ratify such an agreement.[55] Thus, by the end of August the Secretary was convinced that a unilateral pronouncement would be the best tactic, and he doubted that the Senate would interfere.

Several events combined to convince Hay to act. The most important was the Tsar's Ukase of August 15, 1899, declaring Talien a free port. The American Minister to Russia, Charlemagne Tower, assured the Secretary that the Ukase meant that Russia agreed in principle to an "open door to China."[56] Clearly Hay could argue that he was asking from the Russians no more than they already had pledged.

Also important was the support of the ardent anti-imperialist Jacob Gould Schurman, President of Cornell University. In order to alleviate anti-imperialist pressures, McKinley had appointed Schurman to the Philippine Commission and sent him to the islands to investigate events there. The trip apparently alerted the educator to the need for strong United States action in the Far East.[57] Upon his return from the Philippines, Schurman proclaimed that the closing of China was an event which the United States must avoid: "China . . . should maintain its independent position, . . . its door should be kept open."[58] The impact of Schurman's comments, when added to the growing number of influential men urging action in the Orient, was crucial.[59]

Finally, public opinion was shifting in favor of action in the Far East to protect American interests. Hay had labored to help turn the tide of popular feeling in this direction and by the end of August the Secretary could feel confident that he had succeeded.[60] Beresford's book, *The Breakup of China*, as well as A. R. Colquhoun's *China in Transformation* were receiving wide circulation in the United States.[61] Newspapers, general circulation magazines, and commercial journals were printing article after article about the breakup of the Celestial Empire.[62] Hay was no longer certain, as he had been in the beginning of August, that his attempt to take action regarding the situation in China would be "foredoomed to failure."[63]

Although concerned with "Alaska, and Samoa and China, and Nicaragua and the other outlying nurseries of woe and worry," Hay focused on China.[64] On August 24, 1899, he requested Rockhill and Hippisley to outline their plan on the subject of an open door.[65] The memorandum which Hippisley formulated was essentially the same one which Rockhill sent to Hay. Some scholars maintain that Hay's Notes were merely a copy of Rockhill's August 29 memorandum.[66] However, the difference between what Hippisley and Rockhill suggested and the document which the Secretary of State ultimately issued was significant. The Rockhill memorandum urged the acceptance of existing spheres of influence and demanded only equality of trading opportunity within them.[67] In fact, Rockhill underlined that "the spheres of influence *are an accomplished fact.*"[68] Rockhill emphasized that the powers could not be expected to relinquish their extraterritoriality. Hay did not accept this argument. Perhaps the United States could not convince the other nations to give up their spheres at once, but the State Department did not have to legitimize the powers' rights to these areas. The Secretary reasoned that by refusing to recognize the spheres of influence, the United States could retain a lever for the future. Thus Hay's Open Door Notes, issued on September 6, 1899, asserted that "the United States will in no way commit itself to a recognition of exclusive rights of any power within or control over any portion of the Chinese Empire under such agreements as have within the last year been made."[69]

Hay, of course, did not imagine that his circular would convince

France, Germany, Russia, Japan, Italy, and England to relinquish their portions of China. Instead, he asked those nations (whose spheres he refused to recognize) to pledge that in their districts "the current Chinese treaty tariffs would apply, that duties would be collected by the Chinese Government and that equality of harbor and railroad rates would obtain for merchandise and vessels of all nations."[70] In short, he demanded equality of economic competition for all nations trading and investing in China. He was certain that in such free competition the United States would generally be the victor and that point was not missed by those other powers active in China. The reaction to the Notes by those nations was hardly enthusiastic.

Received with "disquiet" in England, and with qualifications there and elsewhere, negotiations continued through the fall. The most common reaction was similar to that of Great Britain, which would assent only if the others agreed to the "general principle." The British, however, would not return Kowloon which bordered on Hong Kong.[71] Russia replied at first that it would agree only if France would.[72] But when France's reply went further than Russia meant to go, the latter retreated to a vague statement which clearly was meant to exclude all of Manchuria.[73] In February, after repeated attempts to remove some of the "strings," as Rockhill called them, the State Department settled for the fact that Russia would allow herself to be interpreted as having responded "favorably" to the American notes, and would agree that "all privileges accorded to any nation within the Russian sphere of interest should be accorded also to the United States."[74] In a circular on March 20, 1900, Hay announced the "final and definitive" agreement of all the powers, and no one chose to contradict him.[75] As Rockhill described it to Hippisley, "none of the European Powers are prepared to have this question made a subject of heated debate and controversy. . . ."[76] "Peace hath her victories,/ No less renowned than war," quoted William R. Day in his congratulations to Hay. "By moving at the right time and in the right manner, you have secured a diplomatic triumph in the open door' in China of the first importance to your country, and [added] greatly to your personal credit and renown."[77] The press echoed Day's sentiments.[78]

The Open Door Notes also may be seen as an attempt on Hay's part to bypass the Senate, and the divisive effects of a congressional debate upon American foreign relations in an election year. As his initial letters to the American ambassadors made clear in 1899, the legal basis of American trading in China rested upon treaties with China whereby America was granted concessions equal to those of the "most favored nation." If China were destroyed, so also would be the legal basis of American trade. Another alternative would have been for the Secretary to negotiate treaties with all the powers holding leases and claiming spheres of influence in China. But to obtain the same privileges as "the most favored nation," from each of them would have entailed some yielding on the part of the United States—such as an extension of the "open door" to the Philippines. But concessions were not feasible. " 'Give and take'—the axiom of diplomacy to the rest of the world is positively forbidden to us, by both the Senate and public opinion," as Hay wrote Reid. "We must take what we can, and give nothing—which greatly narrows our possibilities."[79] Hay therefore tried to achieve by public "assurances" what he could not have achieved by treaty.

At a minimum the Notes demonstrated that America intended to have a stronger voice in Far Eastern affairs. That voice had been given resonance by the earlier annexation of the Philippines. In the summer of 1900 the policy had its first major test. In the midst of the Boxer uprising against foreigners in July of 1900, Hay took two of the weakest elements of his original notes a giant step further. Having originally stated that the United States did not recognize the "exclusive" rights of the Powers in their "so-called 'spheres of interest,' " and having requested that the Powers allow the Chinese government to maintain a clear right of sovereignty—the collection of customs duties in each sphere—Hay announced in a circular note that the policy of the United States favored safeguarding the administrative and territorial integrity of China and extension of the principle of the Open Door to all her parts.[80]

Clearly, Hay hoped that the Boxer Rebellion would not be used as an excuse to close China to American commerce. None of the powers chose to contradict the assumptions of his circular of July 3, yet he well knew that all were making military preparations and he suspected that most were making private agreements which would violate whatever was left of the Empire's sovereignty. No word had come from the besieged European legations in Peking for a month. The world knew that the German Minister had been killed, and with the breakdown of communications it believed that the legation had been massacred. This belief offered ideal justification for the final spoilation of China. The Chinese Ambassador, Wu Ting-fang, brought Hay a communication from the government at Peking on July 11.[81] Hay moved quickly. If China could get word out, then China could get word in. Here was her chance to prove that there existed a responsible government—some tangible basis for American support for her "integrity." Hay drew up a cipher telegram to his Minister in the besieged legation at Peking, Edwin Conger. Handing the telegram to Ambassador Wu the afternoon of July 11, he asked Wu to "devise means to get it to Conger & obtain an answer."[82] Then he waited, while continuing efforts to "localize the storm" to the area of the uprisings, and safeguard central and southern China from European invasion and pillage. "If I looked at things as you do in the light of reason, history and mathematics," he wrote Adams, "I should go off after Lunch and die. . . . But I take refuge in a craven opportunism. I do what seems possible every day—not caring a hoot for consistency or the Absolute—and, so far, I sleep o'nights, in spite of universal war and a temperature of 99° steady."[83] On the nineteenth of July he signed Rockhill's commission to go to China; even if Conger were alive, Hay wanted more accurate information on Chinese affairs and someone there with a firmer grasp and understanding of his policy than the Minister had.[84] Then, on the twentieth, Ambassador Wu jubilantly brought Hay the long-awaited answer to his telegram to Peking. The foreigners in the legations were alive.[85]

Hay released the news immediately to the press, despite his own doubts of its authenticity.[86] He could not afford to discredit news which supported his policy assumptions of China's governmental integrity.[87] On August 3, all suspicions were allayed, Conger's wire was proved genuine, and the tensions were over.[88]

Hay alone publicly held out against the universal and convenient belief of the total collapse of the Chinese government and the massacre of the legations.[89] He now pushed the point and asked of China "immediate and free communication" by all countries with their ministers, suggesting that the imperial authorities give full information about the legations and cooperate with the relief expedition in the liberation of the ministers and the restoration of order.[90] Those in control in China grasped Hay's point.[91] Communications were restored and the authenticity of Conger's message was verified to the world. On August 14 the relief expedition of American, British, Russian, Japanese, and French troops arrived and the legations were delivered.[92] Congratulations poured upon Hay from every quarter.

To the world it looked as if John Hay had curbed the European plundering of China, saved the lives of the foreign diplomats, and produced a "concert of powers" from a wrangling group bent upon the "mutilation" of China—but Hay knew better.[93] First of all, five thousand American troops had to be sent (mostly from Manila) to China to save the United States Legation during the rebellion.[94] The Secretary persuaded McKinley to keep the troops in Peking after the immediate crisis had passed in order to insure that the other nations involved would not employ their military presence to dismember China.[95] Thus the open door, paradoxically, depended upon American military involvement. While Hay realized "the inherent weakness" of attempting to maintain the open door under such conditions,[96] he told Reid that he was determined "to hold on like grim death to the Open Door."[97] The American press, however, in a chauvinistic mood, praised Hay's actions, in both the July 3 circular and in his sending of troops to Peking, as humanitarian gestures, neglecting the fact that they had earlier urged intervention for more practical reasons.[98] The way the press and often the Secretary viewed things, the extension and protection of American commerce were both moral and humanitarian. Hay well knew that it was not his moral stance that had induced the powers to agree to his proclamations about equality of opportunity and the territorial integrity of China. "The talk about 'our preeminent moral position giving us the authority to dictate to the world,'" he wrote Adee, "is mere flapdoodle."[99] The other nations had listened because the United States had sent troops and because those nations distrusted each other so thoroughly that Hay's Notes and actions gave them a basis upon which to check the aggrandizement of one another.

The Open Door Notes and the July circular established a potential, rather than a real, position of authority for the United States. Yet Hay believed them to be an essential statement of American foreign policy. With an open door in China he hoped to retain the best of two worlds; for the policy promised the benefits of commercial expansion without colonial entanglements in China. In a free competitive atmosphere, the belief was that the United States would win out. Yet, some colonial entanglements had underpinned the open door from the very first, such as the annexation of the Philippines, Hawaii, and military presence in Samoa. And, while the open door promised to provide a way to maintain American interests in China and to avoid armed intervention, it led to military intervention as the Boxer Rebellion revealed. Most clear, however, was the fact that China was to be the object in all of this. Hay had demanded the territorial integrity of the Empire, not for its own sake, but as the best way to protect American interests there. In a sense, his open door was more selfish than the policy of spheres of influence. Most of the powers were willing to settle for a slice; Hay wanted the whole pie.

Many present-day historians argue that Hay's Open Door Policy was a failure, in that it ultimately did not preserve the territorial integrity of China and because the China market remained a mythic, rather than a real, area for American commercial expansion.[100] While such criticisms are accurate, they seem to miss the real significance of Hay's policy. First, the Open Door Policy is important, not in relation to its success or failure in China, or even in its possibility of success, but as a key to understanding the thinking of American policymakers during this period. Hay, McKinley, and others believed that the open door was essential to America's long-range survival and American foreign and domestic decisions were formed and effected in that context. Secondly, the central assumption of the Open Door Policy—that commercial and investment benefits could be maintained and extended without direct military and political involvement by supporting the political integrity of states who offered equality of commercial opportunity—did not die with its failure in China, rather it grew to be a cornerstone of United States foreign policy.

CHAPTER 7

An Informal Alliance

THE other issues John Hay handled as Secretary of State were much less dramatic than his Open Door Notes, but they were not less revealing. Hay's policy and attitude toward Great Britain remained as they had been, cooperative when interests were mutual, as almost always Hay believed them to be. Nevertheless, he willingly employed Britain's involvement in the Boer War to press American claims for the abrogation of the 1850 Clayton-Bulwer treaty binding the United States to refrain from building a trans-Isthmian canal without British consent. Hay's primary goal continued to be the erection of an informal alliance between the two English-speaking nations in order to spread America's commerce, values, and power around the world. Yet other aims figured in his policy. Just as America had wasted its strength and weakened its institutions in Civil War, so would liberalism be vulnerable if divided against itself. The emerging nations had not followed the American republican model, and among the powers, England and America alone seemed committed to the notion, as Lincoln put it, "That popular government is not an absurdity." They thus had a mission, a "partnership in beneficence." It was a task which had grown more urgent with the increasing strength of Germany and Russia.[1]

While the Congress, especially the Senate, as well as influential Republican leaders, such as Lodge and Roosevelt, often disagreed with Hay's tactics toward Great Britain, they did not dispute his goals. Although he often argued bitterly with the Senate and others in his party, those disagreements should not be overemphasized in analyzing the thrust of his foreign policy. In a sense much of the internal debate among policymakers over foreign relations during this period seems trivial today because those arguments were not substantive. Rather than review every diplomatic event of the

115

McKinley Administration—which, in any case, has been done by others in greater detail than space here allows[2]—this chapter will concentrate on Hay's policy toward gaining exclusive rights in building a canal in Central America and its relation to general Anglo-American affairs. These negotiations, similar to those surrounding the Open Door Notes, illustrate clearly his policy and world view as McKinley's Secretary of State.

After several false starts, the United States and Great Britain agreed to establish a Joint High Commission to resolve disputes between the United States and Canada.[3] Disagreements remained over pelagic seal fishing in the Bering Sea, the Canadian-Alaskan boundary, the Newfoundland fisheries, and trading reciprocity. The discovery of gold in the area of the disputed Alaskan boundary two years before and the subsequent building-up of a series of claims and counterclaims by the population of the gold lands made the issue potentially explosive. Any hopes for quick solutions which Hay may have had began to deteriorate in October, 1898, when the American commissioner, John A. Kasson, reported from Quebec that negotiations were becoming "tedious" with much discussion and little accomplishment. The problem was that the Canadians were inadequately prepared, "unsettled," and "indefinite" about their claims.[4]

The commission opened its Washington phase in December, and Hay discovered that the Lord High Chancellor of England, Baron Farrer Herschell, appointed to "smooth down the asperities of the Canadians," as Henry White phrased it, was in reality dedicated to sharpening Canada's arguments and strengthening her claims.[5] Hay wrote White in London to do what he could with Colonial Secretary Joseph Chamberlain toward pressuring Herschell; for contrary to the hopes of those who had suggested and approved his appointment, Herschell was "by far the worst member of the Commission to deal with, [he was] technical sharp often violent and shows the narrowest kind of lawyer's attitude on everything."[6] White contacted the Colonial Secretary immediately, quoting large sections of Hay's remonstrance. He wired the Secretary that Chamberlain was quite willing to accept suggestions "privately" for settlement of the points in dispute, and wanted to know exactly on what points "he might bring pressure on the Commissioners."[7] Hay's response was quick: "In the case of Alaska, it is hard to treat with patience the claim set up by Lord Herschell that virtually the whole coast be-

longs to England. . . . We are absolutely driven to the conclusion,"
he protested, "that Lord Herschell put forward a claim that he had
no belief or confidence in, for the mere purpose of trading it off for
something substantial. And yet, the slightest suggestion that his
claim is unfounded throws him into a fury."[8]

Herschell, however, believed in the Canadian case he had so
carefully formulated and staunchly defended, and made the Alaskan
boundary the *sine qua non* of the commission's work. Refusing to
treat or settle the eleven other matters on which there was a substantial basis of agreement, he adjourned the commission in February, 1899, and thus closed down not merely the negotiations on
which the commission was concerned, but the negotiations between
Hay and the British Ambassador, Sir Julian Pauncefote, over an
interoceanic canal treaty as well. The Canadians were convinced
that the continued existence of the Clayton-Bulwer treaty was their
major source of leverage against the United States. The Dominion
government successfully urged upon Salisbury that to settle a new
interoceanic canal agreement before the Canadian claims were settled would be unfair to Canada.[9]

If the acquisition of the Philippines made American trade in the
Far East more significant, it also made more urgent the building of a
canal in Central America. Of all the controversies preventing
Anglo-American understanding, the Clayton-Bulwer treaty was the
biggest, for in order to prevent England from building an Isthmian
Canal, America, in effect, had prohibited herself from doing so.
Getting rid of that restriction was a paramount aim of the McKinley
Administration.[10]

Hay's policy showed its consistency with that of his predecessors.
In November, 1898, he obtained from former Secretary of State
Richard Olney permission to use the memoranda and materials
which had resulted from Olney's canal discussions with Pauncefote.[11] If Hay was to get a treaty through the Senate, he would need
many Democratic votes and might more easily obtain them if the
work of Democrat Olney were incorporated into the treaty.[12]

The former Secretary's cooperative reply to Hay granting full use
of the materials included a memorandum he had made in 1896: "The
canal shall always be free and open in time of war as in time of peace
to vessels of commerce and of war. The canal shall never be subjected to the exercise of the right of blockade."[13] Thus Olney's
thinking, and presumably Cleveland's, had followed the precedent

of the Suez Canal negotiations, as well as the Clayton-Bulwer treaty's principle of neutralism.

Considering Olney's memorandum, Pauncefote's personal experience in the Suez Canal Convention negotiations in Paris in
1885, and Hay's strong preference for the use of concerts of international power in lieu of American military force, the resulting convention which Hay and Pauncefote agreed upon in 1899 should not
have been a surprise. It removed the restrictions imposed by the
Clayton-Bulwer treaty against an American-built American-owned,
and American-operated canal, and like the Olney memorandum, it
retained the Clayton-Bulwer treaty's neutrality provisions. As in the
case of Suez, the canal's neutrality was to be guaranteed not only by
England and America, but also by inviting other nations to agree.
By this convention, America could build an international, unfor-
tified waterway, open to all nations on an equal basis "in peace as in
war."[14]

There is no evidence in the Hay papers or letters concerning
Hay's thinking about the canal which is contrary to the resulting
convention. He submitted it to the scrutiny and suggestion not only
of Olney but also of his predecessor William R. Day, McKinley, and
the international lawyer John Bassett Moore.[15] Having achieved his
major point of removing the prohibition against America's building a
canal, the Secretary was satisfied.[16] It is unlikely that he ever considered fortifying the waterway. Hay believed that a canal is a very
vulnerable outstanding hostage—one bomb can render it useless.
Like Suez, the American canal would be located in foreign territory,
and it would depend largely for its safety upon the goodwill of the
people through whose lands it passed. The Suez precedent of a
neutral canal, the neutrality of which was guaranteed by international agreement, appealed to McKinley and Hay as realistic and
compatible with their Open Door Policy.[17] Ostensibly, the gains
from the convention were all American; for Britain gave up a great
deal and received no more than any other nation. The canal would
benefit American trade more than English commerce. There was
certainly nothing in the treaty to cause Great Britain to hurry in
signing it. Nor did she.

With the failure of the Joint High Commission in the winter of
1899, negotiations of the canal treaty faltered, for Britain understood that in obtaining concessions from the Americans in the settlement of other problems her strongest pressure came from the

continued existence of the Clayton-Bulwer treaty. And Hay, in February, 1899, was furious when Henry White informed him that the English would not sign a canal convention as long as the Alaskan boundary remained unsettled. But events in South Africa in 1899 favored Hay's hopes.[18]

No doubt these occurrences convinced the London government in October, in the face of strong Canadian objections, to accept Hay's *modus vivendi* [temporary agreement] on the boundary dispute.[19] Britain's involvement in the Boer War, beginning in October, 1899, proved the importance of external pressures for Anglo-American amity. Hay's proclamation of the traditional American policy of neutrality operated to the advantage of Great Britain—the power controlling the sea. A neutral America might also encourage the neutrality of other nations.[20]

While officially the United States remained impartial, it would be difficult to characterize Hay's activities as evenhanded. He strongly supported the administration's efforts to prevent the Republican Presidential Nominating Convention from passing a plank supporting the Boers, and he actively discouraged all attempts by the Transvaal Free Orange representatives to gain his support in negotiating an end to the war.[21] Privately, the Secretary compared the British actions in South Africa to his own country's policy toward the Philippine rebels.[22] He wrote to his son Adelbert, who was serving as United States Consul in Pretoria, that the British would be victorious. In personal letters to Adelbert and to others Hay betrayed his enthusiasm for the British cause as well as his fears of the consequences their defeat would bring.[23]

In September of 1900, Hay wrote White enclosing a letter which he asked to have shown to Arthur Balfour, but instructed White: "do not let him keep it, and do not let it be copied . . . I wish no record of it to remain." The enclosure was dated January 8 and referred to a visit to Hay from the German Ambassador, who wished a joint German-American demonstration against Great Britain on seizures of ships made during the Boer War in Delagoa Bay. "The Secretary of State declined—saying cases were dissimilar. The Ambassador did not seem unfriendly to England: but rather agreed with Secretary of State who said, "a definitive defeat of British Army would be a calamity to the whole civilized world."[24]

That Hay intended whatever aid to Britain American neutrality offered is very clear from his private statements. "The serious thing," he wrote Adams, "is the discovery now past doubt—that the British have lost all skill in fighting: and the whole world knows it, and is regulating itself accordingly. It is a portentous fact, altogether deplorable in my opinion, for their influence on the whole made for peace and civilization. If Russia and Germany arrange things, the balance is lost for ages."[25]

Hay, however, was not above playing on the Boer War to press his nation's claims, and he expected that the British would prove more flexible given American policy during the war. For instance, Hay chose the annexation of the Transvaal in September, 1900, as the occasion for sending Balfour the copy of the United States' response to the German request for condemnation of the British actions at Delagoa Bay. Hay hoped this might persuade the London government to approve the Hay-Pauncefote agreement and to pressure the Canadians to resume negotiations on the Alaskan boundary. Nevertheless, the British resisted signing the canal treaty. Some members of Congress threatened direct action to obtain an Isthmian canal. While Hay complained to Henry White that the Senate's action would destroy any chance for an agreement with Britain, he simultaneously urged Senator James T. Morgan, the bill's sponsor, to continue to press for a bill revising the Clayton-Bulwer treaty. Hay told Morgan that he saw "no reason why your work on the bill should be checked."[26] Morgan's bill passed in January, 1899, and the Secretary vigorously congratulated the Senator.[27] The bill, however, was stalled in the House of Representatives. In December, 1899, Congressman Peter Hepburn introduced legislation in the House, which like Morgan's, called for the building of a canal and the ignoring of the Clayton-Bulwer treaty.[28] It seemed likely that Morgan's proposal would be combined with Hepburn's.

Hay informed the British that he might not be able to deter Congress from unilaterally abrogating the Clayton-Bulwer treaty. In January, 1900, he urged both Pauncefote and Choate to make strong representations to Lord Salisbury to approve the Hay-Pauncefote agreement before the Congress acted.[29] Ambassador Choate reported to Hay on February 2 that he had told the Prime Minister that "the country was getting urgent for the building of a canal, and that if he decided to sign the concert it would go to the Senate at once, and probably be acted on promptly—before the discussion of any legislation."[30] Choate's warning was supported by Pauncefote's letter to Salisbury of January 19, which, after reviewing the case, ended simply: "America seems to be our only friend just now and it would be unfortunate to quarrel with her."[31] The Prime Minister agreed and instructed his Ambassador to sign the canal treaty and on February 5 Hay and Pauncefote affixed their signatures to the agreement.

"Mutilated" and "mangled" by amendments, the treaty passed the Senate December 20, 1900, and Hay detailed its misadventures the next day to Choate.[32] Submitted the preceding spring, it had immediately caused fears among the Republican leaders. What Hay had thought would be a brilliant asset to McKinley's election campaign of 1900, Republicans on the Senate Foreign Relations Committee, wary of the anti-British sentiment, were loath to touch. They debated, added an amendment canceling the prohibition against fortifying the canal in cases of American national interest, and adjourned.[33] After McKinley's victory in November, new forces had gathered in opposition to the treaty, all of whom Hay abused bitterly. To obtain passage, more amendments were added, and the Secretary feared that the British would, with justice, reject the treaty. He further suspected that the rejection would cause the Congress to override a presidential veto of outright abrogation of the Clayton-Bulwer treaty. Despite the amended treaty's flaws, Hay urged its acceptance by Britain and hoped she would see that the "substance is, after all, unchanged," and say, "Take your treaty, Brother Jonathan, and God send you better manners."[34] But the British found that the substance *was* changed and rejected the amended treaty in March, 1901. The amendments placed the United Kingdom under a handicap in time of war; unlike any other nation, she would not only have to respect the neutrality of the canal but protect it.[35]

Hay was furious with the Senate; its action surprised even him. He wrote to White, "I have never seen such an exhibition of craven cowardice, ignorance, and prejudice [and] . . . it never entered into my mind that anyone out of a madhouse could have objected to the Canal Convention."[36] Nevertheless, he believed that a canal treaty was essential if Anglo-American commercial cooperation was to be continued in the Far East and around the world.[37] That the United States would build a canal was inevitable; Hay wanted it built with

Britain's blessing, but, of course, under America's control. Thus he put his pride to one side and tried to develop a treaty which would please both the Senate and the British.

What did the Senate want? The amendments, the opposition press, and Senate debate reflected a demand for United States control over an American canal. The Senate and the press seemed perfectly willing to open it on an equal basis to the ships of all nations, "in time of peace," but not "in time of war." And they were not at all prepared to invite agreement from other nations. That had been a useful device by which to protect American interests in China, but in Latin America such a course was considered to be a violation of the Monroe Doctrine. Lastly, sentiment demanded that the Clayton-Bulwer treaty not be revised, but abrogated. All of these points Hay carefully included in the new treaty, and just as carefully explained in his letter presenting the treaty to both Senator Shelby M. Cullom and Lord Pauncefote.[38]

The British government had not objected to the treaty, but to the treaty as amended; and since Senate ratification of any treaty necessitated the inclusion of its amendments, Hay's task was not simple. Perhaps from his long association with Julian Pauncefote, added to the lucid picture of British policy contained in Ambassador Choate's dispatches and his own understanding of the men and the problems involved, the Secretary gained his insights.[39] From whatever sources they came, they seemed accurate. The essence of Britain's resistance originally had been pique. They were conceding a great deal by giving up the Clayton-Bulwer treaty at a time when they had many unsettled claims with America, and this generous gesture had been unappreciated. The Senate had dismissed their concession in "a clause," and then, without consultation or further negotiation, had released America and all other nations from the principle of neutrality "in time of war," but left Great Britain bound.[40]

Hay began resolving conflicts by soothing British sensibilities. Removing the abrogation of the Clayton-Bulwer treaty from the relative unimportance of a clause, he gave it the dignity of article one. The United Kingdom agreed that the United States could own, build, operate, and control a canal for which America alone assumed the "burden" of maintaining neutrality and security. Having assumed this burden, the United States could fortify the canal.[41] The words "in time of peace and in time of war" were deleted; thus, during war, both parties could revert to their natural rights of self-defense. In deference to the Monroe Doctrine, other nations would not be called upon to join the convention, but all nations using the canal were held to its rules of neutrality and equality of use, and in article six, the canal was declared to "enjoy complete immunity from attacks or injury by belligerents."[42]

Hay had found a way all could follow, and then set about getting others to see and approve it. The British were pleased at a solution to the controversy.[43] The Senate was consulted and was satisfied that its intentions had been recognized, and during the summer it sent unofficial representatives to England for consultation.[44] No one desired a canal controversy—everyone wanted a canal. Even Theodore Roosevelt, so major and voluble an opponent of the first treaty, worked for the passage of the second.[45] Henry Cabot Lodge "broke his back" getting it through, as Hay wrote White after ratification.[46] The Second Hay-Pauncefote Canal Treaty, presented April 25 to Great Britain, and passed December 16, 1901, by the Senate with a vote of seventy-two to six, was the result of his labors.[47]

Hay added to the general favor toward negotiations and conciliations by presenting to Lord Pauncefote on May 5 two drafted conventions for solution to Alaskan controversies which the two men had been patiently working out since Lord Herschell's death in 1899.[48] The three proposed treaties thus separated the areas of contention and pointed different ways to their solutions.[49] The Alaskan boundary *modus vivendi* stabilized the area adequately until the Senate ratified the agreement by which the boundary could be determined on February 17, 1903.[50] It was a most successful spring's work. Alone and with others, Hay had separated the issues causing friction between Britain and America, and set forces in motion for their solution. He had also united Senate action with administration purpose.

The failure of the first canal treaty reaffirmed Hay's view of the Senate as an outdated institution, for he still considered the Senate the enemy which had hampered Lincoln's leadership and which had checked and slowed many of his own plans. The upper house remained a vestige of the principle of states' rights incarnate, a small minority thwarting the good of the whole nation. When Lodge defeated the Newfoundland Treaty in 1902 because it was unacceptable to the fishermen of one town—Gloucester, Massachusetts—he merely underlined Hay's point.[51] And when in 1904 the Senate refused to allow Hay to accept the Medal of the Legion of Honor, voted by the French Republic to honor America's role in maintaining world peace, it made the point personal.[52] Committed to the Union, Hay served the Executive, not the Senate. Until his death on June 2, 1905, he was negotiating and signing arbitration treaties, which the Senate refused to pass. With the arbitration treaties he hoped to remove many international disputes from the scene of senatorial contention.[53] They might not pass during his tenure, but his friend and chosen successor, Elihu Root, would get them through.

The successful and popular passage of the canal treaty made 1901 a year of triumph for Hay; it was also the most tragic year of his life. To demonstrate American neutral conduct during the Boer War, President McKinley, unknown to the Secretary of State, had chosen Hay's eldest son, Adelbert, to represent the United States in the delicate post at Pretoria, the Boer capital in the Transvaal.[54] On Adelbert's return from this mission in the spring of 1901, McKinley had asked him to become his private secretary and thus begin the path to public affairs on which his father had started forty years before. Hay's pride was very great; even greater was his grief in June when his son died.[55] What must have plagued him was the senselessness of Adelbert's death; he allegedly had fallen from a window while sleeping on its wide ledge. "He was a part of all our lives; our hopes, our plans, our pride, our affections were all so bound up in him, that we find wherever we turn, something broken, crippled, shattered, torn," Hay confided to Reid.[56] Reeling from the loss, he limped through the summer's work on the canal and peace in China. Then in September, the President was assassinated; it was the third assassination of a President in Hay's lifetime. McKinley's death on September 14 was followed by that of Hay's oldest friend, John Nicolay, twelve days later.[57] In December, his beloved friend Clarence King succumbed to tuberculosis in Arizona.[58] With some ruefulness the Secretary must have viewed Theodore Roosevelt's Christmas greeting: "I am very, very sorry; I know it is useless for me to say so—but I do feel deeply for you. You have been well within range of the rifle fires this year—so near them that I do not venture to wish you a merry Christmas."[59]

Despite his grief, his age, and illness, Hay, like all the other members of the Cabinet, had offered his resignation or his services to the new President upon McKinley's death.[60] The night before

McKinley's funeral, Hay met Roosevelt's train in Washington, and wrote of their interview to Adams:

> . . . in the station, without waiting an instant, [he] told me I must stay with him—that I could not decline nor even consider. I saw, of course, it was best for him to start off that way, and so I said I would stay, forever, of course, for it would be worse to say I would stay a while than it would be to go out at once. I can still go at any moment he gets tired of me, or when I collapse.[61]

As McKinley's Secretary of State Hay had accomplished much of what he had set out to do. Anglo-American cooperation, Hay's goal since his term as Ambassador to Great Britain, was placed on a solid foundation. The Open Door Notes and the Second Hay-Pauncefote Canal Treaty were personal triumphs that reflected Hay's view that foreign policy decisions must be tied to domestic realities. His actions in both the issuance of the Open Door Notes and the canal treaty mirrored his belief that the growing industrial structure required expanding foreign markets. He had hoped that in gaining access to new areas the United States could maintain economic advantages without direct political involvement. Such a policy also aimed at lessening the chances of direct conflict with the other major industrial powers of the world. The Senate often seemed to Hay to be the greatest obstacle to achieving either of those goals. Therefore, he continued to urge strengthened executive power over the exercise of foreign relations.

His service under McKinley was personally satisfying in that Hay had been intrusted with the management of America's foreign relations. With the help of Adee, Choate, White, Rockhill, and others, he had directed the State Department. With McKinley's death that began to change. For increasingly Hay was overshadowed by Theodore Roosevelt. Yet, he remained to serve the new President, for Roosevelt's actions fit what Hay had demanded since his association with Lincoln—strong executive leadership unhampered by legislative restraints.

CHAPTER 8

Policy and Tactics: The Final Years

TEN days after John Hay's death in July, 1905, President Theodore Roosevelt wrote to Senator Henry Cabot Lodge that
Hay's "name, his reputation, his staunch loyalty, all made him a real
asset of the Administration. I had to do all the big things myself, and
the other things, I always feared would be badly done or not done at
all."[1] Roosevelt's harsh judgment of Hay, however, was more reflec-
tive of the stylistic differences between the two men than of Hay's
performance as Secretary of State.

The personal relationship between John Hay and Theodore
Roosevelt was an ambivalent one. Hay was of Theodore's father's
generation, and during the 1880s and 1890s the generational lines
had been distinctly drawn between the two men. In the years immediately preceding his ascension to the presidency, Roosevelt's
views of Hay's diplomatic abilities were contradictory. The younger
man often wrote gushing letters of praise to the older man. For
instance, In February, 1899, he congratulated Hay for his "great
work" as Ambassador to England and as Secretary of State which
"your children's children will recall with eager pride. You have led a
life eminently worth living, oh writer of books and doer of deeds!"[2]
However, he was much less enthusiastic about Hay's performance
when writing to others.[3] When, as Governor of New York, he
openly criticized Hay's handling of the first Hay-Pauncefote Treaty
as "a great error," Hay exploded.[4] In a terse letter he asked
Roosevelt, "Cannot you leave a few things to the President and the
Senate, who are charged with them by the Constitution?" He angrily instructed Roosevelt: "Please do not answer this—but think
about it awhile."[5]

Hay thought Roosevelt too immature and too quick in judgment
to be trusted with the vice-presidency, let alone with the presidency. When rumors began to circulate around the capital that
126

Roosevelt might receive the vice-presidential nomination in 1900, Hay deprecated the idea. In a letter to Henry Adams, Hay mockingly described Roosevelt's intrigues in pursuit of high office. "Teddy has been here: have you heard of it? He was more fun than a goat."[6]

Nevertheless, when Roosevelt was nominated, Hay quickly sent off a letter of congratulations which showed none of his earlier displeasure: "You have received the greatest compliment the country could pay you. . . . Nothing can keep you from doing good work wherever you are—nor from getting lots of fun out of it."[7] When Roosevelt was subsequently elected, Hay betrayed other feelings on the matter to his friend Henry Adams. After all, he conceded, it could have been worse, Bryan could have been elected and he ". . . is quite too halcyon and vociferous. He would be worse than Teddy; yes, I tell you worse. For Teddy will probably want to occupy his chair [as President of the Senate] a good deal, and so must hold his tongue."[8]

When Roosevelt was elevated to the presidency through the death of McKinley, Hay wrote to the new President that "If the Presidency had come to you in any other way, no one could have congratulated you with better heart than I."[9] His tone was more frank with Henry Adams: I "shuddered at the awful clairvoyance of" your phrase "about Theodore's luck. Well, he is in the saddle again."[10]

Generally, Hay and Roosevelt maintained a proper and often friendly relationship with one another. To third parties, however, each revealed ambiguous feelings about the other. Nevertheless, this ambivalence was truly one of temperament and personal style. No doubt these differences were evident in each man's tactical approach to particular foreign policy issues; yet these tactical differences should not be accorded more importance than they merit. For on general policy issues, as well as on broader ideological questions, there was no real distance between them. Roosevelt might think Hay too cautious and Hay might believe Roosevelt too reckless, but both men agreed that an interoceanic canal must be built, that the door to American commerce must be kept open in China, that Anglo-American ties should be strengthened, and that the military and naval power of the United States should continue to grow. They differed only on how to pursue such goals most effectively.

Roosevelt understood this perhaps as well as anyone. Although after Hay's death the President's own statements often added to the speculation that the split between the two men was serious,[11] Roosevelt noted "how futile it was for . . . my enemies to try to draw the distinction between what Hay did and what I did." The President explained, "The same people who, not because they cared for Hay, but because they hate me, insisted that everything of which they approve in the management of the State Department was due to him . . . hope thereby to damage or irritate me."[12] No doubt, Roosevelt was so annoyed by such rumors that he often became his own enemy.

Yet from the very first the President wanted Hay to stay on as his Secretary of State.[13] In later years, he claimed that he had retained Hay only because "In the Department of State his usefulness to me was almost exclusively the usefulness of a fine figurehead."[14] While it is true that after 1903 Hay's illnesses made it almost impossible for him to function as Secretary of State on a day-to-day basis, his decreasing control over foreign affairs was not due, as Roosevelt claimed, to Hay's "moral timidity which made him shrink from all that was tough in life."[15] Rather, his loss of power resulted from the President's belief that if something were to be done correctly, Roosevelt must do it himself.[16] In fact, it was fear of Roosevelt's arrogance, in part, that convinced the ill and aging John Hay that he must stay on as Secretary of State in order to restrain the young President from wrecking through enthusiasm what Hay and others had built through patience. As Hay wrote to Adams, Teddy "told me I must stay with him—that I could not decline or even consider. I saw, of course, that it was best for him to start off that way."[17]

Initially Hay had some limited success in guiding the robust President, or at least his letters and diary betray the fact that Hay thought he had succeeded in controlling Roosevelt's passion. In September of 1902 King Edward VII of England wished to induct Roosevelt into the Royal Regiments as an Honorary Colonel. Hay discreetly stopped the movement before the President could find out about it. He congratulated himself for avoiding a "nasty" Senate debate over British "merits."[18] In December, 1902, the German government invited Roosevelt to arbitrate the German dispute with Venezuela over Venezuelan debts to Germany. The Secretary of State was alarmed that Roosevelt might accept since the United States also had unsettled claims against Venezuela.[19] Hay quickly and quietly arranged to have the Hague Court arbitrate the

German-Venezuelan dispute. When his plans were within hours of being accepted, he was alleged to have exclaimed, "I have it all arranged. I have it all arranged. If Teddy will keep his mouth shut until tomorrow noon!"[20]

Hay's ability to divert Roosevelt from controlling the State Department was shortlived, if not stillborn. By the middle of 1903 the Secretary of State complained to his wife of the President's attitude and actions in ignoring Hay's advice: "McKinley . . . gave me all his time until we got through: but I always find T. R. engaged with a dozen other people, and it's an hour's wait for a minute's talk—and a certainty that there was no necessity in my coming at all." Mrs. Hay obviously did not carry out her husband's instruction to "destroy this mutinous and disloyal letter as soon as you have read it."[21]

Even when Hay got his way with Roosevelt, the victory led to exasperation. In the summer of 1902 Hay persuaded the President to submit the Alaskan boundary dispute to a six-man tribunal (consisting of three Americans, two Canadians, and one Englishman), even though Roosevelt had consistently resisted such a proposal.[22] However, the three American commissioners appointed by the President—Senator Henry Cabot Lodge, Secretary of War Elihu Root, and former Senator George Turner—did not meet the intent of the Hay-Herbert Treaty of 1903, which specified that the tribunal be made up of "six impartial jurists."[23] The Secretary of State was angered at what he considered to be Roosevelt's breach of faith in appointing Lodge, Root, and Turner. Angrier still was the Canadian Prime Minister Sir Wilfred Laurier, who urged Hay to persuade the President to reconsider his choices and appoint "impartial jurists" since Lodge and Turner had "both in public and private speeches widely circulated . . . practically proclaimed that they could not approach the question with an open mind."[24] The London Government, which was not adverse to having the boundary resolved in a manner favorable to the United States, was annoyed at Roosevelt's heavy-handed action. Chamberlain protested to Henry White that "it would have been so much easier and would have commanded so much influence" if Roosevelt "had appointed judges or lawyers who were not connected with the Government or who had not committed themselves publicly against the Canadian claims."[25] Officially Hay defended the President's choices, but privately he protested loudly to Roosevelt.[26] To White, Hay wrote that he could "well appreciate" the Canadian and British objections: "The presence of

Lodge on the Tribunal is from many points of view regrettable.[27] Roosevelt took a different view of his Secretary of State's dissent. To the President this was only more evidence that Hay "could not be trusted where England was concerned."[28] The entire affair so exasperated the Secretary that he offered his resignation to Roosevelt.[29] Roosevelt, however, asked him to continue.[30]

In any case, while the British stalled in protest over Roosevelt's appointments, they finally agreed to convene the tribunal in September, 1903.[31] The Canadians appointed two commissioners and the British appointed one, Lord Chief Justice Alverstone. The British government realized that if the tribunal failed to reach a boundary settlement the earlier *modus vivendi* might fall apart and the entire boundary issue might never be resolved. Such an inconclusive state would surely result in serious clashes between America and Canada. Lord Alverstone therefore voted to support the position of the United States as did, to no one's surprise, Lodge, Root, and Turner.[32] The tribunal's decision was one that both Hay and Roosevelt had desired. What separated them was an argument over the best tactics to achieve it. In the end, no doubt, both Hay and Roosevelt were convinced that the other man almost had dashed all hopes for a favorable settlement.

More important, the handling of the Alaskan boundary dispute clearly demonstrated that Roosevelt intended to assume direct control over the State Department. The President's success extended even to weakening the Senate's ability to interfere in the process of foreign relations, except in those cases where he welcomed such interference. Hay had called for increased executive control over foreign affairs ever since his days as Lincoln's secretary. Thus it was ironic that he proved to be a victim of sorts of his own policy and vision. He no doubt understood the irony, and perhaps that fact explains his willingness to remain as Roosevelt's Secretary of State and to support the President publicly long after his own influence over State Department policy had diminished.

An example of this is to be found in Hay's defense of Roosevelt's actions when the government of Colombia refused to agree to his terms for the proposed Isthmian canal. The President wished to "at once occupy the Isthmus anyhow and proceed to dig the canal."[33] A United States backed revolution soon broke out in Colombia, and a new nation, Panama, was established. Panama willingly agreed to Roosevelt's terms for the canal, including the cession of a six-mile-wide piece of territory across the Isthmus of Panama. The press castigated Hay as well as the President for their part in the Panamanian revolution. Hay maintained the fiction that Roosevelt had acted legally. He wrote to Root in February, 1904, that the President had followed a "perfectly regular course" as required by "the Constitution, the laws, and the treaties."[34] In private, however, he was more forthright. Having preferred the route through Nicaragua, he was quoted as telling one friend that he was "disgusted with the necessity of dipping into endless turmoils involved by bolstering up the spectres of government in these homes of anarchy."[35] Nevertheless, he had spent a good deal of his own time during the McKinley Administration obtaining the right of the United States to build an interoceanic canal. That he was persuaded of the necessity for such a waterway cannot be doubted.[36] Again, he may have quarreled with Roosevelt's tactics, but he had no wish to reverse the result.

Hay believed that reciprocity treaties could be an important lever for the expansion of American commerce, while simultaneously protecting domestic American industrial and commercial production. They would also have the added benefit of making nations so interdependent that the possibilities of wars would be lessened.[37] Therefore, as Secretary of State he hoped to establish a pattern of reciprocal treaties as a model for future Secretaries. The test came with his negotiation of a reciprocity treaty with Newfoundland in the fall of 1902. He wished to renew and to expand the 1890 treaty which Secretary of State Blaine had negotiated, allowing the free entry of certain Newfoundland fish into the United States in return for free bait for American fishermen and the free entry of specified American manufactured goods into Newfoundland.[38] Moreover, Newfoundland-Canadian relations were less than cordial, and he hoped that the Newfoundland government would support the United States in its claims against the Dominion.[39] Sir Robert Bond, Governor of Newfoundland, negotiated with Hay a five-year extension and expansion of the Blaine-Bond Convention. The Hay-Bond agreement included a free entry of Newfoundland salted cod into the United States.[40] Senate Foreign Relations Chairman Henry Cabot Lodge objected to this new treaty, since the Newfoundland fish would come into direct competition with cod from his own state, particularly from Gloucester, Massachusetts. Also, Lodge's son-in-law, Robert Gardner, was a candidate for a congressional seat in that district, and Lodge feared the Hay-Bond Treaty might cost Gardner his seat in the November election.[41] Hay was furious at what he viewed as Lodge's narrow and personal self-interest deterring a policy of profound national significance.[42] Roosevelt, however, seeing the dispute as a private affair between Hay and Lodge, remained neutral, thus leaving Hay alone to fight the Senate, where the treaty was stalled until January, 1905, and ultimately amended in such a manner as to insure Newfoundland's rejection.[43] Roosevelt was disturbed by the entire affair and blamed Hay: "The Newfoundland business is most unlucky. No treaty ought to have been attempted," he wrote Lodge. "I am to blame for not having discouraged Hay. And Hay is to blame for refusing to consult anyone who knew anything of the subject."[44] The Secretary was embittered by this defeat, which served to reaffirm his belief that the Senate's main function in foreign relations was to destroy creative policies.[45]

Perhaps the Newfoundland reciprocity treaty issue was one instance in which Hay believed he had a substantive rather than a tactical difference with the President. Yet Roosevelt had instructed Lodge not to scrap the treaty entirely: "Where there are good objections to the treaty, amend it; but show a real purpose of trying to get it."[46] Nonetheless, Hay was convinced that the tactical differences in this matter between himself and Roosevelt and Lodge were serious enough to disrupt shared policy goals.

Of all the Presidents Hay served, Roosevelt was probably the most influenced by Hay's own work. It had been Hay who issued the Open Door Notes, which led to Roosevelt's arbitration of the Russo-Japanese War. And it was Hay's diplomacy with Great Britain which paved the way for the Panama Canal. Indeed, Roosevelt's whole reliance upon an Anglo-American understanding, and the many alternatives which that reliance afforded, were due in major part to the work of John Hay since 1897. While Hay lost the personal battle for control over foreign affairs to the President, in most cases, he could hardly complain about the results—the strengthened Executive, a canal connecting the Atlantic with the Pacific, and the end to the Canadian-American disputes over the Alaskan boundary. Moreover, he often could not disagree with Roosevelt's tactics.

For years the State Department had been harassed by missionary societies whose missionaries were kidnapped or mistreated and who demanded redress. Turkey was one of the worst offenders. Files of correspondence had been built up protesting the Turkish government's inability or unwillingness to protect foreigners. Hay had no love of missionaries and was delighted that Roosevelt might remind them that there was "a certain element of martyrdom" in their task and that the government could not "make their lives and their comfort absolutely secure."[47] He did not forget that avenging the death or kidnapping of missionaries had been a favorite device of Christian countries in their development of "spheres of influence" in China. On the other hand, it rankled him that Middle Eastern governments continued to ignore what he saw as their responsibilities and the just claims of America against them.[48] To support the unsuccessful negotiations of the American consul in Beirut, in the summer of 1903, Hay suggested that since the fleet was going around the world, it might be useful in Turkish waters.[49] It was very useful, for a short while.[50] By the next year matters had again deteriorated, and when the Tangierian rebel Raizuli kidnapped Ion H. Perdicaris, Hay not only sent the fleet, but a "growl"—as he called it—as well.[51] After several diplomatic attempts at freeing Perdicaris, he wired on June 22, "We want Perdicaris alive or Raizuli dead." Two days later, the American consul received Perdicaris alive.[52]

When the French government voted in 1904 to give Hay the medal of the Legion of Honor in recognition of his work for world peace, the Secretary demurred.[53] He feared that the debate over it in the Senate would disturb friendly Franco-American relations on which he had based whatever leverage he could bring to bear on France's ally, Russia.[54] Roosevelt urged his acceptance. The honor, he argued, would encourage Russia and Japan to seek Hay's help and thus measurably add to American chances of open trade in the Far East, and it would also add to the political prestige of the Roosevelt administration in an election year.[55] Hay reluctantly bowed to Presidential pressures and received the honor July 14, 1904.[56]

While the President may have undervalued Hay's diplomacy abroad, he did not underestimate the Secretary's worth for "diplomacy" at home. Roosevelt used Hay mercilessly throughout the 1904 presidential campaign.[57] Hay's speeches, personal appearances, and moderating influence were of great advantage, as the President told him after the election and Hay recorded in his diary:

The president sent for me this morning. He spoke in very warm terms of my work in the campaign, and the effect, even greater, he said, of my personal

influence on public opinion. He quoted Moody as saying that "Hayism" was
one of the most telling subjects he could use on the stump. The President
repeated that he considered my willingness to remain in the Cabinet (which
I have never expressed) had something to do with our success. He added
that it meant much to his 'personal comfort.'[58]

And indeed it did, particularly with the press and the old guard
Republicans, suspicious of the "young upstart" Roosevelt. As a
former writer and editor of the *New York Tribune*, Hay had great
respect for the power of the American press, and the members of
the press had respect for him. He had been one of them. Many have
commented on the generally favorable newspaper response given
foreign policy during his tenure of office despite strong anti-
imperialist and anti-English feelings in the country. It is true that
criticism of administration policy may have been blunted by the fact
that Hay had many friends among the most critical writers. But it is
more important that he recognized the power of the press and used
it. Watching Lincoln's careful dealing with "the press gang" and
their powerful editors—men like James Gordon Bennett and
Horace Greeley—as well as his own years in journalism had taught
Hay a good deal. As Secretary of State, he returned to methods he
had found useful when serving as Assistant Secretary of State under
Hayes. Then he had provided the *Tribune* with editorials written by
himself and the bureau chief, Adee.[59] During his own Secretaryship, Hay inaugurated a stream of information from the Department
of State to leading editors. His correspondence contains adroitly
written letters of information and congratulations sent when he approved of a paper's policy, and equally adroit corrections and
suggestions when he saw need for clarification of policy or room for
strengthening popular support for the administration's measures.[60]
Then, too, he himself made news; he spoke quotably and did news-
worthy things. Under his guidance, Americans saw themselves assuming the dramatic, if giddy, heights of world leadership. All this
was not lost on Theodore Roosevelt.

Another of Hay's "comforts" as a colleague for the new President
lay in his association with Lincoln and the critical older members of
the Republican party, who, like Root, were uncertain that the bois-
terous Teddy was "fit" for high office.[61] This understanding may
underlie Roosevelt's later ungenerous assessment of Hay's service as
a "figurehead." If so, the "figurehead" was Lincoln as well as Hay.

For the older man thought Roosevelt needed to soften his roughness and blunt the contempt of party elders. In the "softening" Hay consistently used Lincoln as an instrument to restrain intemperateness and to reward strength of purpose. He began by giving the young President a set of the Lincoln *History*, from which Roosevelt confessed that he derived not only the glory of being "descended" from the political line of Lincoln but also a notion of how petty were his problems compared with those of the Civil War President.[62] Using Lincoln's example of firmly leading but not alienating Congress, Hay advised Roosevelt not to make an angry Senate irrevocably hostile over the issue of the arbitration treaties.[63] "Let them die," he urged, "there is nothing to be gained by a battle over the corpse."[64] Equally helpful was the Lincoln example to the Secretary when he applauded Roosevelt's Labor Day address of 1903 as "flawless." "No man has ever spoken to so called 'working men' with such dignity and such truthful unreserve," wrote Hay. "So high a compliment has not been paid them since Lincoln spoke in a similar tone."[65]

With the Lincoln theme so strongly running through Hay's last years, it is not surprising that on Roosevelt's inauguration in 1905 he wore a ring, of which the Secretary retained a copy, presented by Hay and containing the locks of Lincoln.[66] It was a macabre Victorian convention turned to practical account.

With the party firmly behind him after 1904, Roosevelt still needed Hay for his agility in working with the British and as an object of international trust and prestige. Again Hay was keeping a diary, and its daily accounts testify not only to the rifts between the President and his Secretary of State but to the consultations in Hay's home when he was too ill to go to the office and to an underlying respect and fondness between the men of different generations and styles. On a May Sunday in 1904 Hay recorded: "The President was reading Emerson's *Days* and came to the wonderful closing line: 'I, too late, Under her solemn fillet saw the scorn.' I said, 'I fancy you do not know what that means.' 'O, do I not? Perhaps the greatest men do not, but I in my soul know I am but an average man, and that only marvelous good-fortune has brought me where I am.'" Then he broke out, 'I want to see St. Gaudens' bust of you. Mrs. R[oot] says it is splendid.' So we walked over to the studio. He was delighted with it—but getting around to the side said there was not power enough in the jaw. St. Gaudens afterwards smiled and said

the president projected his own powerful jaw on the universe. . . ."
A month earlier, Roosevelt was somewhat surprised on his arrival in
Yosemite's wilds to discover from the guide that Hay and Adams had
been there years before him. Roosevelt wrote to his Secretary of
State, "I wonder if you realize how thankful I am to you for having
stayed with me. I owe you a great debt, old man."[67] And as Hay had
to admit to Adams, "He has plenty of brains, and as you know, a
heart of gold."[68] Thus, although often irritated, Hay stayed "in har-
ness" to serve yet another leader with a mission.

To Hay the office of Secretary of State was not an independent
force, but an extension of power. The power of the President derived from the whole people—the ultimate symbol of authority in a
republic. And since 1860 Hay had served as an instrument of that
office: first in the task of achieving union, then in the reform and
maintenance of union, and finally in the representation of its power
and policies to the world. His search for repose and health in
Europe in 1905 had been dogged at every step by invitations from
nations eager to honor and to confer with the American Secretary of
State.[69] Looking back over the years and service begun in the cruci-
ble of the Civil War, it is difficult to conclude, as so many authors
have, that Hay was an overwrought, hypersensitive, and reluctant
servant of the republic. He spent twenty-one years in public life,
actively sought and vigorously defended political position, and did
so consistently at critical times. Hay had not shunned controversy,
but he had always brought to controversy the appearance of tradition, harmony, and unity by which it might be mitigated or resolved. His strongest convictions had been derived from his father
Charles and his uncle Milton. The time he spent in Lincoln's service
reinforced and refined those views. His years with Lincoln were the
source of his political concerns and provided the pattern of his
ideology. His closest confidant, Henry Adams, understood the relationship when he wrote of Hay's policy: "the hand is the hand of
Hay, but the temper, the tone, the wit and genius bear the birth-
mark of Abraham Lincoln."[70]

Hay could not consciously make such a comparison, or perhaps he
did not see the connection. But, during a banquet honoring him for
his service to peace in 1903, he had described himself in Lincoln-
esque terms:

I was born in Indiana, grew up in Illinois, I was educated in Rhode Island
and it is no blame to that scholarly community that I know so little. I

learned my law in Springfield and my politics in Washington, my diplomacy in Europe, Asia and Africa. I have a farm in New Hampshire and desk room in the District of Columbia. When I look to the springs from which my blood descends the first ancestors I ever heard of were a Scotchman, who was half English, and a German woman who was half French. Of my immediate progenitors, my mother was from New England and my father was from the South. In this bewilderment of origin and experience I can only put on an aspect of deep humility in any gathering of favorite sons, and confess that I am nothing but an American.[71]

Unconsciously, however, Hay made the connection between himself and Lincoln, and it came forth in a dream. On the return voyage from Europe and his unsuccessful search for health in the spring of 1905, Hay wrote one morning in his diary:

I dreamed last night that I was in Washington and that I went to the White House to report to the President who turned out to be Mr. Lincoln. He was very kind and considerate, and sympathetic about my illness. He said there was little work of importance on hand. He gave me two unimportant letters to answer. I was pleased that this slight order was within my power to obey. I was not in the least surprised at Lincoln's presence in the White House. But the whole impression of the dream was one of overpowering melancholy.[72]

John Milton Hay died on July 1, 1905; he was sixty-seven years old. It had been his father's ambition to found a family—to make the Hay name live in history. John Hay could die knowing that he had fulfilled his father's hopes.

Selections from Hay's Letters and Diaries

THE major sources for any study of John Hay are his own letters and diaries. Hay was a prolific writer and letters from him may be found in the manuscript collections of almost all important post–Civil War Americans. The largest collection of his letters and papers is housed at the John Hay Library at Brown University. During the Civil War Hay began a diary which he continued to keep until 1870. In 1904 until his death in 1905, Hay again kept a diary. The original copy of this diary is in the Library of Congress in Washington, D.C., as is Hay's correspondence as Assistant Secretary and Secretary of State.

One cannot get the full flavor of John Hay without reading some of his letters and extracts from his diaries. Hay's letters often reveal his attempt at playing off his many roles to suit the expectations of those to whom he wrote. While this convention of letter writing is not unique, John Hay was an expert at the craft. Even in this small sample from his letters and diaries, he emerges in all his complexities as a man who in attempting to control and direct his destiny simultaneously ascribed his successes to fortune. Perhaps this too was a convention of the nineteenth century, but he clearly urged luck on with all his resources.

Finally, we offer the following selections to provide the reader with a glimpse of a more personal side of John Hay, an aspect that any text invariably obscures.

TO MARY HAY[1]

Springfield–March 5th 1854

My Dear Sister

The receipt & perusal of your last, conferred great pleasure upon me. I am glad to learn that our little village is assuming the habits and appearance of a city: for in my opinion, all the sentimental talk we hear from the poet & novelist, about the simplicity & quiet ease of village life, is all humbug. The city is the only place to gain a knowledge of the world, which will fit a man for entering upon the duties of life. I also wish you & your coadjutors the best success in your praiseworthy enterprise. The grave yard at Warsaw is a beautiful place, in the summer, when the trees are covered with their rich foliage, affording a pleasant shade to any one who may wish to wander in the cool paths, or to sit at the foot of some spreading oak, to read or meditate. But I object to the propriety of allowing the same privilege, to the cows and hogs who may be passing by.

In your opinions in regard to poetry, I fully agree, I think, with you, that it is one of the noblest faculties of our nature, and should be cultivated to its fullest extent. The true poet, *will* cultivate this gift. One who is so highly gifted, can no more keep silent, and withhold from pouring out a flood of song, than can the songsters of the grove, refrain from warbling their notes of praise, or the rivulet refuse to flow. His thoughts and meditations are not in common with other men; his studies are not the everyday concerns of life. This imagination soars above the dark & gloomy real, to mingle with the bright & ever glorious ideal creations of his own fancy, and converses with kindred spirits of the past. His book is not the counting house ledger, or even the page of philosophic lore; but the great book of Nature is ever open before him, & from this he draws, the most priceless stores of Wisdom. To him there is exquisite happiness in contemplating the grandeur of the hoary mountain, the calm solitude of the forest, the roar of the boundless ocean, the headlong career of the torrent, and the merry laugh of the dancing rill.

There are few to whom this great and glorious gift is granted and the names of Milton, Byron, Moore & Burns are familiar, to every admirer of the beautiful. These I almost worship. There is nothing I so much *love*, as good poetry. But if real, sterling, heart-moving poetry is good, I think there is nothing worse than bad rhymes. (Such as the one enclosed).

The Legislature adjourned yesterday. During the session, I went several times, to the Hall, but heard nothing of any interest, except on one day when there was quite an animated debate on the Nebraska Bill.

We are still studying Latin, Greek, Rhetoric & Algebra. We are now reading the odes of Horace which are beautiful. Tomorrow we commence the Iliad of Homer. We are busy every night with our studies except Sunday & Friday nights. On Friday our Society meets for the purpose of debating, reading original essays, and criticizing. I manage to come in as often as possible, for speaking, which takes up no time in the week. How is your friend Mr. Cooley. Has he established himself in an office yet; or does he continue to write the fancied misfortunes of romantic youth? Does the perfume of his Regalia continue to penetrate the neighboring houses, or has he returned to his own native Maryland discouraged & grieved at the reception which his brilliant talents & commanding appearance met with among the Western Barbarians? Am I too hard on him?

Give my respect to all inquiring friends (If I have any). My best love to Ma with an earnest request to write one or two lines if no more. Although I can hardly expect it, as she has so much to occupy her time. My love to Charlie with a positive injuction to write, To Ella

Yours fraternally

J. M. Hay

TO HIS FAMILY[2]

Brown University, November 28, 1855

My Dear Friends:—

To-morrow is Thanksgiving. We have no lessons this week and many of the students have gone home. I thought that when this time came I would have plenty of time to catch up with my correspondence and make some excursions to the surrounding country. But here half the week is gone and I have done nothing at all. The fact is, I am so much occupied with my studies that when a few days of release come I cannot make a rational use of my liberty. You know I entered the Junior Class behind the rest, and consequently have several studies to make up before I can be even with them. And as the prescribed studies are about as much as I can attend to, I do not know whether I can finish the course, with justice, in two years. I think I can graduate in that time, but will not stand high, or know as much about the studies as if I had been more leisurely about it. Again, if I go through so hurriedly, I will have little or no time to avail myself of the literary treasures of the libraries. This is one of the greatest advantages of an Eastern College over a Western one.

This matter, however, I leave for you and Pa to decide; but you may be assured that whatever time I remain here I am determined to show you that your generous kindness has not been misapplied or ungratefully received. I am at present getting along well in my class. The Register tells me that I stand in the first class of honor, my average standing being 18 in 20. The life here suits me exactly. The professors are all men of the greatest ability, and what is more, perfect gentlemen. They pursue a kind and friendly course toward the students as long as they act in a manner to deserve it, but any violations of the rules of the institution are strictly punished. There have been several expulsions and suspensions since I came here.

I have no acquaintances out of the college, consequently know very little of the city. There is not much excitement here on any occasion, except Thanksgiving and Training-Day, and then it is a quiet Yankee excitement as much as possible unlike the rough, hearty manner of the West.

I heard Oliver W. Holmes deliver a poem here last week, which (was) a splendid thing; also a lecture by Professor Huntingdon. Thackery will be here before long and I expect to hear him lecture.

It is getting very late and I close this excuse for a letter with my best regards for all the family and all my friends in Springfield.
P.S. Thursday morning.—I have just received and read with pleasure Aunt D.'s and Cousin S.'s letter. Augustus has only written once to me since I have been here. I am anxious to hear from him.
P.P.S. Please remit at your earliest convenience some of "the root of all evil," alias, "tin," alias, Pewter.
P.P.P.S. Some one write soon and I will answer likewise.
P.P.P.P.S. I will return good for evil and answer Cousin Sarah on a whole sheet, instead of a few lines at the end of this.
P.P.P.P.P.S. I received a letter from Dad lately.
P.P.P.P.P.P.S. That is all.

Yours truly,

J.M. Hay

TO NORA PERRY[3]

Warsaw,

January 2nd, 1859

Let me hope, Nora, that your Christmas was merrier than mine. Whatever be your fortune, you are happy in yourself and in your friends. You have the poetic soul that can idealize common things till they stand before you in transfigured vitality. Permit me to say also that you have what is better than all poetry, the warm and catholic love of a woman for everything that is beautiful or good. The world must be very fair as seen through the rosy atmosphere of luxuriant youth and maidenhood. Memory paints warm pictures of the past, to adorn the gay revels of the present, and the mind goes a-gypsying into the future. You are much to blame if you are not happy, lighted through pleasant places by the soul of a poet,
"Singing alone in the morning of life,
In the happy morning of youth and of May,
A passionate ballad, gallant and gay."
If you loved Providence as I do you would congratulate yourself hourly upon your lot. I turn my eyes eastward, like an Islamite, when I feel prayerful. The city of Wayland, and Williams that smiles upon its beauty glassed in the still mirror of the Narragansett waves, is shrined in my memory as a far-off mystical Eden where the women were lovely and spirituelle, and the men were jolly and brave; where I used to haunt the rooms of the Athenaeum, made holy by the presence of the royal dead; where I used to pay furtive visits to Forbes' forbidden mysteries (peace to its ashes!), where I used to eat Hasheesh and dream dreams. My life will not be utterly desolate while memory is left me, and while I may recall the free pleasures of the student-time; pleasures in which there was no taint of selfishness commingled, and which lost half their sin in losing all their grossness. Day is not more different from night than they were from the wild excesses of the youth of this barbarous West.

Yet to this field I am called, and I accept calmly, if not joyfully, the challenge of fate. From present indications my sojurn in this "vale of tears," as the elder Weller pathetically styles it, will not be very protracted. I can stand it for a few years, I suppose. My father, with more ambition and higher ideals than I, has dwelt and labored here a lifetime, and even this winter does not despair of creating an interest in things intellectual among the great unshorn of the prairies. I am not suited for a reformer. I do not like to meddle with moral ills. I love comfortable people. I prefer, for my friends, men who can read. In the words of the poet Pigwiggen, whom Neal has immortalized in the "Charcoal Sketches," "I know I'm a genus, 'cause I hate work worse'n thunder, and would like to cut my throat—only it hurts." When you reflect how unsuitable such sentiments are to the busy life of the Mississippi Valley, you may imagine then what an overhauling my character must receive—at my own hands. too.

There is, as yet, no room in the West for a genius. I mean, of course, of the Pigwiggen model. Impudence and rascality are the talismans that open the gates of preferment. I am a Westerner. The influences of civilization galvanized me for a time into a feverish life, but they will vanish before this death-in-life of solitude. I chose it, however, and my blood is on my own head.

I received Mrs. Whitman's very kind letter a day or two ago. To have friends, esteemed like her, welcome me so cordially back to life is something worth being sick for. I will seize the privilege of writing to her soon. When I last wrote I promised to send her something saved from the wreck that burnt in my stove last winter. But I concluded not to look back, and so will request you to hand her the enclosed affair, being the only fruit of so many months of exile. If you can read it, look upon it, not with justice but mercy. I wrote it the other morning because I felt like it, and I don't know whether it is passable or execrable. I add another somewhat dissimilar. I am at once flattered and grateful for the favor you conferred upon me and my lines at the Phalanstery. I, alas! have no audience out of my own family to read your beautiful poems to, but they all admire them equally with me. . . .

TO MILTON HAY[4]

Warsaw, Illinois, Jan. 28th, 1859.

My Dear Uncle,

Although I have very little to say, I write according to your request to let you know how I am getting along. I am not making the

most rapid progress in the law. I have, as you advised, read all of
Hume consecutively, and, to speak with moderation, remember
some of it. I would then immediately have made an attack upon
Blackstone, had I not been prevented for a while by the general
worthlessness induced by the distemper that has troubled me more
or less all the season. During the last few weeks I have been occupied in making preparations for a lecture before the "Literary
Institute" in this town. I delivered it last Saturday evening to the
best house I have ever seen in Warsaw. I think it was well received.
People did not expect much from a boy, and so were more than
satisfied. I have been asked to write again but shall not. It is too
great an expenditure of time for no pay but nine days' glory.

It has had one effect, at least. It has convinced my very pious
friends in this place that there is no sphere of life, for me, but the
pulpit. I have been repeatedly told by lawyers here that I will never
make my living by pettifogging. This is, of course, very encouraging, but I think, if my manifest destiny is to starve, I prefer to do it
in a position where I will have only myself to blame for it. I would
not do for a Methodist preacher, for I am a poor horseman. I would
not suit the Baptists, for I dislike water. I would fail as an Episcopa-
lian, for I am no ladies' man. In spite of my remonstrance, however,
I am button-holed in the street daily, and exhorted to enter into
orders. Our minister here has loaded me with books which he inno-
cently expects me to read—as if my life was long enough. I find it
the easiest way to agree with everything they say and to follow the
example of the shrewd youth in the parable, who "said, 'I go,' and
went not."

I have a quiet room here to myself in which I can do as much as I
could anywhere, alone. I suppose that I miss the personal superintendence of a preceptor, but hope that I can make up for that loss
hereafter. If you think, at any time, that I can engage in anything
profitable, either to myself or others, by coming to Springfield, I am
ready to come. You spoke of a possibility of my succeeding, in case
of a vacancy, to a berth in the Auditor's office. That would be especially pleasant, as I suppose it would give me free access to the
Libraries in the State House. However, I am very easily contented,
in whatever sphere I may be placed, and can always wait for the tide
of circumstances without any inconvenience. Meanwhile, I will go
on and read Blackstone at home. It is as pleasant as possible in
Warsaw now. . . .

I send you what our paper has to say about my lecture.
Please remember me to all the family, especially to Grandfather.

John M. Hay

TO WILLIAM L. STONE[5]

Springfield May 20th 1859

My Dear Friend,

I would hold myself inexcusable for having delayed to so late a day, a reply to your kind letter, if it were not for the peculiar circumstances of the case. When I received it, I was in a state of great uncertainty about my future action. The life of listless apathy which I had been leading ever since we parted, was growing distasteful at last & I began to consider seriously the expediency of an immediate course of study. Before long I decided & left, for the last time perhaps, the green hills of my home, the birthplace of my mind, the Pastures of my earliest revelations. (Pardon me I am not going to inflict any sentiment on you.) For several weeks since I have been wandering like an Ishmaelite through the dark places of Missouri, getting up extempore romances in the villages, & dreaming away the hours in the excitement of the cities. I am stranded at last, like a weather-beaten hulk, on the dreary wastes of Springfield—a city combining the meanness of the North with the barbarism of the South. Let the cry of your mourning go up continually for your brother of old time, for he hath fallen upon evil days. There is no death so sad as this. The sky is forever leaden with gloomy clouds, or glowing with torrid fervors. But the Aborigines are contented & happy. If the air is a furnace, they say "Powerful nice weather for the wheat." If the day weeps in sad-coloured showers they shake the rain from their hats & grin, "This is given to send the corn up amazin." Yet these barbarians are men of large substance, & "marvellous witty fellows." Dogberry ought to have been an Illinoisan. Yet such as it is, for the present Springfield is my home. I am settled here—a student of the Law, an't please you,—& here shall I abide for many days to come.

I did not write all this because my thoughts were of any importance, but merely to tell you why I could not write before, & why I cannot see you, if you take the trip you mentioned, up the towering flood of the Father of Waters. But if the course of your western wanderings (and how my imagination lovingly follows your progress, each step of which is hallowed, each hour of which is tinged with the coloring divine granted but once in a life-time) you should happen to pass over the prairies that lie along the path way of the Alton & Chicago Rail Road, I need not say to you who know me how delighted I shall be to grasp with an old-fashioned grip, the hand of "Benidick, the married man." What can I say, my Dear Stone, worthy of me or of you, upon the subject which lies nearest your hearts. For to one whose past life has been & whose future shall be, so solitary as mine, there is not granted a conception of joy as holy & intense as pervade a heart around which floats this roseate halo of young & happy love. I can gaze upon your happiness with the sad joy that the reluctant Peri felt, standing in tearful trance before the chrystal bar of Eden.

Yet with my whole heart I give you joy in the Name of God. May you be as happy as you deserve to be. Only we who know you & love you, can appreciate the fulness of that prayer. And you will be. You are thrice happy. There will be scattered in the path of every man, those lurking shadows that lay in wait to strangle the few sunbeams in this infinite bore of a world. But you can meet any fate, with defiant calm. For where love is, there can be no weariness. Love is an armlet, that blunts every dart aimed against the heart that contains it. Love will gild sorrow, as sunset paints clouds. Love will tinge with gold the sands of time. Leave the future to its own soil. Dream in the present out of the full fruition of perfected Love. If you appreciate the worth & excellence of this warm-tinged dawn of life, you will, in the happy days which are to come so soon, lay up a treasure of opulent joy with which to face bravely the cares of manhood & the challenge of Fate. God's blessing & Love's blessing (which are one) be with you & yours.

John Hay

DIARY (1861)[6]

November 11. Tonight Bleaker's Germans had a torchlight procession in honor of McC. [General George McClellan] promotion. I never saw such a scene of strange and wild magnificence as this night-march was. Afterwards we went over to McC[s] and talked about the Southern flurry. The President thought this a good time to feel them. McC. said, "I have not been unmindful of that. We will feel them tomorrow." The Tycoon and the General were both very jolly over the news.

November 13. I wish here to record what I consider a portent of evil to come. The President, Governor Seward, and I, went over to McClellan's house tonight. The servant at the door said the General was at the wedding of Col. Wheaton at General Buell's, and would soon return. We went in, and after we had waited about an hour, McC. came in and without paying any particular attention to the porter, who told him the President was waiting to see him, went up stairs, passing the door of the room where the President and Secretary of State were seated. They waited about half-an-hour, and sent once more a servant to tell the General they were there, and the answer coolly came that the General had gone to bed.

I merely record this unparalleled insolence of epaulettes without comment. It is the first indication I have yet seen of the threatened supremacy of the military authorities.

Coming home I spoke to the President about the matter but he seemed not to have noticed it, specially, saying it was better at this time not to be making points of etiquette & personal dignity.

SPEECH TO FLORIDIANS, Spring, 1864[7]

. . . If there could be one lingering relic of hope for rebellion in the attitude of the border states it would be in that contagion of like social systems that first endangered their loyalty. But that has at last vanished. I should wrong your intelligence and my own sense of honor, citizens of Florida if I should attempt to conceal, in deference to worn-out prejudices what I in common with 9/10 of the people of the United States now think in regard to the national bearing of this dead question of negro slavery. I believe it caused the war and I believe its removal from national politics by its own destruction will under God close the war, and the only argument I care to offer in support of that belief, is the free and dispassionate utterance of those slave states who have been allowed to give their testimony in regard to this momentous issue.

For many years they have cherished this institution as their palladium, their sacred idol. They have forbidden all discussion of its

merits. They have compelled dumb silence or unreasoning praise.
They have fiercely resented comment from without: they have
sternly repressed question or inquiry from within their borders. For
a man to express a doubt as to the expediency or morality of this
system was to involve the risk of his life, and the more dreadful
certainty of social ostracism. The instances of spirits of such eccen-
tric courage were rare. At the beginning of this war the border slave
states could justly claim a united public sentiment in favor of slavery.

The enormous prosperity we had for years enjoyed under the
benign and fostering influences of our Republican government,
which extended to the slave states as well as to the free, gave currency and color of truth to their constant assertion that their prosperity depended on the perpetuation of their system of labor. They
stubbornly refused to recognize the fact that the comparative progress of free and slave communities showed incontestably that they
were prosperous not by means, but in spite of their vicious social
system. An error thus bred of endless fair weather must be dis-
sipated by storm.

The storm came, the awfullest in intensity and terror the world
earth has yet seen: Elemental forces contending in the moral world
atmosphere: good & evil marshalling on either side the prin-
cipalities & powers of the air. Among the wrecks of that tempest
there is nothing we cannot regret. The utter discredit and destruction of the delusion that slavery in any circumstances, is better than
freedom. This foundered in the rough weather. The currents of
men's minds were disturbed. They lost their bearings in the stress of
new events and were forced to take new observations and points of
departure. In the heat of this fury revolution old party ties parted
like cobwebs, and the mists of passion & prejudice vanished &
ceased to cloud the minds of men, sobered by the pressures of issues
greater than any that had ever confronted them before.

To the eternal honor of the men of the border states let it be told
that they rose to the level of the occasion. They did not shirk or seek
to evade the great issues before them. They examined the whole
subject with what calmness and temper they could bring to the
consideration of a matter so near to their hearts. They questioned
what were the influences which could tend to cause them to link
their fate with this causeless and insane revolt. They saw that a
sympathy bred of a similar social system alone impelled their heed-
less and impulsive citizens into that ruinous alliance. . . .

Men's minds were sobered & their tongues freed. And when free discussion once begins it will never end in an intelligent community but in the abatement of the question which has provoked it. You know better than I, that a system of social servitude is incompatible with free discussion. It lives in an atmosphere of repression. It is walled round by silence & darkness. It crumbles when brought to the light and air, as long buried corpses do. . . .

Citizens of Florida, the time has come for you to take your ground upon this matter. The moment of supreme decision is here. It is for you to choose whether you will have a continuance of anarchy and lawless waste and all the hideous concomitants of a state of civil war; or a fixed and stable government bringing with it all the blessings of a well-ordered civilization. It is for you to say whether you will embark your hopes and your interests in the shattered and sinking ship of rebellion, "Built in eclipse & rigged with curses dark," trembling with the final throes of dissolution in the majestic presence of the national power like the fated bark of the eastern fable, before the mountain of Loadstone, losing every belt and bar & rivet in the power stress of that awful attraction, and drifting on helpless, incoherent, and undone to break in disordered fragments on the wavewashed base of the everlasting rocks: or whether, taught by experience and taking counsel of the solemn voices of events, you will wisely adhere to the good ship *Union* whose timbers are staunch and true, whose mighty frame is still defiant of time and chance, whose keel was laid in justice for the perpetuation of liberty, whose helm has been consecrated by the firm hands of dead worthies whose vigilant eyes watch her protectingly from heaven—whose wake is a pathway bright with glory and honor—whose prow is turned forever to the shining shores of limitless wealth and progress in the mists of distant centuries.

TO J. C. NICOLAY[8]

Warsaw Illinois
Aug 25, 1864

My Dear Nico:

I arrived home yesterday, fagged. I have made an examination of something less than a hundred boarding schools and convents and we have at last, after a family council held last night, pretty well settled upon the Convent of the Visitation [for his sister Ellie] at St Louis.

I shall stay here until the term begins & go with Ellie there, and then come at once back to Washington early in September.

We are waiting with the greatest interest for the hatching of the big Peace Snakes at Chicago. There is throughout the country, I mean the rural districts, a good healthy Union feeling & an intention to succeed, in the military & the political contest, but everywhere in the towns, the Copperheads [those calling for peace] are exultant and our own people either growling & despondent or sneakingly apologetic. I found among my letters here, sent by you, one from Joe Medill, inconceivably impudent, in which he informs me that on the fourth of next March, thanks to Mr Lincoln's blunders & follies, we will be kicked out of the White House. The damned scoundrel needs a day's hanging. I won't answer his letter till I return & let you see it. Old Uncle Jesse is talking like an ass—says if the Chicago nominee is a good man, he don't know, &c., &c. He blackguards you & me—says we are too big for our breeches—a fault for which it seems to me either Nature or our tailors are to blame. After all your kindness to the old whelp & his cub of a son, he hates you because you have not done more. I believe he thinks the Ex. Mansion is somehow to blame because Bill married a harlot & Dick Oglesby is popular.

Land is getting up near the stars in price. It will take all I am worth to buy a tater-patch. I am after one or two small pieces in Hancock for reasonable prices; 20 to 30 dollars an acre. Logan paid $70,000 for a farm a short while ago, & everybody who has greenbacks is forcing them off like waste paper for land. I find in talking with well-informed people a sort of fear of Kansas property: as uncertain in future settlement & more than all, uncertain in weather. The ghost of famine haunts those speculations.

You were wrong in thinking either Milt. or Charlie Hay at all Copperish. They are as sound as they ever were. They of course are not quite clear about the currency, but who is?

Our people here want me to address the Union League. I believe I won't. The snakes would rattle about it a little & it w^d do no good. I lose my temper sometimes talking with growling Republicans. There is a diseased restlessness about men in these times that unfits them for the steady support of an administration. It seems as if there were appearing in the Republican party the elements of disorganization that destroyed the Whigs.

If the dumb cattle are not worthy of another term of Lincoln then let the will of God be done & the murrain of McClellan fall on them.

Yours truly
J.H.

TO WILLIAM H. SEWARD[9]

New York
March 4, 1867

My Dear Mr. Seward:

I see by the journals of this morning, that General Dix is confirmèd [as Minister to France]. I am very glad of it, both on the General's account and because I seem to see that the "whip of the overseer" has ceased to be all-powerful in the Senate. I have talked with many people here, and though I hear much bitterness and injustice, I think the talk grows vaguer day by day. I cannot but think that while the people are as fixed as we in their determination that the war shall bring forth its fruits of lasting freedom and security, a more practical and American tone of feeling is beginning to assert itself.

I have thought proper to remain, as long as I have, within hail of Washington. As there will now be no occasion for me to return to Paris I will go West tonight. I have made as yet no permanent business arrangement. I have received several offers. The best are rather indefinite and others are scarcely sufficient for my maintenance. I will remain in the West for a month and then return to the East to begin my work—whatever I decide upon.

I have ceased to think much of the possibility of a diplomatic appointment. I recognize how difficult it must necessarily be for you to make an appointment so exclusively your own as mine would be—having no support except your own choice and judgment. To me, the knowledge that I have been thought worthy of high trust by you, is worth more than any office. I shall go into private life prouder that you proposed my name for a mission than if I had received it by the direction of any other man.

I owe you gratitude for a thousand favors, but I think there is no tinge of personal feeling in the devotion and adherence which I avow for you. That has grown up by the observation of six busy years. I have never known you to despair of the Republic. I have never heard from you a bitter word of any adversary. I have never seen your official action for one moment warped by personal interest. I have seen you deliberately prefer your convictions of duty to the certainty of vast popularity, and sacrifice for a present benefit to the Nation the cheap praise of immediate and unanimous history. I have come to regard you as I know the world will, when the smoke has risen from the battlefields of today, as nearly as one may reach it, the Ideal of a Republican working man—calm without apathy, bold without rashness, firm without obstinacy and with a patriotism permeated with religious faith.

To have done some work under your orders will always be to me a source of pride and gratulation; but the recollection of having enjoyed your friendship and your confidence will be to me in the future among my most precious possessions—raising and dignifying me in my own eyes.

Pardon my making so many words of what I sat down to write— that I thank you for all you have been to me—that I beg you will not allow any consideration of my interests to annoy or embarrass you further (as I shall get on well enough) and that I am

Very devotedly
Your friend and servant,
John Hay.

TO WILLIAM H. SEWARD[10]

Legation of the United States
Vienna. June 8, 1868

My Dear Wm Seward,

Prince Napoleon arrived here on Friday night, and was visited on Saturday by the Emperor and the Imperial family of Austria. On Sunday the members of the Diplomatic Body were informed that as the Prince was travelling *incognito*, he would not formally receive them as a body but would be happy to see any of them who might call. In obedience to this intimation I went the same day to make my compliments. The Prince received me with cordiality and spoke with much animation of his visit to America some years ago. He

referred in terms of especial warmth to his acquaintance with you
and the late President Lincoln.

H. I. Highness will remain here during this week and it is thought
will make a visit to Prague in Bohemia before proceeding on his way
to Pesth and Constantinople. He travels as the Counte de Mendon
until arriving at Constantinople where he will assume his dynastic
name and character, to return the Sultan's visit to Paris, of last year.

His arrival here has given rise to great discussion and conjecture
among diplomatic circles. It is even asserted by some that he comes
to make direct overtures for an alliance with Austria—but this is
incredible in view of his life long opinions—repeated in the cele-
brated speech at Ajacsio—that the Austrian alliance was always
and necessarily fatal to France. Some of the representatives of the
smaller powers here, are filled with almost fantastic hopes of vengeance upon Prussia, based upon conjectured alliances between France
and the Southern German nations. In general, the Prince and his
suite talk as if the sole object of the present journey was information
and amusement. Of course, so clever and experienced an observer
cannot but return from such a tour with views and suggestions of
great value. He receives a great many people here, representatives
of all classes and shades of political opinion in the monarchy.

It now appears that he will not go to Galicia. The Russian Government still keeps up its semi-official publications of an imaginary
insurrection in Poland, which serves as a pretext for the most vigor-
ous measures of repression. But the best information shows these
statements to be absolutely devoid of foundation. Still these rumors
have awakened such an unquiet interest in the entire Polish territory, that it would be obviously unwise for the Prince to arouse
unduly the jealous susceptibilities of Russia by any such journey.

It is probable that he will also give up his trip to Bucharest. The
stories of the organization of insurrectionary armed bands in the
provinces of European Turkey, so current in the last few months,
were doubtless over wrought and exaggerated. But all accounts con-
cur in showing a most nervous and critical state of public feeling in
Bosnia, Servia, Wallachia and Bulgaria. It is possible that with peace
in Europe, the outbreak which is finally inevitable may be long
delayed. But the first spark of war among the great powers will
doubtless kindle into flame the combustible mass which has been so
many years accumulating in the half-barbarous regions between the
Euscine [?] and the Adriatic.

Altogether, I find in every circle here a curious and vague pre-sentiment of war. It does not seem to me founded on reasonable grounds. None of the great powers can give any good reason for fighting—or name any probable advantage at all commensurate with the certain cost. I hear no one predicting with any definiteness when the war will begin, or on what occasion. But an unpleasant uncertainty seems to fill all minds. Europe is ruining itself in armaments—and not a sovereign opens his mouth but to preach peace.

The people no where want war. If they had their way, as they should have, the armies would disband and go to work, and it would be an impertinence for kings to promise peace or threaten war.

I remain with the deepest respect and affection.

Your friend and servant

John Hay

TO ALVEY A. ADEE[11]

New York
November 28, 1874

My dear Alvey

It is a Saturday afternoon. I have been sitting by the window reading some Hawthorne. My wife, who is a large, handsome, and very comfortable young woman, says to me "You *must* write to Mr. Adee today." Some of these days you will learn how the lines are drawn by a gentle voice under that imperative. So I laid my book down and took up my pen to say I am very well and hope you are enjoying the same inestimable blessing.

Yea, verily, old friend, my ways have been those of pleasantness since we parted. I have had one great trouble which I will never get over. The pang is as keen today as it was the day my sister died—it is a pang made of anger, love, pity and regret, for myself and for her, all at once. But the malice of fate was exhausted in that one blow. I have been prosperous in everything else. Both my books got more praise than they deserved. My work in journalism is successful and well-paid. And now my father in law wished me to go into another line of business, which will bring me immediate wealth, if I accept it. But the best of all good luck that would possibly happen to a man I have found in my marriage. It was as much luck as anything. I fell head over heels in love with a pretty face, and gave its owner no peace until we were engaged. She lived in Cleveland and thus our acquaintance was scattering. We were not much known to each other when we were married. But I know her now and I never could have imagined so desirable a wife. I hope there may be another one as good somewhere and that you may find her. You deserve such a one more than I do.

We lived last Winter & Spring in pleasant Bohemian fashion in 25th Street. This year we are more ranges [orderly]. We have a handsome house in 42nd Street (No 11, East) which we have taken until next summer, and I wish we could have you here to tea—and to dinner—and to breakfast. We do not see much company except that of intimate friends and go out scarcely any. But I never have had so good a time as now.

I like to hear of your success in the Legation. You have a gilt-edged character. But I can't help wishing you were at home, so that I could see something of you, and so that you could be exposed to the temptations of matrimony. You have done wisely not to marry in a hurry—I shudder to think "if I had married at 25!"—But I should be sorry to think of your waiting until your life was too fixed.

I send you a picture of my wife taken in her wedding dress—the only one we have.

She sends her love to you and I wish you would write oftener.

Yours affectionately

J. H.

TO ALVEY A. ADEE[12]

506 Euclid Avenue
Cleveland Ohio. Feb. 20, 1877

My dear Adee

I am desolated that I have missent your money. I sent it as soon as I wrote to you, to your Uncle. If it has gone into the [unclear], law and equity combine to say it should be my loss and not yours. I will reimburse as soon as I know. You appear as to have heard of Mr. Witthaus' misfortunes. I know nothing in detail. A private letter from New York simply says "Have you heard of our good friend Witthaus' bankruptcy?" No man owning real estate in New York seems safe. Taxes are already almost equal to rent. It is little better anywhere else. Here in Cleveland, the tax on my house is as much as I could rent it for.

We are in a pretty bad way—but some of us think times will begin to mend after Hayes is inaugurated. You have never seriously thought Tilden was going in—have you? I hope you have not resigned on that supposition—though I cannot help thinking you have stayed about as long as you can afford. If you really enjoy it, stay by all means. There are not too many pleasant situations in the world. If you leave, some Yahoo will get your place. I do not believe in the reform of the civil service under anybody. Human nature and universal suffrage will prevent that among us for many a long year. Think of that herd of wild asses' colts now braying and kicking up their heels in the House of Representatives. What can you expect of a people which chooses such rulers, and likes them best when they are most sonorously asinine?

My boy is not like that. He eats and sleeps—he likes his joke—he gurgles at all my attempts at wit, without too closely considering the quality. He will lie for an hour looking at his handsome mamma and thinking how lucky he is that he is not a congressman, and does not have to roar and brawl and lie to get a slim living out of the votes of cads.

As for me, I shall never, while I have my reason, run for any office in the gift of this or any other people. The depradation is beyond computing. I do not see how a politician coming out of a canvas can ever hope to be clean again.

But why all this Buzz! I am never likely to be asked.

Yours

John Hay

Burn this letter and tell me you have done so.

TO CLARA S. HAY[13]

Nov. 22. 1879

When my letter declining the appointment arrived at the Department, Mr. Evarts [Secretary of State] brought it to Fred. Seward and said, "There! that is just what the President said." So it is evident His Excellency, from a single interview in Cleveland took me for a sensible man who thought too much of home and wife and babies to come away from them on a wild-goose chase to Washington. Alas! how frail we are—and here I am.

I slept well last night and got up early this morning and trotted over to the State Department at nine o'clock. As I was going up in the elevator, with a lot of Department clerks, one of them said to another, "So we are to have a new Assistant Secretary today?" and a lady clerk chimed in "Yes—isn't it too bad!" Seward is greatly loved in the service. I went in and talked with Brown & Adee and after a while, Mr. Seward came in, and I was immediately sworn in, and had a big Commission handed me, for which Adee had a tin case made, all in the course of an hour or two—on which Mr. Seward gave up his room to me formally, and took possession of a little closet-room adjoining to finish up his work in.

I had a great pile of letters of congratulation, and after I had read these, the visits began. Almost every one of the visitors had an ax to grind. I got sick and tired of it very soon. The worst is the ladies who want work, those who are gentle and ladylike and poor. There is not a single clerkship vacant, and yet they come in droves and it is dreadful to send them away.

Mr. Seward took me over to the White House to present me to the President. We went in to the Secretary's room where we saw Webb Hayes. He went into the room adjoining to announce us, and came back with his grave waggish countenance & said "The President is not in, but the Kitchen Cabinet is there." So we went in and Mrs. Hayes rose all smiles to receive us. She chatted away for some time, until Priv. Sec. Rogers came in and engaged Mr. Seward in conversation. Then Mrs. Hayes turned to me and talked about the change in the State Department. She said there was no hope whatever of Mrs. Seward's recovery—but it is very evident that Fred. refuses to give up.

Mr. Evarts seems very kind and amiable. He asked Mr. Seward &

me to take a family dinner with him tomorrow—adding "I don't have dinner parties Sundays."

Good Bye, my dearest heart. I shall spend this evening quietly at home, and go to bed early. I wish—but what's the use? I will try to get through the next six weeks without getting too blue. God bless my darlings.

TO AMASA STONE[14]

> Department of State
> Washington.
> December 4. 1879

Dear Mr. Stone

I have your letter of the 2nd as well as your former one—which I inadvertently omitted to acknowledge.

It seems probable that no measures will be taken by the present Congress to make provision for the gradual retirement of green backs. Very few Democrats are in favor of such a measure and the large majority of the Republicans are also opposed to it, and regret the recommendations of the President, which they say are likely to prove an embarrassment to the party in the coming campaign. The President, having given his opinion, is not disposed to push the matter, and I do not anticipate that any important differences will arise in the party on this subject.

Now that the Congressmen are all here, the raid on this Department for offices has fairly begun. Men not fit for tide-waiters come here with their representatives and Senators and ask for foreign missions and important consulates. Those who have got places find they cannot live on them and want promotions. All are greedy and unreasonable. Thank Heaven! I never asked for an office, and never shall while I live.

The weather here is perfectly delightful. I think a few weeks here would strengthen you in your ideas of owning a residence here. Even if I had no office, I could spend a month or so here with advantage, then go to Cleveland while you came here for February to May.

> Yours affectionately
>
> John Hay

TO E. C. STEDMAN[15]

New York

Aug. 13. 1881

My dear Stedman

Thanks for the paper. They also sent me one. You are like lots of others. You love radicalism and detest radicals. Me—I will put myself in also—adore freedom, but we don't want anybody to make free with us.

The reason, I imagine, is this. I have never met a reformer who had not the heart of a tyrant. Boundless conceit and moral selfishness seem the necessary baggage of the professional lover of liberty.

Many of us think we are Radicals when we are merely Epicureans.

However, catching bass is nobler work than moralizing.

Yours

J. H.

TO RUTHERFORD B. HAYES[16]

Merchants Bank Building

Room 10

Cleveland, O. Oct. 4, 1884

Dear General Hayes:

I do not know whether you think, as I do, that the general admission of girls into Adelbert College will have a tendency to diminish its standing and influence as a school for boys. If you hold the opposite opinion, I have nothing to say. If you agree with me, I hope we may rely on your influential voice at the meeting this month.

On another point I am sure of your support. There is a strong leaning in the Faculty towards Free Trade and Grover Cleveland—a tendency which if not checked will ruin the college. It would be a bitter sight to see Amasa Stone's endowment turned into a Democratic campaign fund.

Yours sincerely

John Hay

TO GEORGE W. CURTIS[17]

800 Sixteenth Street

Lafayette Square

Nov. 23, 1887

Dear Mr. Curtis,

You say the Independents in the late election voted the Democratic state ticket, the success of which is "mainly due" to them. On the same article you enumerate the President's [Cleveland] various lapses from consistency, with that amazing climax of his Fellow's letter which you know of course was not merely the expression of his individual preference for a dishonest man over an honest one but an offer—perfectly well understood by all politicians—to every office holder in New York to work for [the election of John R.] Fellows [for District Attorney of New York City].

Now, will you let me—who am a life long admirer of yours, if I can not presume to claim the title of a lifelong friend, who am not a politician, who will never again be one—ask you if there is *anything* the President can do which would induce the Independents to rebuke him in the only way a man of his mental and moral characteristics understands rebuke?

TO HENRY ADAMS[18]

Washington, Feb. 6, 1895.

Your party wallows still in the trough of the sea. Cleveland's recommendations to Congress are like wisdom crying in the streets—no man regardeth him. My party is nearly as much embarrassed by its victory as is yours by its defeat. Here the Reed [Speaker of the House] men are worse afraid of McKinley than of the devil, and more anxious to beat him. In New York the good people are scared out of their wits for fear Platt should do something they would like, so that they never make up their mind till he moves, and then they jump like sheep for the other thing. Tammany will come back in a year or two with an outfit of seven-fold deviltry. Don [Senator Cameron] is quite nervous about Pennsylvania; he thinks there is a chance of losing the State, in spite of its quarter-million majority. So you may be ready for another big swing of the pendulum.

Everybody seems to admit there will be no financial legislation this session. Perhaps Cleveland will call an extra session—but I doubt it. They can rub along through summer with one or two loans.

TO MARK HANNA[19]

Washington D.C.

Dec. 20, 1895

My Dear Hanna,

I have had a long and intimate talk with [Senator Don] Cameron today, in accordance with your suggestion. The substance of what he says is this. He thinks [Senator Matthew S.] Quay is heading towards McKinley as fast as is desirable. He says he does not think there is any cast-iron combine possible between Quay, [Thomas C.] Platt and others against McKinley such as the newspapers report. He does not think it advisable, even in the interest of McKinley, for Quay and Platt to come out now in his favor. He thinks it would consolidate certain elements against him, if they took him up as their special candidate. He admits the existence of a strong McKinley party in Pennsylvania, says it would be easier for them to carry the state for McK than for any one else. All Quay wants is to control the state organization and to name the 8 delegates at large. He will not oppose the election of McKinley delegates in the Districts, provided they are not personal enemies of his and Cameron's.

Cameron—I find has not absolutely given up all hope of being himself the candidate in certain contingencies. He thinks the war scare will suck all the gold out of the country, that there will be a pressure to sell American stock which will result in a panicky feeling over here and hard times about next June. He says he would make a good "Calamity Candidate" in that case.

Putting himself and his own contingent chances out of the question he seemed to talk as favorably of McKinley as could be expected. He was particularly anxious that we should not go into Pennsylvania and fight him and Quay in the Republican organization. I told him it was the last thing McKinley's friends would wish to do if they were not forced to; that there was a majority of Republican voters there for McKinley and one way or the other they must have a chance to express their preference. I told him if he or Quay were the Pennsylvania candidate that McKinley would not fight him in his own state, but that as against any one else, we felt the vote of the state properly belonged to McKinley. He rather agreed to this but said we would make nothing by forcing things; he thought we would gain all we wanted by waiting and letting it come naturally.

This talk was absolutely confidential and I think I will ask you not mention it to anybody but McKinley himself. I should not like this letter to be exposed to the chance of being lost or picked up—if you will be kind enough either to destroy it or enclose it back to me I will be obliged.

I hope Mrs. Hanna is on the way to complete recovery.

                                        Yours truly,

                                        John Hay

           TO ALBERT LEE, ESQ.[20]

                                   Newbury, N. H.

                                     Sept. 11. 1899

Dear Sir,

My early dreams consisted rather of a desire than of an expectation that I might do some service to the country in the way of politics and diplomacy. Through the favor of fortune and the kindness of friends my opportunities have been far greater than my dreams. For the meagreness of the results, I am alone to blame—and that not for the lack of goodwill, but of ability. Looking back over sixty years I can think of no one who has injured me.

Yours sincerely,

John Hay

TO WHITELAW REID[21]

Sep. 1, 1900.

. . . Neither of the stories about me in the papers is true. The Yellows lied who said I was dying and I lied a little when I saw I was fit as a flea or words to that effect. A contradiction has to be unqualified or it does not contradict. The fact is that my June and July in Washington, with a crisis per hour, and a temperature of 98 used me up considerably. This old tabernacle which I have inhabited for 60 years is getting quite ramshackle in the furnace, the plumbing and the electrical arrangements. But I have had myself pretty thoroughly overhauled and they tell me there is nothing much the matter except antiquity and that I have the right to look forward to a useless and querulous old age. I can't get back to Washington for a while yet, and though I feel like a shirk and a malingerer in putting off my work on Adee and Root, I comfort myself with the thought that they are doing it admirably.

I thank you most cordially for your good words about my work, and I must thank you over again for the able and constant support you have given us, in every time of need. Particularly in this China business, not only the Editor but the Washington representatives of *The Tribune* have held up our hands magnificently. During the darkest days, when the whole world was deriding us for our naivete and credulity, Fearn was almost alone among the men who came to the Department in believing that Conger was alive and that we should save him.

I see nothing ahead but ceaseless work and worry. I can tell you, confidentially, that when I got the news about New Chwang I sent a despatch to Russia, asking what it meant, and intimating that we were not to be shut out from Manchuria, in that or any other way.

They answered very promptly that their occupation of New Chwang was military and temporary, and that they did not purpose any territorial acquisition "in China or Manchuria." This explicit mention of Manchuria was very gratifying. Of course they will not be bound by a promise when it becomes inconvenient but the promise is an excellent thing to have on record.

I take it you agree with us that we are to limit as far as possible our military operations in China, to withdraw our troops at the earliest day consistent with our obligations, and in the final adjustment to do everything we can for the integrity and reform of China, and to hold on like grim death to the Open Door.

DIARY [22]

June, 1905.

I say to myself that I should not rebel at the thought of my life ending at this time. I have lived to be old; something I never expected in my youth. I have had many blessings, domestic happiness being the greatest of all. I have lived my life. I have had success beyond all the dreams of my boyhood. My name is printed in the journals of the world without descriptive qualifications, which may, I suppose, be called fame. By mere length of service I shall occupy a modest place in the history of my time. If I were to live several years more I should probably add nothing to my existing reputation; while I could not reasonably expect any further enjoyment of life, such as falls to the lot of old men in sound health. I know death is the common lot, and what is universal ought not to be deemed a misfortune; and yet—instead of confronting it with dignity and philosophy, I cling instinctively to life and the things of life, as eagerly as if I had not had my chance at happiness and gained nearly all the great prizes.

Notes and References

Preface

1. Richard Hofstadter, *The Age of Reform* (New York, 1955).

2. Ibid., p. 91. Even those who take issue with Hofstadter on many of his arguments about the "Gilded Age" accept his general assumption about the mugwump type. For instance Ari Hoogenboom contends ["Spoilsmen and Reformers," in *The Gilded Age*, ed. H. Wayne Morgan (Syracuse, 1963), p. 80] that the reformer had lost "social and economic power." He was "an outsider, philosophically, as well as politically." John G. Sproat, in his outstanding recent work, *"The Best Men:" Liberal Reformers in The Gilded Age* (New York, 1968), pictures Mugwumps as politically independent elitists whose world view rested upon the assumptions and moralisms of preindustrial America. Unlike Hofstadter, Sproat does not include John Hay, Theodore Roosevelt, or Albert J. Beveridge in his Mugwump-type list.

3. Tyler Dennett, *John Hay: From Poetry to Politics* (New York, 1933).

4. Kenton J. Clymer, *John Hay: The Gentleman as Diplomat* (Ann Arbor, 1975).

Chapter One

1. Charles Hay to Elisabeth Hay, October 3, 1861, John Hay Papers, John Hay Library, Brown University (hereafter cited as Hay Papers, BU).

2. Tyler Dennett, *John Hay: From Poetry to Politics* (New York, 1933), p. 58.

3. Henry Adams, *The Education of Henry Adams* (Boston, 1918), pp. 362, 364–65, 424.

4. William R. Thayer, *The Life of John Hay*, 2 vols. (New York, 1915), I, 314.

5. Dennett, *Hay*, pp. 176–77, see also pp. 12, 69–70.

6. Frederic Cople Jaher, "Industrialism and the American Aristocrat: A Social Study of John Hay and his novel, *The Breadwinners*," *Journal of the Illinois State Historical Society* 65 (Spring, 1972), 69–93. For another view see Anne H. Sherrill, "John Hay, Shield of Union" (Ph.D. dissertation, University of California, Berkeley, 1966), p. 18. A recent biography [Ken-

ton J. Clymer, *John Hay: The Gentleman as Diplomat* (Ann Arbor, 1975)] does not deal with Hay's political career but concentrates on Hay's political thought and diplomatic career.

7. See Dennett, *Hay*, pp. 31–32; also, Caroline Ticknor, ed., *A Poet in Exile: Early Letters of John Hay* (New York and Boston, 1910), pp. 1–11; Thayer, *Hay*, I, pp. 52–73.

8. Dennett, *Hay*, p. 1.

9. Charles Hay to Elisabeth Hay, June 11, 1830, Hay Papers, BU; also see Charles Hay to Elisabeth Hay, July 27, 1829, ibid., and Charles Hay to Nathaniel Hay, July 27, 1829, ibid.

10. Charles Hay to Elisabeth Hay, Sept. 23, 1830, ibid.; also see Charles Hay to Nathaniel Hay, July 17, 1830, ibid.

11. Charles Hay to Elisabeth Hay, Sept. 23, 1830, ibid.; Charles vigorously resisted the suggestion of his father, John Hay, that he (Charles) remove his practice to Springfield. Charles Hay to John Hay, Feb. 20, 1832, ibid.; see also Charles Hay to Nathaniel Hay, May 21, 1834, ibid.

12. Charles Hay to Nathaniel Hay, Feb. 12, 1835, ibid.

13. Charles Hay to Addison Hay, Nov. 3, 1839, ibid.; see also Dennett, *Hay*, p. 11.

14. Dennett, *Hay*, p. 11; Charles Hay to Theodore Hay, May 4, 1843, Hay Papers, BU; Charles Hay to Milton Hay, Jan. 5, 1841, Charles Hay Papers, Illinois State Historical Society, Springfield, Illinois (hereafter cited as C. Hay Papers, ISHS).

15. John Hay, *Dr. Charles Hay* (New York, 1884), p. 13.

16. Charles Hay to Elisabeth Hay, Sept. 23, 1830, Hay Papers, BU.

17. Charles Hay to Nathaniel Hay, July 15, 1833, ibid.; Charles Hay to Elisabeth Hay, August 3, 1833, C. Hay Papers, ISHS.

18. Charles Hay to William Graham, Aug. 7, 1839, Hay Papers, BU.

19. Charles Hay to Nathaniel Hay, July 17, 1830, ibid.

20. Charles Hay to Elisabeth Hay, Oct. 17, 1831, ibid.; Charles Hay to Nathaniel Hay, Feb. 12, 1835, ibid.

21. Charles Hay to William Graham, Aug. 7, 1839, ibid.

22. Charles Hay to Addison Hay, June 7, 1837, ibid.

23. Charles Hay to Elisabeth Hay, Oct. 17, 1831, ibid.

24. Dennett, *Hay*, pp. 6–9.

25. Ibid., p. 9.

26. Charles Hay to Nathaniel Hay, Oct. 4, 1831, Hay Papers, BU.

27. Charles Hay to Elisabeth Hay, Nov. 2, 1830, ibid.

28. Lorenzo Sears, *John Hay: Author and Statesman* (New York, 1914), p. 5.

29. Dennett erred on the date of John's birth. On John's second birthday, his eldest brother, eight-year-old Edward Leonard, died. Both of Milton Hay's sons also died as children. The entire family's subsequent behavior suggests that the deaths of these children caused them to show

greater concern for the least strong child—John. John's brothers and sisters were Edward Leonard (born November 9, 1832, died October 8, 1840), Augustus Leonard (born December 2, 1834, died November 12, 1904), Mary Pierce (born December 17, 1836, died March 21, 1914), Charles Edward (born March 23, 1841, died January 15, 1916), and Helen Jemima (born September 13, 1844, died June 19, 1873). Dr. Charles Hay died on September 14, 1874, and his wife Helen Leonard Hay, died on February 18, 1893. See John Hay, *Letters of John Hay and Extracts from his Diary*, 3 vols. (Washington, 1908), I, v–vi; Thayer, *Hay*, I, 5; Dennett, *Hay*, p. 10.

30. Charles Hay to Nathaniel Hay, July 15, 1833; May 21, 1834, Hay Papers, BU. In 1848 when John was ten years old Charles wrote that he had twelve children in his family; in addition to his own five children, "5 regular boarders, and Mrs. Parke [Nancy Leonard Parke] and two children." Charles Hay to Theodore Hay, May 9, 1848, ibid.; also see Charles Hay to Elisabeth Hay, August 3, 1833, C. Hay Papers, ISHS.

31. John Hay, "The Press and Modern Progress," May 19, 1904, *Addresses of John Hay* (New York, 1907), pp. 244–45.

32. For instance see Twain's boyhood views of sitting along the banks of the Mississippi cited in Albert B. Paine, *Mark Twain, A Biography*, 3 vols. (New York, 1912), pp. 49–50. Also see Dixon Wecter, *Sam Clemens of Hannibal* (Boston, 1952).

33. Charles Hay to Addison Hay, Nov. 3, 1839, Hay Papers, BU.

34. A. S. Chapman, "The Boyhood of John Hay," *Century* 56 (July, 1909), 446; Thayer *Hay*, I, 14–19; Dennett, *Hay*, p. 13.

35. Thayer, *Hay*, I, 19. John was very close to his older brother Augustus, whom John apparently outshown in every intellectual endeavor, even though Augustus was four years older than John. See John Hay to Theodore Roosevelt, Nov. 16, 1904, ibid., pp. 14–16.

36. Thayer, *Hay*, I, 16.

37. Chapman, "Boyhood of Hay," pp. 447–49.

38. Dennett, *Hay*, pp. 14–16. For more on Milton Hay see John G. Nicolay and John Hay, *Abraham Lincoln, A History*, 10 vols. (New York, 1890), I, 167–72, 214.

39. In 1857 Milton's wife died and he moved to Springfield, joining the firm of Stephen Logan as a junior partner. See Dennett, *Hay*, pp. 15–16.

40. Charles Hay to Elisabeth Hay, March 30, 1854, Hay Papers, BU; also see, Sherrill, "Hay," p. 3.

41. John Hay to Mary Hay, March 5, 1854, Hay Papers, BU.

42. Hay to Family, Sept. 30, 1855, Nov. 28, 1855, ibid.

43. Dennett, *Hay*, p. 19.

44. Hay to Family, Nov. 28, 1855, Hay Papers, BU.

45. Ibid.

46. John Hay to Milton Hay, March 30, 1856, ibid.; Charles Hay to Sisters, Dec. 14, 1856, C. Hay Papers, ISHS.

47. Thayer, *Hay*, I, 33.
48. F. Burge to William L. Stone, n.d., Hay Papers, BU.
49. Dennett, *Hay*, p. 21. In his last year Hay was ill only six days.
50. Thayer, *Hay*, I, 35.
51. Hay to Family, Nov. 28, 1855, Hay Papers, BU.
52. Thayer, *Hay*, I, p. 34; Dennett, *Hay*, p. 20.
53. Chapman, "Boyhood of Hay," p. 450.
54. Some of Hay's classmates claimed that he was "a young Dr. Johnson without his boorishness, or a Dr. Goldsmith without his frivolity," see Thayer, *Hay*, I, 41.
55. Thayer, *Hay*, I, 40–41, 47; Dennett, *Hay*, p. 22. Also see Hay to Leandor Manchester, July 23, 1857, Hay Papers, BU; and Hay to Edgar R. Morris, Feb. 7, 1858, ibid., for more on Hay's fraternity life.
56. *Brown Alumni Magazine* 6 (July, 1905), 29.
57. John Hay, *A College Friendship, A Series of Letters from John Hay to Hannah Angell* (Boston: Privately printed, 1938), pp. iii–iv.
58. See John Hay to Hannah Angell, June 2, 1858: June 26, 1858; July 6, 1858; July 19, 1858, *College Friendship*, pp. 3–26; also see introduction, ibid., p. vi.
59. Nora Perry was five or six years older than Hay. John, although serious in his relations with Hannah, also grew infatuated with Nora. In fact, John had a reputation among his classmates as a youth who easily became infatuated with pretty girls. One of his classmates at Brown recalled that if Hay "was smitten with the charms of a pretty girl, he raved and walked the room pouring out his sentiment in a flood of furious eloquence." Chapman, "Boyhood of Hay," p. 450.
60. Hay to Nora Perry, Jan. 2, 1859, Hay Papers, BU.
61. Dennett, *Hay*, p. 31; Clymer, *John Hay*, p. 7; Sherrill, "Hay," pp. 7–9.
62. Hay to Nora Perry, Aug. 30, 1858, Hay Papers, BU.
63. Hay to Nora Perry, Oct. 12, 1858, ibid. He wrote to Mrs. Whitman that he feared "that if I remain in the west I will entirely lose all the aspirations I formerly cherished." Hay to S. H. Whitman, Aug. 30, 1858, ibid.; also see Hay to S. H. Whitman, Dec. 15, 1858, ibid.; and, Hay to Hannah Angell, Aug. 13, 1858, *College Friendship*, pp. 26–28.
64. Hay to H. Angell, July 19, 1858, ibid., pp. 15–19.
65. Hay was capable of fairly morbid poetry while still in Providence. In a poem written in 1858 entitled "In The Mist," the poet contemplates suicide. This poem was composed during a period which all Hay's biographers see as the happiest period of his life. In sending the poem to Hannah, John warned, "Do not think that *I think I think* everything in it. It is merely an attempt to describe a mood of a misanthropic boy. . . ." Hay to H. Angell, Aug. 3, 1858, *College Friendship*, pp. 19–26. Hay's biographers were certain that due to its tenor, the poem must have been written in

Warsaw in 1859. (See, for instance, Clymer, *John Hay*, pp. 6–7.) Actually Hay contributed to this misunderstanding by sending a copy of the poem to Nora Perry in Jan., 1859, implying that he had composed it in his grief at being removed from Providence. See Hay to Nora Perry, Jan. 2, 1859, Ticknor, *Poet in Exile*, pp. 27–35.

66. Hay to Nora Perry, Jan. 2, 1859, Hay Papers, BU.

67. Hay to Hannah Angell, Oct. 20, 1858, *College Friendship*, p. 34.

68. Hay to Hannah Angell, Dec. 11, 1858, ibid., p. 38.

69. Hay to Hannah Angell, Jan. 17, 1859, ibid., p. 40.

70. Hay to Nora Perry, Jan. 2, 1859, Hay Papers, BU.

71. Hay, *Dr. Charles Hay*, p. 13.

72. Charles Hay to Milton Hay, Sept. 6, 1859, Hay Papers, BU.

73. Ibid.

74. Ibid.

75. Ibid.

76. Ibid.

77. Milton Hay's letter to his nephew has been destroyed, but its contents are referred to in John Hay to Milton Hay, Jan. 28, 1859, Hay Papers, BU.

78. Ibid.

79. Hay to William Stone, May 20, 1859, ibid.

80. Hay to Nora Perry, May 15, 1859, ibid.

81. Hay to Hannah Angell, July 27, 1859, *College Friendship*, p. 48; also, Hay to Hannah Angell, July 1, 1860, ibid., pp. 49–51.

82. Again recent scholarship has accepted Hay's rhetoric. Jaher ["Industrialism and the American Aristocrat," pp. 77–78] contends that during this period "In attitude, if not origin, Hay was more typical of the East."

83. Lincoln, Stephen Douglas, Judge David Davies (later of the Supreme Court), Samuel H. Trent, O. H. Browning, Lyman Trumbull, Senator James Shields, Stephen Logan, John T. Stuart, E. D. Baker, Albert T. Bledsoe, and John Alexander McClernand all resided in Springfield during this period. Nicolay and Hay, *Abraham Lincoln, A History*, I, 214, 299–301; Thayer, *Hay*, I, 74–76.

84. For more on this point see Howard I. Kushner, " 'The Strong God Circumstance': The Political Career of John Hay," *Journal of the Illinois State Historical Society* 67 (September, 1974), 362–84.

85. Dennett, *Hay*, p. 25.

Chapter Two

1. Hay to Nicolay, August 7, 1863, Hay Papers, BU.

2. Tyler Dennett, *John Hay: From Poetry to Politics* (New York, 1933), pp. 35–37. While admitting that Lincoln's relationship to Hay was that of father to son (p. 39), Dennett dismisses the impact of these years on Hay as an "episode" (p. 49).

3. All of Hay's biographers have seen the appointment as a great stroke of luck. Dennett states that the appointment cannot be explained (*John Hay*, pp. 33–34). Thayer ascribes the appointment to fortune: "Thus Fortune opened her door to the young man of twenty-two. Instead of condemning him to perpetual banishment in the 'West', she led him to the East, Washington. . . ." William R. Thayer, *The Life of John Hay*, 2 vols. (Boston and New York, 1915), I, 87–88.

4. Thayer, *Hay*, I, 86–88.

5. Nicolay to unknown person, March 10, 1861, quoted in Dennett, *John Hay*, p. 35. See also David C. Mearns, *The Lincoln Papers*, 2 vols. (New York, 1948), I, 22.

6. See diaries, John Hay Papers, Library of Congress, Washington, D.C. (see journals I and II; diaries will hereafter be cited as JHP:LC:J).

7. John Hay, "E. E. Ellsworth," *Atlantic* 8 (July, 1861), 119–25; Hay diary, April 20, 22, 24, 26, 30, 1861; May 1, 2, 7, 9, 1861, JHP:LC:JI. John George Nicolay and John Hay, *Abraham Lincoln, A History*, 10 vols. (New York, 1886–1890), IV, 312–15, 320 (hereafter cited as Nicolay and Hay, *Lincoln*).

8. Hay, "Ellsworth."

9. Ibid., p. 120.

10. Ibid., p. 125.

11. Hay to Hannah Angell, August 12, 1861, in John Hay, *College Friendship: A Series of Letters from John Hay to Hannah Angell* (Boston: Privately printed, 1938), p. 61.

12. Hay diary, November 13, 1861, JHP:LC:JI. For more on Lincoln's relationship with McClellan see Hans L. Trefousse, *The Radical Republicans: Lincoln's Vanguard for Racial Justice* (New York, 1969), pp. 177–202. For a recent compilation of Hay's views on the Union's generals see George Monteiro, ed., "John Hay and the Union Generals," *Journal of the Illinois State Historical Society* 69 (February, 1976), 46–66.

13. John Hay, "Colonel Baker," *Harper's* 24 (December, 1861), pp. 103–110.

14. Ibid., pp. 104, 109.

15. John Hay, "Rhymes," *The Complete Poetical Works of John Hay* (Boston, 1916), pp. 268–69.

16. Salmon P. Chase, *Inside Lincoln's Cabinet, The Civil War Diaries of Salmon P. Chase*, ed. David Donald (New York, 1954), September 11, 1862, pp. 132–35; Gideon Welles, *Diary*, 3 vols., ed. H. K. Beale (New York, 1960), September 16, 1862, I, 130–39.

17. Hay to Helen Hay [mother], April 23, 1863, Hay Papers, BU; Lincoln to David Hunter and Samuel F. Dupont, April 14, 1863, *The Collected Works of Abraham Lincoln*, 9 vols., ed. Roy P. Balser (New Brunswick, N.J., 1953), VI. 173–74 (hereafter cited as Lincoln, *Works*).

18. Hay to Nicolay, April 23, 1863, *Lincoln and the Civil War in the*

Diaries and Letters of John Hay, ed. Tyler Dennett (New York, 1939), p. 62 (hereafter cited as Hay, *Civil War Diaries*); also see Lincoln, *Works,* VI, 174. Hay diary, April 9, 1863, JHP:LC:JIV.

19. Hay to Grandfather, May 2, 1863, Hay Papers, BU; Hay to Nicolay, April 8, 1863; Hay, *Civil War Diaries,* pp. 56–57.

20. Hay to Helen Hay, April 23, 1863, Hay Papers, BU; Charles Hay to John Hay (Dr. Hay's father), March 29, 1863, ibid.

21. Hay diary, April 24, 1863, JHP:LC:JIV.

22. Ibid., April 24–27, 1863.

23. Ibid., May 22, and April 26, 1863.

24. Hay diary, 1862; July 18, 1863; July 1, 1864, JI. Thayer, *Hay,* I, 10–18, 150. For more on Hay's views on slavery see Kenton J. Clymer, *John Hay, The Gentleman as Diplomat* (Ann Arbor, 1975), pp. 69–70. For more on Lincoln's attitude toward emancipation see Trefousse, *The Radical Republicans,* pp. 202–30, 237–38, 284–86.

25. Hay to Helen Hay, March 19, 1863, Hay Papers, BU: also see Nicolay and Hay, *Lincoln* VI, 124, 443.

26. Hay diary, April 19, 1863, JHP:LC:JIV.

27. Ibid., April 19, 25, 26, and May 23, 1863.

28. Ibid., May 21, 1863.

29. Ibid., May 19, 22, 23, 1863.

30. Ibid., (JI), September 15, 1862.

31. Hay to Nicolay, August 7, 1863, Hay Papers, BU.

32. Hay diary, July 14, 1863, JHP:LC:JI.

33. Ibid., July 31, August 1, 1863.

34. Ibid., July 31, 1863.

35. Ibid., July 23, August 6, 10, 1863; also see Nicolay and Hay, *Lincoln,* VIII, 224–29.

36. Hay diary, July 21, August 14, 1863, JHP:LC:JI.

37. Ibid., August 14, October 22, 1863.

38. For Lincoln's plans for reconstruction see J. G. Randall and David Donald, *The Civil War and Reconstruction,* 2nd ed. (Boston, 1961), pp. 552–55; and William B. Hesseltine, *Lincoln's Plan of Reconstruction* (reprint, Chicago, 1967); Trefousse, *The Radical Republicans,* pp. 266–89.

39. Dennett, *John Hay,* pp. 43–44; Hesseltine, *Lincoln's Reconstruction,* pp. 108–9.

40. Hay diary, December 28, 1863, JHP:LC:JII.

41. Ibid.

42. Ibid., December 29, 1863; also see Lincoln to Major General Quincy A. Gilmore, January 13, 1864; Lincoln, *Works,* VII, 126; (by the end of the war, Hay's rank was colonel). Hay diary, January 20, 1864, JHP:LC:JVI.

43. Hay diary, February 15, 1864, JHP:LC:JVI.

44. Ibid., February 17, 1864.

45. Ibid., February 18, 1864.

46. Ibid., February 21, 22, 24, 28, and March 10, 1864.

47. *New York Herald,* February 22, 24, 28, 1864.

48. Hay diary, March 10, 1864, JHP:LC:JIV; Hay to Charles Halprine, April 23, 1864, Hay Papers, BU; also see Hay (n.d.), untitled address to the people of Florida, JHP:LC:JVI.

49. Hay diary, June 17, 1864, JHP:LC:JII.

50. Ibid.; Lincoln to Hay, June 10, 1864; Lincoln, *Works,* VII, 386.

51. Lincoln to Rosecrans, June 10, 1864, Lincoln, *Works,* VII, 386; Hay diary, June 10, 11, 12, 13, and 14, 1864, JHP:LC:JII; see also Edward C. Kirkland, *The Peacemakers of 1864* (New York, 1927), pp. 43–44, 116, 131–32.

52. Hay diary, June 17, 1864, JHP:LC:JII; see also Lincoln, *Works,* VII, 386–88.

53. Ibid.

54. Greeley to Lincoln, July 7, 1864; Lincoln, *Works,* VII, 435–36. The other proposals listed by Greeley were: A complete amnesty for all political offenses; payment of four hundred million dollars to the slave states for their slaves; representation for former slave states in Congress based on total population; and a national convention to be called at once.

55. Shelby M. Cullom, *Fifty Years of Public Service* (Chicago, 1911), p. 101.

56. Hay diary, June 30, July 1, 4, 8, 9, 10, 11, and 13, 1864, JHP:LC:JI; also see Trefousse, *The Radical Republicans,* pp. 289–98.

57. Lincoln to Greeley, July 15, 1864; Lincoln, *Works,* VII, 440–41; Hay diary, July 21, 1864, and Hay to Mr. ? McNeil, July 14, 1864, JHP:LC:JV.

58. Hay diary, July 21, 1864, JHP:LC:JV; Cullom, *Fifty Years,* p. 101; also see Randall and Donald, *The Civil War and Reconstruction,* pp. 470–72; Kirkland, *Peacemakers,* pp. 68, 73, 76; Dennett, *John Hay,* pp. 45–46.

59. Hay to Mrs. James Coggeshall (Hannah Angell), July 31, 1864, and August 25, 1864, *A College Friendship,* pp. 62–63; Hay to Nicolay, August 25, and September 7, 1864, Hay Papers, BU.

60. Hay to Nicolay, August 25 and 26, 1864, ibid.

61. Hay to Nicolay, August 25, 1864, ibid.

62. Nicolay to Hay, August 25, 1864, quoted in Helen Nicolay, *Lincoln's Secretary* (New York, 1949), p. 212.

63. Hay to Nicolay, August 25 and 26, 1864, Hay Papers, BU.

64. Ibid.; see also Hay to Nicolay, September 7, 1864, ibid., where Hay is more optimistic about Lincoln's chances.

65. Hay diary, May 24, October 2, 7, 8, and 11, 1864, JHP:LC:JII, JIII.

66. Ibid., October 2, 1864; Welles, *Diary,* November 26, 1864, II, 181–187. Holt declined the offer.

67. Hay to Nicolay, August 25, 1864, Hay Papers, BU.

68. Hay diary, November 28, 1863, and December 12, 1863, JHP:LC:JII.

69. Ibid., July 1, 4, 11, and 12, 1864, JI; see also entry for May 14, 1864, JII.

70. Ibid., November 18, 1863.

71. Ibid., September 26, 1864, JIII.

72. Ibid., October 7, 1864.

73. Ibid., November 12, 1864, entry written November 16, covering events of November 13–16.

74. Ibid.

75. Nicolay to Therena Bates, February 4, 1865, quoted in Nicolay, *Lincoln's Secretary*, p. 222. See also Hay to Charles Hay (Brother), March 31, 1865, Hay Papers, BU.

76. Nicolay, *Lincoln's Secretary*, pp. 223–24.

77. Nicolay to Therena Bates, March 12, 1865, ibid., p. 225.

78. Hay to Charles Hay, March 31, 1865, Hay Papers, BU.

79. Nicolay to Therena Bates, March 28, April 1, 17, and 19, 1865, in Nicolay, *Lincoln's Secretary*, pp. 228–33.

80. Nicolay and Hay, *Lincoln*, see vol. x, chap. 14. See also Nicolay to Therena Bates, April 24, 1865; Nicolay, *Lincoln's Secretary*, p. 233.

Chapter Three

1. For a general discussion of Hay's literary associations see Kenton J. Clymer, *John Hay: The Gentleman as Diplomat* (Ann Arbor, 1975), pp. 1–29.

2. The other charter members were Howells, Twain, Stedman, Augustus Saint Gaudens, John LaFarge, and Edward McDowell. James and Adams were elected later by the original seven members. See George Monteiro, *Henry James and John Hay: The Record of a Friendship* (Providence, Rhode Island, 1965), pp. 40–43.

3. Clymer, *Hay*, p. 8; Monteiro, *James and Hay*, p. 43.

4. Hay's career is often presented as two careers at odds. See for instance, Tyler Dennett, *John Hay: From Poetry to Politics* (New York, 1933), especially pp. 24–34; Clymer, Hay, pp. 13–16. Also see Henry Adams, *The Education of Henry Adams* (Boston, 1918, 1931 edition), pp. 364–65, 424–25. Lorenzo Sears, *John Hay, Author Statesman* (New York, 1914), pp. 71–72.

5. The careers of John L. Motley and James Russell Lowell also fit this pattern. For more on Hay's relationship with Bigelow see Dennett, *John Hay*, pp. 59–60; see also Anne H. Sherrill, "John Hay: Shield of Union" (Ph.D. dissertation, University of California, Berkeley, 1966), pp. 213–14, 218–19.

6. See for instance, Clymer, *Hay*, pp. 42–44. Granville Hicks, "The Conversion of John Hay," *The New Republic* 63 (June 10, 1931), 100–101.

7. For an interesting discussion on this point see Michael Paul Rogin,

Fathers and Children: Andrew Jackson and the Subjugation of the American Indian (New York, 1975), especially pp. 126–34; 298–301.

8. Leslie A. Fiedler, *Love and Death in the American Novel*, 2nd ed. (New York, 1966), pp. 26–31.

9. While we do not wish to argue one way or the other in the debate over whether the Civil War was a revolution, we do wish to make the point that Hay increasingly believed that the war's results were revolutionary. For more on the Civil War as a revolution see Barrington Moore, Jr., *Social Origins of Dictatorship and Democracy: Lord and Peasant in the Modern World* (Boston, 1966), pp. 111–55; William Appleman Williams, *The Contours of American History* (Chicago, 1966), pp. 284–300; Richard D. Brown, "Modernization and the Modern Personality in Early America, 1600–1865," *Journal of Interdisciplinary History* 2 (Winter, 1972), 201–28.

10. Hay, *Civil War Diaries*, February 11, 1867, p. 273.

11. Ibid.

12. John Hay, "Sunrise at the Place de la Concorde," *The Complete Poetical Works of John Hay* (Boston, 1916), pp. 29–34.

13. Hay, "The Sphinx of the Tuileries," ibid., pp. 35–37.

14. Hay, "A Triumph of Order," ibid., pp. 63–65.

15. For instance see Hay diary, September 8, 1867, where Hay refers to the Roman Church as "non-producing and all consuming." John Hay Papers, Library of Congress, Journals, volume VII (Hereafter cited as JHP:LC:JVII).

16. Hay, "The Monks of Basle," *Complete Poetical Works*, pp. 47–51.

17. Hay diary, July 12, 13, and 15, 1867, JHP:LC:JVII.

18. Ibid., September 8, 1867. Also see diary for September 9, 11, and 15, December 18, 22, 26, and 30, 1867; January 5, 18, February 18, March 23, April 10, 23, 1868, for observations on the aristocracy and the Church in Austria. For Hay's views on those institutions in Spain see his *Castilian Days* (New York, 1871), especially the chapters entitled "Red Letter Days," "The Influence of Tradition on Spanish Life," and "Spanish Living and Dying." Also see Hay to Bigelow, April 27, 1868, Hay Papers, BU.

19. Hay diary, September 9, 1867, JHP:LC:JVII. For Hay's impressions of Europeans in Washington during the war, see diary, October 10, 12, 1861; September 10, 1863, JHP:LC:JI; April 24, 1864, JHP:LC:JII.

20. Ibid., September 8, 9, 11, October 28, December 16, 22, 1867, January 18, March 23, 1868.

21. Ibid., September 9, 1867.

22. Ibid., September 25, 1866. See also September 10, 1867.

23. Hay, "The Curse of Hungary," *Complete Poetical Works*, pp. 44–46.

24. Hay diary, September 8, 1867, JHP:LC:JVII.

25. Hay to Bigelow, April 27, 1868, Hay Papers, BU.

26. Hay, *Castilian Days* (Boston, 1871).

27. Hay, *Castilian Days* (Boston, 1903 edition), p. 88.

28. Ibid. (1871) edition), see especially pp. 210, 404–8.

29. Hay, "Address to the Citizens of Florida" (Spring, 1864), JHP:LC:JVI.

30. Hay diary, September 8, 1867, JHP:LC:JVIII.

31. Hay, *Castilian Days* (1871 edition), p. 25.

32. See for instance, Dennett, *John Hay*, pp. 77–80.

33. Hay, "Jim Bludso of the Prairie Belle," *Complete Poetical Works*, pp. 3–5.

34. Hay, "Little Breeches," ibid., pp. 6–9.

35. Hay, "Banty Tim," ibid., pp. 10–13.

36. Hay, "The Pledge at Spunky Point," ibid., pp. 21–25.

37. Hay, "Esse Quam Videri," ibid., p. 134.

38. See Hay to Seward, March 9, 1867, Seward Papers, Hay to Motley, [Summer, 1869], Hay Papers, BU; also see Hay, *Complete Poetical Works*, p. 134.

39. They both began their publishing careers in the same volume of the *Atlantic*. Both Hay's "Ellsworth" essay and Adams' "A Field Night in the House of Commons" appeared in volume 8 of the *Atlantic* (1861).

40. Hay diary, September 10, 1867, JHP:LC:JVII.

41. See Hay's articles on Ellsworth and Baker discussed in chapter 2 as well as his 1864 "Address to the Citizens of Florida."

42. See Adams, *Education*, p. 266. For a recent interpretation of Adam's ideas see James G. Murray, *Henry Adams* (New York, 1974).

43. Hay to Bigelow, August 19, 1869, Hay Papers, BU.

44. Hay to Robert Todd Lincoln, January 6, 1886, ibid.

45. See Howard I. Kushner, " 'The Strong God Circumstance': The Political Career of John Hay," *Journal of the Illinois State Historical Society* 67 (September, 1974), 372–73.

46. Hay diary, February 28, 1867, February 24–March 5, 1867, JHP:LC:JVII; Hay to Nicolay, February 14 and March 18, 1867, Hay Papers, BU.

47. Hay diary, November 7, 1861, JHP:LC:JI. We will discuss Hay's views on "free trade" more fully in chapter 6. Two works which discuss the complex and changing meanings of free trade in the late nineteenth century are Edward Chase Kirkland, *Dream and Thought in the Business Community, 1860–1900* (Ithaca, 1956) and Tom E. Terrill, *The Tarriff, Politics, and American Foreign Policy, 1874–1901* (Westport, Conn., 1973), especially, pp. 81–83, 118–25, 136, 159–83.

48. Hay diary, February 12, 1864, JHP:LC:JVI.

49. Hay diary, July 19, 1863, December 9, 1863, JHP:LC:JII; Dennett, *John Hay*, 127–28 (quoting parts of Hay's speech of October 15, 1879), John Hay, untitled manuscript speech [1892], Hay Papers, BU.

50. Hay's opposition to what he thought were Radical Republicans runs all through the diary entries for 1863 and 1864. See also February 7, 1867 JHP:LC:JVII. For views on hopeful passage of British Reform Bill of 186̃

see ibid., July 12, 13, 1867, and Hay to John Bigelow, April 27, 1868, Hay Papers, BU.

51. See John Hay, "A Prefatory Sketch," pp. iii–ix, 1899 *Harper's* edition of *The Bread-winners*. Note also the demeaning depiction of the strike in the novel (pp. 185–96, 215–19, 237–43) as a "Holiday," called without cause or conviction and ended by one groups acceptance of the bosses' offer and by anothers acceptance of their wives' collective remonstrance that "their lazy picnic had lasted long enough, that there was no meat in the house, and that they had got to come home and go to work." (p. 241).

52. J. C. Levinson, *The Mind and Art of Henry Adams* (Boston: Houghton Mifflin Co., 1957), pp. 290–91, 336–37; Hay to Adams, April 25, 1894, JHP:LC.

53. *The Bread-winners* was originally published in installments in the *Century* magazine from August, 1883, to January, 1884. The manuscript copy of the work in the Houghton Library of Harvard University is dated 1882 and gives evidence of very few changes between Hay's facile first draft and the published version. He had trouble with one point. How virile should the gentlemanly Arthur Farnham be? The final version is much tamer than the original. The book had many purposes and themes. As "A Social Study," it delineated Hay's and his characters' varying ideas of American social classes and their behavior. The book was also a love story and tribute to his wife who was the daughter of a successful former carpenter and a seamstress. Finally, as many have pointed out, it was a response to Henry Adams' *Democracy* and its conclusion that political activity by the "better sort" was futile.

54. Hay, *The Bread-winners*, pp. 8–9, 50–51, 98, 163, 188–89, 193–94, chapters 14, 15.

55. Hay to Amasa Stone, August 23, 1877, Hay Papers, BU.

56. John Hay, *The Bread-winners: A Social Study* (New York, 1883); also see *The Life and Works of John Hay*, ed. Brown University Library (Providence, 1961), p. 36.

57. See Granville Hicks, "The Conversion of John Hay," *The New Republic* 63 (June 10, 1931), 100–101.

58. See chapter 1 for a discussion of Dr. Charles Hay's views of Andrew Jackson.

59. See, for instance, Edward Pessen, "The Egalitarian Myth and the American Social Reality: Wealth, Mobility, and Equality in the 'Era of the Common Man,'" *American Historical Review* 76 (October, 1971), 1004–29; Rogin, *Fathers and Children*, especially chapter 8, "The Market Revolution," pp. 251–79.

60. Hay, *The Bread-winners*, p. 82.

61. Herbert G. Gutman, "Work, Culture, and Society in Industrializing America, 1818–1919," *American Historical Review* 78 (June, 1973), 531–87.

62. Hay, *The Bread-winners*, p. 85.

63. See Richard Hofstadter, *Social Darwinism in American Thought* (Boston, 1946), pp. 41–43.

64. Edward J. Shriver (letter to editor), *The Century* 27 (November, 1883), 157–58.

65. John Hay (letter to editor), ibid., p. 158.

66. See Clymer, *Hay*, pp. 37, 42; Frederic Cople Jaher, "Industrialism and the American Aristocrat: A Social Study of John Hay and His Novel *The Bread-winners*," *Journal of the Illinois State Historical Society* 65 (Spring, 1972), 62–93.

67. Clymer, *Hay*, pp. 42–44.

68. While most of the research for these volumes was done by Nicolay, Hay concerned himself with the thesis and the style of the work. Portions of the manuscript written by Hay are in the Houghton Library, Harvard University. See Dennett, *John Hay*, p. 137.

69. Ibid., pp. 133–34.

70. Clymer unfortunately ignores *Lincoln: A History* in his otherwise interesting study of John Hay.

71. Hay believed that a dead leader could become a very potent symbol. Thus Hay wrote in 1867 that it was his hope that Garibaldi would "free Rome . . . and then die." Hay noted that "John Brown is a saint now. Had he lived he would have been a [undecipherable] malignant Rad, and people would have tired of him." Hay diary, September 10, 1867, JHP:LC:JVII.

72. Nicolay and Hay, *Lincoln* X, 349.

73. Ibid.

74. Hay, "Liberty 1" (1880) Scrapbook, Hay Papers, BU.

75. Hay, "Liberty," *Current Literature*, August, 1905; also in *Complete Poetical Works*, pp. 107–8.

76. See Carlton J. H. Hayes, *A Generation of Materialism* (New York, 1941), on the *Kulturkampf*, pp. 66–87.

77. Hay diary, two untitled poems at the end of entries for June 10–16, 1864, JHP:LC:JIV. One of the sinners is "the rambling wreck from poverty," unemployed and given to drink, the other is a prostitute.

78. Hay diary, April 19, 1863, JHP:LC:JIV.

79. Henry James, *The American* (New York, 1922), p. 2.

80. See Thayer, *Life of Hay*, I: 4–5, 22; Dennett, *John Hay*, pp. 17, 18, 28–30.

81. Hay to Milton Hay, January 28, 1859, Hay Papers, BU; Hay to Hannah Angell [postmarked July 19, 1858], *A College Friendship*, pp. 15–18. The John Hay Papers, New York Public Library, Manuscript Collection, contains a scrapbook of clippings of criticism of "Jim Bludso" on religious grounds, JHP:NYPL:Scrapbook.

82. Hay, "Jim Bludso," *Complete Poetical Works*, p. 5.

83. Hay, "Little Breeches," ibid., p. 6.

84. Caroline Ticknor, *Poe's Helen* (New York, 1916), p. 25.

85. Hay, "Mount Tabor," *Complete Poetical Works*, p. 116.
86. Hay, "The Monks of Basle," ibid., pp. 47–51.
87. Hay, "The Prayer of the Romans," ibid., pp. 42, 43.
88. Hay, "God's Vengeance," ibid., pp. 162–63.
89. Hay, "Religion and Doctrine," ibid., p. 119.
90. Hay, "Banty Tim," ibid., p. 12.
91. Hay to Nicolay, August 10, 1885, Hay Papers, BU.

Chapter Four

1. Tyler Dennett, *John Hay: From Poetry to Politics* (New York, 1933), p. 58.
2. John Hay, "Una," *Complete Poetical Works* (Boston, 1916), pp. 173–75.
3. Henry Adams, *The Education of Henry Adams* (Boston, 1918), pp. 362, 364–65, 424.
4. Thayer, *Life of Hay*, I, 314.
5. Dennett, pp. 176–77, see also pp. 12, 69–70.
6. Frederic Cople Jaher, "Industrialism and the American Aristocrat: A Social Study of John Hay and his novel, *The Bread-winners*," *Journal of the Illinois State Historical Society* 65 (Spring, 1972), 69–93. Jaher contends that "Although Hay was a Republican, his refusal to enter political life carried the tone of mugwump fastidiousness. He showed the distaste of eastern bluebloods for the methods of politics and, like them, was prepared to sacrifice power for style and principle" (p. 832). Kenton J. Clymer, *John Hay: The Gentleman as Diplomat* (Ann Arbor, 1975) does not deal with Hay's political career, but concentrates on Hay's political and social thought and diplomacy.
7. Hay to Amasa Stone, Dec. 4, 1879, in Brown University Library, ed., *The Life and Works of John Hay* (Providence, 1961), p. 40.
8. Hay to Charles Hay, March 31, 1865, *Letters of John Hay and Extracts from His Diary*, 3 vols. (Privately printed, Washington; 1908), I, 253.
9. See for instance Hay, *Civil War Diaries* ed. Sept. 5, 1862, p. 49; Nov. 22, 1863, pp. 124–25; Dec. 19, 1863, p. 139; June 18, 1884, p. 194; July 8, 1864, pp. 207–8. In many ways Hay's later policies as Secretary of State were a working out of Seward's own goals. For background on Seward's foreign policy see Howard I. Kushner, "Visions of the Northwest Coast, Gwin and Seward in the 1850's," *Western Historical Quarterly* 4 (July, 1973), 295–306 and Ernest Paolino, *The Foundations of American Empire: William Henry Seward and U.S. Foreign Policy* (Ithaca, 1973).
10. See William Marsh to Hay, Oct. 30, 1863, William H. Seward Collection, Rush Rhees Library, University of Rochester, Rochester, New York; Hay to Seward, Oct. 30, 1863, ibid. (hereafter cited as Seward Papers).

11. Helen Nicolay, *Lincoln's Secretary* (New York, 1949), pp. 222–27. See also Hay to Seward, July 26, 1865, Seward Papers in which Hay wrote to Seward from Paris, "I wanted to . . . thank you again for all your goodness to me."

12. Hay to Charles Hay, March 31, 1865, *Civil War Diaries*, I, 253.

13. Bigelow resigned as Minister to France in July, 1866. The State Department, while accepting Hay's resignation, requested that he remain until January, 1867, in order to aid Bigelow's successor. Hay to Seward, July 17, 1866, Seward Papers; Seward to Hay, Aug. 7, 1866, ibid.

14. Hay diary, Feb. 2, 1867, *Civil War Diaries*, p. 261.

15. Hay diary, Feb. 3, 1867, *Civil War Diaries*, pp. 261–64.

16. Thayer, *Hay*, I, 256–57.

17. Hay, *Civil War Diaries*, Feb. 4, 1867, Feb. 10, 1867, pp. 265, 270–72.

18. Hay, *Civil War Diaries*, Feb. 6, 1867, pp. 265–66.

19. Ibid., Feb. 7, 1867, pp. 267–68; Feb. 8, 1867, p. 269.

20. Ibid., Feb. 8, 1867, pp. 269–70; Feb. 9, 1867, p. 272; Feb. 11, 1867, pp. 272–73.

21. Ibid., Feb. 10, 1867, pp. 270–73.

22. Hay to Seward, March 4, 1867, Seward Papers.

23. Hay to Nicolay, Feb. 14, 1867, Hay Papers, BU.

24. Hay to Seward, March 4, 1867, Seward Papers. The next day Hay also wrote a letter of thanks to the Assistant Secretary of State, Frederick W. Seward, see Hay to F. W. Seward, March 5, 1867, ibid. In April Hay, apparently losing hope that the State Department would find him a place, wrote a long letter to Secretary of War Edwin M. Stanton asking Stanton if he [Hay] "could be profitably employed" by the War Department. Hay to Stanton, April 22, 1867, Stanton Papers, Manuscript Div., Library of Congress. Over the years Hay had attempted to cultivate the Secretary of War's friendship. Not above the use of flattery, Hay wrote Stanton in July, 1866 that "the readers of history a hundred years hence will know . . . that if any human names are to have the glory of this victory, it belongs to you among the very few who stood by the side of him who was gone to his better reward. . . ." Hay to Stanton, July 26, 1865, ibid. This praise went unrewarded; the Secretary of War did not offer Hay a position in April, 1867.

25. Hay, *Civil War Diaries*, June 11, 1867, pp. 281–82; Hay to John Bigelow, June 11, 1867, Hay Papers, BU; Hay to Elisabeth Hay, June 12, 1867, ibid.; Thayer, *Hay*, I, 278–80; Dennett, *John Hay*, p. 64.

26. See Hay to Seward, Aug. 12, 1868, Seward Papers.

27. Thayer, *Hay*, I, 315.

28. Hay to Nicolay, Dec. 8, 1868, Hay Papers, BU.

29. Ibid.

30. Hay to Sumner, March 13, 1869, Dennett, *John Hay*, p. 65.

31. Hay to Nicolay, March 14, 1869, *Civil War Diaries*, pp. 298–99.

32. John Bigelow, *Retrospections of an Active Life*, 5 vols. (New York, 1909–1913), IV, 294–95; Dennett, *John Hay*, pp. 65–66.

33. Hay to General Daniel Sickles, May 1, 1870, Hay Papers, BU.

34. As early as October, 1869, Hay informed Nicolay of his plans of "coming home next Spring." Hay to Nicolay, Oct. 7, 1869, ibid.

35. Dennett, *John Hay*, p. 69.

36. Hay, of course, had known both Reid and Greeley for several years as a result of Hay's duties as presidential secretary. See chapter 2. Also see Hay to Nicolay, Dec. 8, 1868, Hay Papers, BU. Also see Hay to O. M. Hatch, April 12, 1870, ibid., where Hay, still in Spain, noted that he had "a sort of good offer in New York"; presumably at the *Tribune*. See also Reid to Hay, Sept. 21, 1870, ibid.; Hay to Nicolay, Dec. 12, 1870, ibid.; Reid to Hay, Dec. 23, 1870, ibid. Hay's salary was quickly increased from an initial $50 per week to $65 per week.

37. Thayer, *Hay*, I, 424; Hay to Nicolay, Dec. 12, 1870, Hay Papers, BU.

38. Hay to Nicolay, Jan. 30, 1870, Hay Papers, BU; Hay to John Bigelow, May 9, 1870, ibid.; Hay to Edward King, June 18, 1870, ibid.; Dennett, *John Hay*, p. 120.

39. See for instance Hay to Reid, August 1, 1872, Hay Papers, BU: "If we carry Pennsylvania and Indiana the prospects here [Illinois] will be vastly increased." Also, Hay to Reid, Aug. 4, 1872, ibid., referring to Greeley's campaign, "The good work is going on beautifully here." Also Hay to Reid, Nov. 27, 1872, ibid. Hay did not vote in 1872. Dennett, with no evidence, attributes this fact to Hay's fear of voting against the Regular Republican Administration and Hay's dilettantish views toward politics (Dennett, *John Hay*, p. 121). In light of Hay's general activities, Dennett's view is very questionable.

40. Hay voted for the Democrat Tilden apparently without any pathological side effects. See Dennett, *John Hay*, p. 123.

41. *New York Tribune*, Nov. 19, 1870, p. 5; Semiweekly *Tribune*, Jan. 6, 1871. Lecturing was one of the most remunerative of nineteenth-century activities. For a picture of the Lyceum lecturers with whom Hay was associated, see Dennett, *John Hay*, illustration opposite p. 82. Hay's topics included "The Progress of Democracy in Europe," and "Phases of Washington Life, or the Heroic Age in America."

42. *Atlantic Monthly*, vols. 27, 28 (Jan.–July, 1871). Hay had begun criticism of Spain while at his diplomatic post. See Hay to Howells, February 26, March 3, 1870, Hay, *Civil War Diaries*, pp. 310–11; Hay to David Gray, March 4, ibid., p. 311.

43. Dennett, *John Hay*, p. 71. See chapter 3 for a more complete discussion of Hay's literary works.

44. Thayer, *Life of Hay*, I, 451. For a recent biography of Reid, see

Bingham Duncan, *Whitelaw Reid, Journalist, Diplomat, Politician* (Athens, Georgia, 1975), especially pp. 51–78.

45. *New York Tribune*, December 15, 1870, p. 2; see also ibid., October 8, 1870, p. 2, article on Dumas datelined "Warsaw, Ill.," and Hay to Nicolay, October 13, 1879, Hay Papers, BU.

46. *New York Tribune*, May 5, 1873, p. 2.

47. George Monteiro, *Henry James and John Hay: The Record of a Friendship* (Providence, Rhode Island, 1965), pp. 8, 14–15, 53–55; Dr. Charles Hay to sisters, November 23, 1873, Charles Hay Papers, Illinois State Historical Society, Springfield, Illinois (hereafter cited as C. Hay Papers, ISHS).

48. See Reid to Hay, December 24, 1872, Hay Papers, BU, where Reid raises Hay's salary to one hundred dollars a week; Hay to Charles Hay, December 11, 1872, ibid. Hay also continued to purchase *Tribune* stock and in 1877 he was appointed a trustee of the *Tribune*. See Bayard Taylor to Hay, August 5, 1872, ibid.; and Reid to Hay, January 17, 1877, ibid.

49. Hay to Mrs. John Bigelow, December 23, 1871, ibid.

50. Hay to Charles Hay, December 11, 1872, ibid.; Hay to Adee, November 28, 1874, ibid.

51. Hay to Reid, August 14, 1873, Whitelaw Reid Papers, Library of Congress (hereafter cited as WRP:LC). For information on Amasa Stone, see John Hay, *Amasa Stone, Born April 27, 1818, Died May 11, 1883* (New York: Privately printed, 1883).

52. Hay to Nicolay, August 27, 1873, Hay Papers, BU; Clara Louise Stone, twenty-four years old at her marriage, was born in 1849.

53. Hay to Reid, March 15, 1875, ibid. The Hay's children were Helen Hay, born 1875 (married Payne Whitney in 1902) and died in 1944; Adelbert Stone Hay, born November 1, 1876, and died in June, 1901; Alice Hay born in 1880 (married James Wolcott Wadsworth in 1902) and died in 1959; and Clarence Leonard Hay born December, 1884, and died in June, 1969.

54. For more on the *Tribune* during the period Hay worked on it see Royal Cortissoz, *The Life of Whitelaw Reid*, 2 vols. (New York, 1921). Also see, Dennett, *John Hay*, pp. 96–102.

55. Hay to Reid, July 24, 1876, WRP:LC; and Charles Hay to his sister, August 29, 1875, C. Hay Papers, ISHS.

56. Dennett, *John Hay*, pp. 96–102.

57. See Hay, *Amasa Stone*, pp. 1–8.

58. Hay to Reid, Sept. 24, 1875, Hay Papers, BU.

59. Dennett, *John Hay*, pp. 123–25.

60. Hay to Reid, March 14, 1876, Hay Papers, BU.

61. Hay to Reid, April 1876, ibid. Dennett finds Hay's support of Blaine strange. Yet for many Republicans in 1875–1876 Blaine was seen as a champion of reform. In 1876 Blaine was the candidate advanced by the

anti-Grant faction at the Republican convention. Blaine's main opposition came from the Grant stalwarts who engineered the nomination of the dark horse Governor of Ohio, Rutherford B. Hayes, see John G. Sproat, *The Best Men: Liberal Reformers in the Gilded Age* (New York, 1968), p. 93.

62. Descriptions of Hay's illness are found in Hay to Nicolay, June 23, 1876, November 6, 1876, Hay Papers, BU; Dr. Richard H. Derby to Hay, March 8, 1878, ibid.; Fordyce Barker to Hay, June 25, 1878, ibid.

63. For more on Charcot see Henri F. Ellenberger, *The Discovery of the Unconscious: The History and Evolution of Dynamic Psychiatry* (New York, 1970), pp. 89–101; also see Hay to Clara Hay, June 24, 1878, Hay Papers, BU. Neurological troubles continued to bother Hay. In 1883 he complained of "nausea, some dizziness, deep depression toward evening, a sense of uncertainty in my gait—irregular pulse after any muscular effort." He also was bothered by difficulty in hearing. These symptoms appeared at irregular intervals and none of the specialists who examined him could uncover any somatic cause for his complaints. This fact has led some of Hay's biographers to conclude that he was a hypochondriac. Another diagnosis may be suggested by the recurrent and multiple nature of Hay's disorders, all of which were neurological in character. Hay may have suffered from some form of demyelinating disorder of the central nervous system, possibly multiple sclerosis, which coincidentally was a disease first diagnosed in 1870 by Dr. Jean Charcot. For additional reports on Hay's symptoms see Hay to Dr. Wier Mitchell, June 10, 1883, Hay Papers, BU; Dr. C. H. Burnet to Wier Mitchell, February 23, 1884, ibid.; Hay to R. Johnson, March 31, 1891, ibid.; Hay to Nicolay, September 16, 1891, ibid.; Dr. Leroy M. Yale to Hay, August 24, 1892, ibid.

64. Reid to Hay, March 20, 1879, WRP:LC.

65. Hay to Reid, March 30, 1879, Thayer, *Hay*, I, 456; Dennett, *John Hay*, p. 126.

66. Hay to Reid, Aug. 20, 1879, Thayer, *Hay*, I, 432.

67. Hay to Reid, Aug. 25, 1879, Oct. 6, 1879, ibid., pp. 433–34.

68. *New York Tribune*, Oct. 7, 1879, p. 5; The *Tribune* added that "great numbers of the Republican Party in the XXth District are looking to him [Hay] as the man of all others to run for Congress next year."

69. *New York Tribune*, Oct. 9, 1879, p. 2.

70. Hay to Howells, Feb. 20, 1877, Hay Papers, BU.

71. *New York Tribune*, Oct. 15, 1879.

72. Hay to Reid, Oct. 1, 1875, p. 5; Thayer, *Hay*, I, 426–27.

73. Dennett, *John Hay*, p. 129.

74. Evarts to Hay, Oct. 24, 1879, Hay Papers, BU.

75. Hay to Evarts, Oct. 28, 1879, ibid. Hay to Reid, Nov. 3, 1879, Thayer, *Hay*, I, 434. Dennett suggests that Hay went through a serious trauma deciding whether or not to assume public office again. Dennett [p. 129] said, "It was a case for the psychologists—a mind at war with itself."

76. Hay to Reid, Nov. 3, 1879, Thayer, *Hay*, I, 434.

77. Thayer, *Hay*, I, 436–437.

78. Dennett, *John Hay*, p. 129; Jaher, "Industrialism and the American Aristocrat," [p. 83] supports his view, though he mistakenly has Garfield appointing Hay Assistant Secretary of State in 1878. Garfield wasn't elected President until 1880, and it was Hayes who appointed Hay in 1879 not 1878.

79. Also see Dennett, *John Hay*, p. 129. Hay's and Clara's son, Adelbert, had been born in 1875, Alice was born in 1880, and Clarence Leonard in 1884.

80. Hay to Reid, March 31, 1880, Thayer, *Hay*, I, 438.

81. See ibid., pp. 437–39.

82. Hay to Howells, May 24, 1880, *Letters*, II, 46.

83. Don Cameron had married into a most powerful social set with his wedding to the beautiful amd much younger Elizabeth Sherman of the Ohio Shermans (General and Cabinet members). Elizabeth's closest friends were the Adamses and Henry Cabot Lodge's wife, Anna. Hay was also adopted into this group.

84. *New York Tribune*, Aug. 1, 1880, p. 3; The *Tribune* reprinted the entire speech which took up a full page. Also see *New York Times*, Aug. 1, 1880, p. 1.

85. Dennett, *John Hay*, p. 131.

86. *New York Tribune*, Aug. 1, 1880, p. 3.

87. For instance see Jaher, "Industrialism and the American Aristocrat," p. 83.

88. Hay to Garfield, Oct. 18, 1880, Dec. 25, 1880, Hay Papers, BU.

89. See for instance Hay to Garfield, Dec. 6, 1880 and Dec. 22, 1880, in which Hay urged Garfield to appoint Blaine Secretary of State, ibid.; Hay to Garfield, Oct. 8, 1880, Dec. 25, 1880, ibid.

90. Adams, *Education*, pp. 323–24.

91. Hay to Garfield, Oct. 18, 1880, Hay Papers, BU.

92. Hay to Garfield, Dec. 25, 1880, ibid.

93. Hay to Reid, Dec. 29, 1880, WRP:LC.

94. Ibid.; Hay to Garfield, Dec. 31, 1880, Hay Papers, BU.

95. See Hay to Reid, Aug. 4, 1880, *Letters*, II, 47–49; Hay to Howells, May 24, 1880, Aug. 9, 1880; ibid., pp. 46, 50–51; Hay to Rhodes, July 10, 1880, ibid., pp. 49–50.

96. See Thayer, *Hay*, I, 450–55.

97. See Hay to Reid, May 26, 1881, Thayer, *Hay*, I, 451–52.

98. Due to the suicide of Hay's father-in-law, Amasa Stone, in May of 1883, Hay and his wife inherited $3.5 million jointly. Hay also replaced Stone on the Board of Directors of Western Union Telegraph Company, a position he retained until he was appointed Secretary of State in 1898. Dennett, *John Hay*, p. 106. Also see Marian Adams to Dr. R. W. Hooper,

May 13, 1883, *The Letters of Mrs. Henry Adams*, ed. Ward Thoron (Boston, 1936), p. 450.

99. Gilder's company was going to publish Nicolay and Hay's *Lincoln: A History*. Hay to Gilder, June 30, 1884, Richard Gilder Papers, New York Public Library.

100. Hay to Howells, Sept. 16, 1884, Hay Papers, BU. Hay characteristically apologized for his role in the campaign to Howells: "I did not intend to do anything but pay my subscription, but I was caught the day I got home, and made to preside at the biggest meeting I ever saw in the square the other night." Hay added, somewhat incongruously that he had met with ex-President Hayes on Blaine's behalf and gained Hayes' "hearty . . . support of Blaine."

101. Hay to Gilder, July 11, 1884, Gilder Papers, N.Y. Pub. Lib. Hay and Blaine had maintained an exceedingly close relationship for years. All during the 1884 campaign Hay kept in personal touch with Blaine. See for instance Hay to Blaine, June 21, 1884, in David S. Muzzey, *James G. Blaine, A Political Idol of Other Days* (New York, 1934), p. 253; Hay to Blaine, Nov. 5, 1884, James G. Blaine Papers, Manuscript Division, Library of Congress.

102. For instance see Hay to Rhodes, Feb. 14, 1885, *Letters*, II, 89–90.

103. Before appearing in its final ten-volume version in 1890, the work appeared in installments from November, 1886, to February, 1890, in the *Century* Magazine. On reasoning behind serialization, see Hay to Reid, July 17, 1886, WRP:LC. The *Century* paid fifty thousand dollars for the installments.

104. Theodore Roosevelt to Hay, July 22, 1902, quoted in Dennett, *John Hay*, p. 141.

105. Hay's house was designed by Henry Hobson Richardson, and shared a wall with the house of Hay's friend Henry Adams. For more on the house see Mark Friedlander, "Henry Hobson Richardson, Henry Adams, and John Hay," *Massachusetts Historical Society Proceedings* 81 (1969), 137–66.

106. Marian Adams to Dr. R. W. Hooper, May 13, 1883, *The Letters of Mrs. Henry Adams*, p. 450; Adams to Charles Gaskell, June 10, 1883, Henry Adams Papers, Massachusetts Historical Society, Boston, Mass. (hereafter cited as HAP:MHS); see Frank H. Mason to Hay, August 8, 1883, Hay Papers, BU concerning the settlement of Stone's estate. Also see Gould to Hay, July 2, 1883, ibid.; Thomas Eckert to Hay, July 3, 1883, ibid.; Stone's place on the Western Union Board went to Astor and Hay was appointed to the next vacancy thanks to the support of Gould and Eckert.

107. See Gould to Hay, February 22, 1884, Hay Papers, BU; and Sherman to Hay, February 10, 1884, ibid.

108. Vanderbilt to Hay, December 29, 1883, ibid., and Hay to Clara Hay, May 27, 1884, ibid.

109. Brayton Ives to Hay, June 17, 1886, July 20, 1886, ibid.; Samuel A. Raymond to Hay, June 9, 1890, ibid.; and D. O. Mills to Hay, December 24, 1891, ibid.

110. For a picture of Washington life during the period and descriptions of the circle in which Hay moved see Sir Cecil Spring-Rice. *The Letters and Friendships of Cecil Spring Rice*, 2 vols., ed. Stephen Gwynn (Boston, 1929), I, 52–120; Adams, *Education*, xxi–xxiv; Ernest Samuels, *Henry Adams, The Middle Years* (Cambridge, 1965), especially chapter 5; Augustus Saint-Gaudens, *The Reminiscences of Augustus Saint-Gaudens*, 2 vols., ed. Homer Saint-Gaudens (New York, 1913), I, 209–12, 348–93, II, 328–45.

111. For a tribute to King see John Hay, "Clarence King," n.d., Hay, *Addresses of John Hay* (New York, 1906), pp. 343–53. The essay is reprinted from an earlier work, *Clarence King, Memoirs,* compiled and written by his friends after his death, and published by the Century Company; for more on King see Thurman Wilkins, *Clarence King: A Biography* (New York, 1958).

112. For Adams' introduction of Hay to English society, see Samuels, *Adams, The Middle Years*, pp. 175–77, quoting from letter from Adams to Robert Cunliffe, November 12, 1882, HAP: MHS; Dennett, *John Hay*, p. 167.

113. See Hay to George W. Curtis, Nov. [23], 1887, Hay Papers, BU.

114. *New York Tribune*, Dec. 8, 1887, p. 1.

115. Hay to Blaine, Dec. 8, 1887, Muzzey, *Blaine*, p. 367; see also Blaine to Hay, July (?), 1887, ibid., p. 359.

116. Hay to Reid, March 16, 1888, *Letters*, II, 144; Hay to Adams, June 25, 1888, ibid., p. 150; Hay to Sherman, June 25, 1888, Dennett, *John Hay*, pp. 171–72.

117. Hay to Adams, June 25, 1888, *Letters*, II, 150; Hay to Sherman, June 25, 1888, John Sherman Papers, Manuscript Division, Library of Congress; Hay to Reid, Aug. 3, 1888, WRP:LC Hay told Sherman that Harrison won the nomination because "of the corruptions, the self-seeking, . . . which were everywhere present." Harrison, noted Hay, was "a man universally regarded as second-rate. . . ." Hay to Sherman, June 27, 1888, Hay Papers, BU.

118. Hay to Harrison, Oct. 1, 1888, Benjamin Harrison Papers, Manuscript Division, Library of Congress.

119. Hanna to Hay, Oct. 19, 1888, Hay Papers, BU; Hay to Reid, Nov. 7, 1888, WRP:LC.

120. Adams, *Education*, p. 234; Thayer, *Hay*, II, 132–33.

121. Hay to Adams, Dec. 17, 1891, *Letters*, II, 231; see also ibid., pp. 193–249.

122. See Hay to Robert Lincoln, April 21, 1890, *Letters*, II, 190.

123. Hay to Adams, Oct. 9, 1890, *Letters*, II, 200; Hay to Adams, Dec. 12, 1890, Dec. 30, 1890, *Letters*, II, 202–4, 209.

124. Thayer, *Hay*, II, 133.

125. Hay to Adams, Aug. 26, 1892, *Letters*, II, 245; see also Hay to Adams, Aug. 18, 1892, ibid., p. 243.

126. Hay to Adams, June 16, 1892, HAP:MHS.

127. See Hay, undated [1892] speech, JHP:LC; Hay to Reid, Oct. 20, 1892, Thayer, *Hay*, II, 134.

128. Hay to Adams, Nov. 9, 1892, *Letters*, II, 248; Hay to Reid, Nov. 10, 1892, Thayer, *Hay*, II, 134–35.

129. Hay to Adams, Aug. 29, 1893, Oct. 2, 1893, *Letters*, II, 261, 264; Hay to Nicolay, Jan. 26, 1894, ibid., p. 277.

130. Hay, "Esse Quam Videri," *Complete Poetical Works*, p. 134.

131. See chapter 3 for more on this point.

132. Hay, *The Bread-winners* (New York, 1883).

133. Hay to Reid, Oct. 12, [1893], WRP:LC.

134. Hay to Reid, March 9, 1894, ibid.

135. Hay to Adams, May 24, 1894, HAP:MHS.

136. Hay to Reid, Oct. 12, 1894, WRP:LC.

137. John Hay, Memorandum, n.d., Hay Papers, BU.

138. Hay to Reid, Oct. 24, 1891, ibid.

139. See Thayer, *Hay*, II, 138.

140. Ibid.

141. McKinley to Hay, Feb. 26, 1893, Hay Papers, BU; from that time on Hay and McKinley worked closely to secure McKinley's nomination. See McKinley to Hay, Nov. 10, 1894, ibid., in which McKinley thanked Hay for his pledge to aid McKinley in obtaining the 1896 presidential nomination.

142. Hanna to Hay, April 15, 1895, Hay Papers, BU; McKinley to Hanna, April 13, 1895, William McKinley Papers, Library of Congress (hereafter cited as WMcKP:LC); McKinley to Hay, April 13, 1895, Hay Papers, BU; McKinley to James A. Gary, April 13, 1895, WMcKP:LC.

143. Hay traveled to Virginia and New Jersey in order to convince key Republicans to support McKinley. See Hanna to Hay, April 15, 1895, Hay Papers, BU.

144. Hay to Hanna, Dec. 20, 1895, Hay Papers, BU; Hay to Hanna, Jan. 27, 1896, WMcKP:LC; Hanna to Hay, March 24, 1896, Hay Papers, BU.

145. Hay to Reid, August 4, 1895, Hay Papers, BU.

146. Adams to Brooks Adams, May 14, 1896, Cater, *Adams*, pp. 368–69; Hay to Reid, April 17, 1896, WRP:LC; Charles Milness Gaskell to Adams, January 9, 1896, HAP:MHS; Adams to Gaskell, January 23, 1896, February 17, 1896, ibid.; Adams to Elizabeth Cameron, February 21, 1896, ibid.

147. Olney to Bayard, July 20, 1895, NA Rg 59, Instructions, Great Britain (hereafter cited as "Instructions, Great Britain"); Grover Cleveland, 3rd Annual Message, December, 1895, *Messages and Papers of the Presidents,* 11 vols, James D. Richardson (Washington, 1904), IX 656–58. For a discussion of the Venezuela crisis see Walter LaFeber, *The New Empire: An*

Interpretation of American Expansion, 1860–1898 (Ithaca, 1963), pp. 242–83; also see David Healy, *U. S. Expansionism: The Imperialist Urge in the 1890s* (Madison, 1970), pp. 24–28; Robert L. Beisner, *From the Old Diplomacy to the New, 1865–1900* (New York, 1975), pp. 98–103. For another view of Anglo-American relations during this period see Lionel M. Gelber, *The Rise of Anglo-American Friendship, A Study in World Politics, 1898–1906* (New York, 1938), esp. pp. 1–167.

148. Hay to Olney, July 31, 1896, quoted in Dennett, *John Hay,* pp. 175–76; Hay to McKinley, August 3, 1896, WMcKP:LC. Hay to Clara S. Hay, June 7, 1896, and July 31, 1896, Hay Papers, BU. Also see Hay to Reid, June 9, 1896, JHP:LC; Adams to Elizabeth Cameron, June 26, 1896, HAP:MHS.

149. Hay to Olney, July 31, 1896, Dennett, *John Hay,* pp. 175–76.

150. Hay to McKinley, August 3, 1896, WMcKP:LC.

151. Ibid.

152. Hay to Adams, September 8, 1896, JHP:LC.

153. *New York Tribune,* Oct. 6, 1896.

154. Hanna to Hay, Oct. 12, 1895, Hay Papers, BU.

155. Hanna to Hay, March 5, 1896, March 27, 1896, Hay Papers, BU.

156. Hay to McKinley, Aug. 3, 1896, WMcKP:LC.

157. Adams to Elizabeth Cameron, June 20, 1907, W. Ford, ed., *Letters of Henry Adams,* 2 vols. (Boston and New York, 1930, 1938). II, 480.

158. See Duncan, *Whitelaw Reid,* pp. 167–70; also see Anne H. Sherrill, "John Hay: Shield of Union" (Ph.D. dissertation, University of California, Berkeley, 1966), pp. 296–305, and Clymer, *John Hay,* pp. 23–26.

159. Reid to Hay, March 27, 1897, WRP:LC.

Chapter Five

1. Theodore Roosevelt to Henry Cabot Lodge, January 28, 1909, Theodore Roosevelt Papers, Library of Congress (hereafter cited as TRP:LC).

2. See Chapter 3 for more on this point. See also Hay to Reid, August 6, 1887, WRP:LC; Hay to Adams, June 19, 1894, JHP:LC); Hay to Adams, July 17, 1897, HAP:MHS.

3. Hay diary, July 12, 1867, JHP:LC:JVII.

4. Hay to Howells, December 20, 1882, Hay Papers, BU. For a good general survey of Anglo-American relations and attitudes during this period see Bradford Perkins, *The Great Rapprochement: England and the United States, 1895–1914* (New York, 1968), especially pp. 3–156.

5. For more on this see chapter 2. See also Norman B. Ferris, *Desperate Diplomacy, William H. Seward's Foreign Policy, 1861* (Knoxville, Tenna., 1976).

6. For a discussion of the background of the dispute over Venezuela see Walter F. LaFeber, *The New Empire: An Interpretation of American*

Expansion 1860–1898 (Ithaca, 1963), pp. 242–83; see also David Healy, *U. S. Expansionism: The Imperialist Urge in the 1890s* (Madison, 1970), pp. 24–28; Robert L. Beisner, *From the Old Diplomacy to the New, 1865–1900* (New York, 1975), pp. 98–103.

7. John Hay, "Thanksgiving Day Address," November 25, 1897, in *The Addresses of John Hay* (New York, 1906), pp. 68–69.

8. Hay, "A Partnership in Beneficence," April 21, 1898, ibid., pp. 77–78.

9. Hay to John W. Foster, June 23, 1900, in Howard K. Beale, *Theodore Roosevelt and the Rise of America to World Power* (Baltimore, 1956), p. 83. For a discussion of American Anglophobia during this period see Edward P. Crapol, *America for Americans: Economic Nationalism and Anglophobia in the Late Nineteenth Century* (Westport, Conn., 1973).

10. Hay to William McKinley, April 13, 1897, WMcKP:LC).

11. Whitelaw Reid to Hay, March 27, 1897, WRP:LC.

12. Baron von Eckardstein, *Ten Years at the Court of St. James's 1895–1906* (London, 1911), p. 44.

13. Henry Adams, *The Education of Henry Adams* (Boston, 1918), pp. 362–63.

14. Dennett, *John Hay*, p. 182.

15. Hay to McKinley, May 25, 1897, WMcKP:LC; Hay to Adams, May 24, 1897, JHP:LC.

16. Hay to McKinley, July 16, 1897, WMcKP:LC.

17. Hay to Reid, July 9, 1896, JHP:LC; Henry Adams to Elizabeth Cameron, June 26, 1896, HAP:MHS.

18. Hay to McKinley, May 9, 1897, WMKP:LC; Hay to Reid, May 14, 1897, WRP:LC.

19. See Sir Julian Pauncefote to Salisbury, no. 275, December 18, 1895, Public Record Office, Foreign Office, vol. 115, 996, microfilm copy in Library of Congress (hereafter cited as PRO:FO:LC); Bayard to Cleveland, December 18, 1895, Richard Olney Papers, Library of Congress (hereafter cited as ROP:LC); Adams to Olney, December 17, 1895, ibid.; T. Roosevelt to Olney, December 20, 1895, ibid.; Hay to Roosevelt, September 29, 1897, TRP:LC.

20. Hay to McKinley, May 9, 1897, WMcKP:LC.

21. Ibid., italics are Hay's.

22. Hay to Reid, May 14, 1897, WRP:LC.

23. The United States claimed that the seals, though captured on the high seas, were actually United States property since they bred on the Pribiloff Islands (which was United States territory). For more on this see Charles C. Tansill, *Canadian-American Relations, 1875–1911* (New Haven, 1943), pp. 267–352; also see Charles S. Campbell, Jr., *Anglo-American Understanding, 1898–1903* (Baltimore, 1957), p. 80.

24. Sherman to Hay, May 10, 1897, National Archives, Record Group 59. "Instructions, Great Britain". (hereafter cited as "Instructions, Great Britain"). Sherman's instructions to Hay were actually written by John Foster, see Dennett, *John Hay*, p. 186. Also see a second note of that same day: Sherman to Hay, May 10, 1897, "Instructions, Great Britain."

25. Hay to Sherman, May 20, 1897, National Archives, Record Group 59, "Despatches, Great Britain" (hereafter cited as "Despatches, Great Britain").

26. Sherman to Hay, May 21, 1897, "Instructions, Great Britain."

27. "England and the Seals," *New York Tribune*, July 14, 1897, p. 2.

28. Kenton J. Clymer, *John Hay, The Gentleman as Diplomat* (Ann Arbor, 1975), pp. 109–110.

29. Hay to McKinley, July 16, 1897, WMcKP:LC.

30. Hay to Adams, May 24, 1897, HAP:MHS; also see Adams to Hay, May 25, 1897 and July 17, 1897, ibid.

31. Salisbury to Hay, July 28, 1897, U.S. Department of State, *Papers Relating to the Foreign Relations of the United States, 1897*, p. 300.

32. Hay to Salisbury, July 29, 1897, ibid.

33. White to J. Addison Porter, August 31, 1897, Henry White Papers, Library of Congress (hereafter cited as HWP:LC).

34. Hay to Sherman, September 25, 1897, "Despatches, Great Britain"; also see Clymer, *Hay*, pp. 111–12.

35. See Clymer, *Hay*, p. 112; Dennett, *John Hay*, pp. 185–86.

36. Hay to McKinley, September 25, 1897, Hay Papers, BU; H. White to Hay, October 11, 1897, HWP:LC.

37. Dennett, *John Hay*, p. 183.

38. William McKinley, "Inaugural Address," *Messages and Papers of the Presidents*, 11 vols., ed. James D. Richardson (Washington, 1904), x 11–19; McKinley, "Message to Congress," March 15, 1897, ibid., 19–21.

39. See Thomas J. McCormick, *China Market, America's Quest for Informal Empire, 1893–1901* (Chicago, 1967), pp. 21–52; LaFeber, *The New Empire*, pp. 1–61.

40. Sherman to Hay, March 25, 1897, "Instructions, Great Britain"; Hay to McKinley, March 16, 1897, WMcKP:LC.

41. Hay to Reid, May 2, 1895, WRP:LC.

42. Hay to Sherman, May 20, 1897, copy in WMcKP:LC.

43. H. White to McKinley, February 6, 1897, WMcKP:LC.

44. H. White to McKinley, February 6, 1897, WMcKP:LC; Hay to Sherman, "Despatches, Great Britain."

45. Adams to Hay, October 19, 1897, HAP:MHS.

46. The special envoys appointed were Senator Edward O. Wolcott of Colorado, Former Vice President Adlai E. Stevenson, and Colonel Charles J. Paine of Massachusetts. See Dennett, *John Hay*, p. 183; Horace Porter to

Sherman, June 30, 1897, in WMcKP:LC.

47. Hay to McKinley, July 30, 1897, JHP:LC.

48. Ibid.

49. Hay to T. Roosevelt, September 29, 1897, TRP:LC.

50. Edward Wolcott to McKinley, August 6, 1897, WMcKP:LC.

51. This aspect of the problem will be discussed at length later in this chapter.

52. On predictions of prosperity see *New York Times* editorial of July 28, 1897, p. 4: "There is nothing in sight but good times and plenty of business." See also Hay to Reid, June 21, 1898, WRP:LC; for the French attitude see Wolcott to McKinley, August 6, 1897, WMcKP:LC and Hay to Adams, September 23, 1897, HAP:MHS.

53. Hay to Adams, October, 1896, HAP:MHS, italics are Hay's.

54. White to Hay, September 16, 1897, HWP:LC.

55. White to Hay, September 29, 1897, ibid.; and Hay to Clara Hay, September, 1897, Hay Papers, BU.

56. Hay to McKinley, October 11, 1897, WMcKP:LC.

57. Ibid.

58. Henry White to Hay, October 5, 1897, HWP:LC.

59. Hay to McKinley, October 11, 1897, and October 21, 1897, WMcKP:LC; Hay to John Sherman, "Despatches, Great Britain."

60. See especially Tyler Dennett's chapter on Hay's Ambassadorship entitled "At the Court of St. James," especially pp. 182–83. For a more positive view of Hay's Ambassadorship see William R. Thayer, *The Life and Letters of John Hay*, 2 vols. (Boston and New York, 1915), II, 182.

61. Both Thayer and Dennett generally neglect this aspect. On the other hand, Clymer and Campbell do discuss Hay's role in American-China policy while Ambassador to England. See Campbell, *Anglo-American Understanding*, pp. 16–21, 160–63, and Clymer, *Hay*, pp. 149–50.

62. Clymer, *Hay*, p. 143.

63. U. S. Commission to Evarts, November 17, 1880, *Foreign Relations, 1881*, p. 198. Evarts depended heavily on Hay during this time. Also see Brooks Adams, "John Hay," *McClure's Magazine* 19 (1902), 177–78. Adams maintains that Hay actually ran the State Department during this period.

64. Hay, *The Bread-winners*, pp. 313–14.

65. See Clymer, *Hay*, pp. 143–44; also see Edward H. House to Hay, February 6, 1897, JHP:LC; Hay to House, March 25, 1897, Hay Papers, BU; Hay to W. W. Rockhill, April 10, 1897, William W. Rockhill Papers, Harvard University, Cambridge, Mass. (hereafter cited as WWRP:HU); Hay to House, July 25, 1897, Hay Papers, BU. Hay's knowledge of the Orient was considerably enhanced by the copious reports of his friends Henry Adams and John LaFarge during and after their trip in 1886, and by

the service there of Sir Cecil Spring-Rice from 1892 to late 1893. Of importance to Spring-Rice was the growing threat of Russia and Germany.

66. Of course, Hay was not alone in his concern over the closing of China and the need for expansion of American markets as a solution to recurring American domestic problems. The best recent work dealing with the push by policymakers for increased penetration of the China market in the 1890s is Thomas J. McCormick's *China Market;* see especially his chapter entitled "Exporting the Social Question," pp. 21–52. Also see Healy, *U.S. Expansionism*, pp. 164–65. A recent work which argues that Manchuria was seen by many Americans as a new frontier is Michael H. Hunt, *Frontier Defense and the Open Door: Manchuria in Chinese American Relations, 1895–1911* (New Haven, 1973). A study which emphasizes that the rhetoric of the China market was greater than its commercial and financial value is Marilyn B. Young's *Rhetoric of Empire: America China Policy, 1895–1901* (Cambridge, 1968).

67. Charles S. Campbell, Jr., *Anglo-American Understanding*, p. 14; Charles Denby, the American Minister to China, warned that the German seizure of Kiaochou posed a great danger for American business interests. The German action, Denby warned, would encourage the Russians to seek a sphere of their own at Port Arthur and Talienwan. See Denby to Sherman, November 18, 1897, National Archives, Record Group 59, Despatches, China (hereafter cited as "Despatches, China"). Also see Denby to Sherman, December 6, 1897, ibid. The business community (at least that part of it concerned with China) put increasing pressure on McKinley to take strong action. See McCormick, *China Market*, pp. 89–93.

68. *New York Times*, December 23, 1897, p. 1; *New York Tribune*, December 23, 1897, p. 1.

69. Ibid.

70. *New York Times*, December 25, 1897, p. 7; *New York Tribune*, December 25, 1897, p. 1.

71. Ibid.

72. Hay to Sherman, January 11, 1898, "Despatches, Great Britain."

73. Salisbury to Pauncefote, January 12, 1898, PRO:FO:LC.

74. White to Sherman, January 19, 1898, "Despatches, Great Britain."

75. Ibid.

76. Ibid.; also see Sherman to H. White, March 17, 18, 1898, enclosed in Adee to Hay, March 20, 1901, JHP:LC.

77. The British Government was also encouraged by other developments in the United States. See H. White to Sherman, January 19, 1898, "Despatches, Great Britain." On January 5, 1898, *The Philadelphia Press* quoted Senator William P. Frye of Maine (and the Foreign Relations Committee) as having said that "This country is vitally interested in the situation in China. . . . Our interests in the matter cannot be exaggerated. The injury

to us resulting from a partition of the Empire would be almost incalculable." In an editorial on January 4, 1898, the *New York Times* declared that in regard to Great Britain, "Our interests in the Far East are the same as hers." The *New York Herald* claimed that the United States would support Great Britain in the Far East against Germany and Russia because the latter two powers would set up "discriminatory trading areas," January 4, 1898. The *London Times* noted on January 5, 1898, that Great Britain "enjoys the powerful support of the Government of the United States." See Campbell, *Anglo-American Understanding,* pp. 14–15; the British Government was also aware of the business pressures which were mounting on the McKinley Administration. See Charles S. Campbell, Jr., *Special Business Interests and the Open Door* (New Haven, 1951), pp. 32–37.

78. Sherman to A. D. White, February 11, 1898, National Archives, Record Group 59, Instructions, Germany (hereafter cited as "Instructions, Germany"). Apparently by early 1898 the State Department was actually being run on a day-to-day basis by Assistant Secretary of State William R. Day. See Campbell, *Anglo-American Understanding,* p. 19. While acknowledging Day's role, Hay believed that all important decisions were made by McKinley. See Hay to Clara Hay, September 29, 1898, JHP:LC.

79. A. D. White to Sherman, February 28, 1898, National Archives, Record Group 59, Despatches, Germany (hereafter cited as "Despatches, Germany").

80. Lodge to H. White, February, 1898, cited in Allan Nevins, *Henry White, Thirty Years of American Diplomacy* (New York, 1930), p. 166.

81. John Hay, *Letters of John Hay and Extracts from Diary,* 3 vols. (Washington: Privately printed, 1908), III, 112–13; Henry Adams, *The Education of Henry Adams* (Boston, 1918), p. 360.

82. H. White to Hay, March 6, 1898, in Nevins, *Henry White,* pp. 162–63; H. White to Sherman, February 23, 1898, "Despatches, Great Britain."

83. H. White to Hay, March 6, 1898, in Nevins, *Henry White,* pp. 162–63.

84. Hay to H. White, March 15, 1898, JHP:LC.

85. See A. Whitney Griswold, *The Far Eastern Policy of the United States* (New Haven, 1938), pp. 43–44; see John Hay's "Letterbook" of March 17, 1898, which contains enclosure marked March 8, 1898, JHP:LC.

86. Sherman to Hitchcock, March 17, 1898, National Archives, Record Group 59, Instructions, Russia (hereafter cited as "Instructions, Russia"). Hitchcock to Sherman, March 19, 1898, National Archives, Record Group 59, Despatches, Russia (hereafter cited as "Despatches, Russia").

87. Denby to Sherman, March 19, 1898, "Despatches, China."

88. Hay to Sherman, March 25, 1898, "Despatches, Great Britain."

89. Denby to Sherman, March 29, 1898, "Despatches, China."

90. Hay to Lodge, April 5, 1898, *Letters,* III, 119–21.

91. H. White to Hay, April 23, 1898, HWP:LC. Also see White to Hay, April 30, 1898, ibid.

92. *London Daily Chronicle,* April 15, 1898, quoted in Campbell, *Anglo-American Understanding,* p. 17.

93. Hay, "A Partnership in Beneficence," April 21, 1898, *Addresses,* pp. 77–78.

94. Hay to Theodore Stanton, May 8, 1898, Hay Papers, BU.

95. Hay to Day, July 28, 1898, HWP:LC. Hay assured McKinley in July that the British Government preferred that the United States retain the Philippines. Hay wrote to Lodge that he (Hay) wanted to keep the Philippines because Germany wants "the Philippines, the Carolines and Somoa—they want to get into our markets and keep us out of theirs." Hay to Lodge, July 27, 1898, JHP:LC.

96. Alfred L. P. Dennis, *Adventures in American Diplomacy, 1896–1906, From Unpublished Documents* (New York, 1928), p. 122.

97. Hay to Lodge, May 25, 1898, *Letters,* III, 123–26.

98. McKinley to Hay, May 29, 1898, JHP:LC.

99. Hay to McKinley, June 3, 1898, WMcKP:LC.

100. Day to Hay, July 14, 1898, "Instructions, Great Britain."

101. See H. White to Hay, April 30, 1898, HWP:LC; before he left England in August, Hay had a long conversation with Lord Charles Beresford. Beresford, a member of Parliament, was about to leave for China as a special representative of the Associated Chambers of Commerce of Great Britain. Hay and Beresford agreed that China should be kept open to the commerce of all nations on an equal footing. Hay concurred with Beresford's hope that a "commercial alliance between Great Britain and America with reference to the 'open door' in China, may become an absolute fact." Beresford to Hay, November 29, 1898, JHP:LC; also see Dennis, *Adventures in American Diplomacy,* p. 186; R. G. Neale, *Great Britain and United States Expansion, 1898–1900* (Lansing, Mich., 1966), p. 190.

Chapter Six

1. Recent scholarship has redeemed McKinley's reputation as a leader. See particularly H. Wayne Morgan, *William McKinley and His America* (Syracuse, 1963) and Margaret Leech, *In the Days of McKinley* (New York, 1959). For Hay's views on McKinley see Hay to Henry Adams, October 20, 1896, Hay Papers, BU; John Hay, "William McKinley, Memorial Address by Invitation of the Congress," February 27, 1902, in *Addresses of John Hay* (New York, 1907), pp. 137–75; Tyler Dennett, *John Hay: From Poetry to Politics* (New York, 1933), pp. 207–8.

2. Hay believed that the McKinley Tariff of 1890 with its reciprocity clause was both the perfect expression of protection and an excellent solution for overproduction. See Hay to Adams, October 9, 1890, Hay Papers, BU; also see Walter LaFeber, *The New Empire: An Interpretation of*

American Expansion, 1860–1898 (Ithaca, 1963), pp. 115–16, and Tom E. Terrill, *The Tariff, Politics and American Foreign Policy, 1874–1901* (Westport, Conn., 1973), pp. 159–83. For variations on this theme see David Healy, *U.S. Expansionism: The Imperialist Urge in the 1890s* (Madison, 1970), pp. 159–77; Robert L. Beisner, *From the Old Diplomacy to the New, 1865–1900,* (New York, 1975), pp. 17–26.

    3. This point often has been made. For an extreme statement of this argument see William Appleman Williams, *The Tragedy of American Diplomacy* (New York, 1962), esp. pp. 17–50; also see Martin J. Sklar, "Woodrow Wilson and the Political Economy of Modern United States Liberalism," *Studies on the Left* 1 (1960): 27, 44–46; N. Gordon Levin, Jr., *Woodrow Wilson and World Politics, America's Response to War and Revolution* (New York, 1968), pp. 113–14, 237–38, 245–46.

    4. *New York Times* (editorials), February 17, 19, 22, March 11, 15, 1898 (all page 6); also see Leech, *In the Days of McKinley* pp. 154–55; Dennett, *John Hay,* p. 197.

    5. Adams to W. W. Rockhill, October 31, 1898, HAP:MHS: For a view that argues that the 1880s saw a revitalization of the American navy see Kenneth J. Hagan, *American Gunboat Diplomacy and the Old Navy, 1887–1889* (Westport Conn., 1973).

    6. Hay to White, October 2, 1898, JHP:LC); Hay to Adams, May 27, 1898, HAP:MHS; Hay to Choate, December 21, 1900, JHP:LC, Letterbook II (hereafter cited as LB); Hay to H. White, December 23, 1900, March 18, 1901, ibid.

    7. Hay to Choate, August 18, 1899, in Dennett, *John Hay,* p. 237; Hay to J. W. Babcock, April 22, 1900, JHP:LC:LB II.

    8. Hay to Clara Hay, October 7, 1898, JHP:LC; Hay to H. White, October 2, 1898, ibid.; Hay to McKinley, April 10, 1899, ibid.

    9. Hay to Adee, July 12, 1882, Hay Papers, BU; for a recent account of Adee's role in making policy see John A. DeNovo, "The Enigmatic Alvey A. Adee and American Foreign Relations, 1870–1924," *Prologue* 7 (Summer, 1975), 69–80. For Adee's service under Hay see pp. 73–78.

    10. See *New York Times,* August 16, 1898, p. 1; September 2, 1898, p. 6; September 9, 1898, p. 7.

    11. Sir Cecil Spring-Rice to Hay, April 30, 1898, "Annex it now"; Spring-Rice, *Letters,* I, 246–47. Hay to Spring-Rice, May 5, 1898, saying that he fully agreed with "Springy's" analysis of German intentions, and had sent the proposal off to McKinley immediately; ibid., I, 247. Leech, *Days of McKinley,* credits Hay with McKinley's determination of quick annexation (p. 212). The statement in Dennett, *John Hay,* p. 278, that "Hay had no part in the transaction," is not supported by the evidence.

    12. Joseph Chamberlain had threatened to resign from the Cabinet should Britain join the coalition. Spring-Rice was chosen to convey the Cabinet's secret deliberations to Hay. In 1917, he reported the entire affair

in writing to William Roscoe Thayer, Spring-Rice to Thayer, Spring-Rice, *Letters*, I, 253. Spring-Rice to Hay, July 16, 1898, ibid., I, 251–52, informs Hay that he had hopefully squelched German bid for a coaling station in Philippines by telling Count Metternich that Britain "would be opposed to any action on Germany's behalf which would be unpleasant to America."

13. Hay, draft of speech given July 4, 1898, American Society of London, JHP:LC. Same theme in Baker article of December, 1861.

14. Hay to Nicolay, January 30, 1870, Hay Papers, BU; Hay on threat of military in Philippines, see Albert W. Caleb to Hay, March 26, 1899, JHP:LC. Theodore Roosevelt was one of the military men desirous of becoming Secretary of War. Lodge to Roosevelt, September 23, 1898, *Selections from the Correspondence of Theodore Roosevelt and Henry Cabot Lodge*, 2 vols. (New York, 1925), I, 347–48. Henry Adams to Elizabeth Cameron, January 6, 1899, HAP:MHS.

15. Philip Jessup, *Elihu Root*, 2 vols. (New York, 1938), I, 215–17; Hay to H. White, August 11, 1899, quoted in ibid., p. 217.

16. Hay, Memorandum, March 25, 1899, JHP:LC; Hay to McKinley, August 28, 1899, ibid. There was talk of Dewey's running for President in 1900.

17. H. Wayne Morgan, *America's Road to Empire: The War with Spain and Overseas Expansion* (New York, 1965), pp. 75–76; LaFeber, *The New Empire*, pp. 409–10.

18. Charles S. Campbell, Jr., *Anglo-American Understanding, 1898–1903* (Baltimore, 1957), p. 82; Day to Pauncefote, March 30, 1898, National Archives, Record Group 59, Notes to the British Legation (hereafter cited as NA "Notes to British Legation"); John W. Foster was chosen to conduct discussions on the regulation of seal fishing on the Bering Sea, and John A. Kasson to represent the United States on other issues. Also see *New York Times*, July 3, 1898, p. 17.

19. Hay to H. White, January 13, 1899, JHP:LC; Hay to H. White, August 11, 1899, *Letters of John Hay and Extracts from Diary*, 3 vols. (Washington: Privately printed, 1908), III, 160–61.; Hay to Adams, May 27, 1898, HAP:MHS.

20. Hay to H. White, November 21, 1898, Henry White Papers, Library of Congress (hereafter cited as HWP:LC).

21. See Alfred L. P. Dennis, *Adventures in American Diplomacy, 1896–1906, From Unpublished Documents* (New York, 1928), p. 439; Bishop Joseph C. Hartzell to Hay, October 19, 1898, National Archives, Record Group 59, Despatches, Liberia; also see Hay to Day, August 27, 1898, ibid., "Despatches, Great Britain."

22. Hay to John B. Jackson, November 18, 1898, and November 21, 1898, ibid., "Instructions, Germany"; Hay to Horace Porter, June 28, 1899, ibid., Instructions, France (hereafter cited as "Instructions, France").

23. Dennis, *Adventures in American Diplomacy*, p. 440.

24. Jackson to Hay, December 5, 1899, "Despatches, Germany"; see also Dennis, *Adventures in American Diplomacy*, p. 440.

25. See Anne H. Sherrill, *John Hay: Shield of Union* (Ph.D. dissertation, University of California, Berkeley, 1966), pp. 349–50.

26. See Morgan, *America's Road to Empire*, pp. 101–9; see Beisner, *Old Diplomacy to New*, pp. 122–24. Two recent works which emphasize the role of anti-imperialism as a factor in the opposition to the treaty are Robert L. Beisner, *Twelve Against Empire: The Anti-Imperialists, 1898–1900* (New York, 1968), and E. Berkeley Tompkins, *Anti-Imperialism in the U.S., the Great Debate, 1890–1920* (Philadelphia, 1970).

27. Whitelaw Reid, *The Diaries of Whitelaw Reid: Making Peace With Spain*, ed. H. Wayne Morgan (Austin, 1965), p. 237. Evidence exists that a plan for seizing the Philippines had developed long before the war with Spain had been declared. See John A. S. Grenville, "American Naval Preparation for the War with Spain, 1896—1898," *Journal of American Studies* 2 (April, 1968), 33–47.

28. William McKinley, "Second Annual Message," December 5, 1898, *The Messages and Papers of the Presidents, 1789–1905*, 11 vols., ed. James D. Richardson (Washington, 1907), XI, 102–3.

29. Hay to White, November 23, 1898, Hay Papers, BU; see also chapter 5 for more on this point.

30. Hay to Conger, October 3, 1898, National Archives, Record Group 59, Instructions, China (hereafter cited as "Instructions, China").

31. New York Chamber of Commerce to Hay, October 10, 1898, ibid., Miscellaneous Letters of the State Department.

32. Reid to Hay, October 16, 1898, Whitelaw Reid Papers, Library of Congress (hereafter cited as WRP:LC); Samuel E. Williamson to Hay, October 18, 1898, JHP:LC; Everett Frazar (President of the American Asiatic Association) to Hay, December 5, 1898, ibid.; Peppermill Manufacturing Company to Hay, January 3, 1899, ibid. This last letter was signed by many influential businessmen as well as Senator Henry Cabot Lodge. They warned that American commerce was being "shut out from the markets of North China" by Russia. Also see Marilyn Blatt Young, *The Rhetoric of Empire, American China Policy, 1895–1901* (Cambridge, Mass., 1968), pp. 115–23.

33. Hay to Conger, December 23, 1898, "Instructions, China"; Conger to the "tsungli yuman," U.S. Department of State, *Papers Relating to the Foreign Relations of the United States, 1899*, p. 144 (hereafter cited as *Foreign Relations, 1899*); additional pressure came from the British explorer, A. R. Colquhoun, who Hay met in the 1880s. Colquhoun wrote Hay in January that "The process of partition is in full operation, and Britain and the United States should make up their minds which of the two policies they will press for; to couple the two—'open door' and 'sphere' . . . will lead

to failure . . . I trust that . . . action will be taken while there is still time." Colquhoun to Hay, January 12, 1899, "Despatches, China."

34. Pauncefote to Hay, January 8, 1899, JHP:LC.

35. Hay to Rockhill, August 7, 1899, WWRP:HU); Rockhill to Hippisley, August 3, 1899, and August 18, 1899, ibid.; Hay to H. White, September 9, 1899, JHP:LC.

36. Hay to Pauncefote, March 7, 1899, "Notes to British Legation."

37. Colonial Secretary Joseph Chamberlain favored such a move. Chamberlain had first suggested taking a sphere in January, 1898. See H. White to Sherman, January 19, 1898, "Despatches, Great Britain."

38. McCormick, *China Market*, pp. 100–101; A. Whitney Griswold, *The Far Eastern Policy of the United States* (New Haven, 1938), p. 50.

39. Beresford to Hay, November 20, 1898, JHP:LC; Rounseville Wildman (U.S. Consul General, Hong Kong) to Hay, November 25, 1898, JHP:LC; Beresford to Wildman, November 19, 1898, ibid.

40. Beresford to Hay, November 20, 1898, ibid.

41. Ibid.

42. See McCormick, *China Market*, pp. 137–39; Lord Charles Beresford, *The Breakup of China* (New York, 1899), pp. 433–37.

43. McCormick, *China Market*, p. 138; Beresford *Breakup of China*, p. 436.

44. Everett Frazar to Hay, February 20, 1899, JHP:LC; McCormick, *China Market*, pp. 138–39; Beresford, *Breakup of China*, pp. 436–37.

45. Conger to Hay, March 1, 1899, "Despatches, China."

46. Hay to Dana, March 16, 1899, quoted in William R. Thayer, *The Life and Letters of John Hay*, 2 vols. (Boston, 1916), II, 241; also see Dana to Hay, March 15, 1899, JHP:LC. Dana hoped that the government would "exert some influence against China's partition."

47. See Dennett, *John Hay*, pp. 289–90; Paul A. Varg, *Open Door Diplomat: The Life of W. W. Rockhill* (Urbana, Illinois, 1952), p. 22.

48. Dennett, *John Hay*, pp. 289–90; see also Thayer, *The Life of Hay*, II, 244.

49. Hay to Rockhill, June 1, 1899, WWRP:HU.

50. Griswold, *Far Eastern Policy*, p. 65.

51. Ibid.

52. Hippisley to Rockhill, July 25, 1899, WWRP:HU; Rockhill to Hippisley, August 3, 1899, ibid.

53. Hay to Rockhill, August 7, 1899, ibid.

54. Hay to H. White, August 11, 1899, "Instructions, Great Britain."

55. Ibid., also see Rockhill to Hippisley, August 3, 1899, WWRP:HU; Hay to Rockhill, August 7, 1899, ibid.

56. Tower to Hay, August 23, 1899, National Archives, Record Group 59, Despatches, Russia (hereafter cited as "Despatches, Russia").

57. McCormick, *China Market*, pp. 140–41.

58. *New York Times*, August 16, 1899, p. 1.

59. Rockhill to Hippisley, August 18, 1899, WWRP:HU; Rockhill noted that "Dr. Schurman's views, as expressed . . . in the papers, will exercise very great influence on the discussion of the Administration."

60. Hay to Rockhill, August 24, 1899, WWRP:HU, Rockhill to Hippisley, August 29, 1899, ibid.; Hay to M. Schuyler, August 30, 1901, Hay Papers, BU.

61. Both books were published earlier that year (1899). See McCormick, *China Market*, p. 138; Rockhill to Hippisley, August 28, 1899, WWRP:HU.

62. McCormick, *China Market*, pp. 138–41.

63. Hay to Adams, August 5, 1899, *Letters*, III, 456–57.

64. Hay to Adee, August 10, 1899, JHP:LC.

65. Hay to Rockhill, August 24, 1899, WWRP:HU.

66. Griswold, *Far Eastern Policy*, p. 74; George F. Kennan, *American Diplomacy, 1900–1950* (Chicago, 1951), pp. 23–37.

67. See Appendix of Griswold, *Far Eastern Policy* (pp. 484–85) for complete copies of the original drafts of both the Hippisley and Rockhill memorandums.

68. Ibid.

69. *Foreign Relations, 1899*, p. 132.

70. Ibid.

71. Rockhill, Memorandum, n.d. (October, 1899), WWRP:HU; Hay to James Angell, July 18, 1900, JHP:LC:LB I; "Notes Published with Final Replies," *Foreign Relations, 1899*, pp. 128–42. Also see Hay to Choate, November 14, 1899, "Instructions, Great Britain"; Hay to Horace Porter, December 8, 1899, "Instructions, France"; also see Campbell, *Anglo-American Understanding*, pp. 165–67.

72. Hay to Tower, Jan. 22, 1900. "Instructions, Russia," copy in WWRP:HU; Tower to Hay, February 12, 1900, JHP:LC; also see Tower to Hay, February 9, 1900, ibid.

73. Ibid.; see also Dennett, *John Hay*, p. 293. For a recent study which details U.S. interest in Manchuria see Michael H. Hunt, *Frontier Defense and the Open Door: Manchuria in Chinese-American Relations 1895–1911* (New Haven, 1973).

74. Hay to Tower, January 22, 1900, copy in WWRP:HU; Tower to Hay, February 12, 1900, JHP:LC.

75. *Foreign Relations, 1899*, pp. 128–42; Hay to Angell, July 18, 1900, JHP:LC:LB I.

76. Rockhill to Hippisley, January 16, 1900, WWRP:HU.

77. Day to Hay, January 24, 1900, JHP:LC.

78. *New York Sun*, March 29, 1900, p. 6; H. White to Hay, May 16, 1900, Henry White Papers, Library of Congress (hereafter cited as

HWP:LC); Everett Frazer to Hay, November 24, 1899, JHP:LC, containing clippings from *New York Tribune*, November 9, 1899, and *New York Herald*, November 11, 1899.

79. Hay to Reid, September 20, 1900, WWRP:HU.

80. Hay to Pauncefote, July 23, 1900, NA "Notes to British Legation."

81. Wu to Hay, July 11, 1900, JHP:LC; see also Dennett, *John Hay*, pp. 304–5; *Foreign Relations, 1900*, pp. 155–56.

82. Wu to Hay, July 11, 1900, JHP:LC.

83. Hay to Adams, July 8, 1900, JHP:LC:LB I.

84. Hay to Rockhill, July 19, 1900, *Foreign Relations, 1900*, p. 156; Adee to Hay, September 3, 1900, and September 4, 1900, JHP:LC. Their code for Conger was "eel."

85. Conger to Hay, July 16, 1900, *Foreign Relations, 1900*, p. 156; Wu to Hay, July 20, 1900, JHP:LC.

86. Adee to Hay, July 24, 1900, JHP:LC.

87. Hay to Thurlow Weed Barnes, July 23, 1900, JHP:LC.

88. Hay to Wu, August 3, 1900, JHP:LC:LB I; Adee to Hay, August 4, 1900, ibid.

89. Choate to William Choate, August 5, 1900, in *The Life of Joseph Hodges Choate as Gathered Chiefly From His Letters*, 2 vols., ed. E. S. Martin (London, 1920), II, 150; *New York Sun*, August 7, 1900 (lead editorial), p. 6; Kasson to Hay, August 8, 1900, JHP:LC; H. White to Hay, August 11, 1900, HWP:LC; Pauncefote to Hay, August 22, 1900, JHP:LC; Reid to Hay, August 25, 1900, WRP:LC.

90. Hay, manuscript, July 28, 1900, letter from the President of the United States to the Emperor of China, JHP:LC; see also Hay to McKinley, July 29, 1900, ibid.

91. Adee to Hay, August 9, 1900, enclosing a copy of telegram from the Japanese Minister of Foreign Affairs to Japan's Minister to the U.S., Takahira, JHP:LC.

92. Conger to Hay, August 14, and August 16, 1900; *Foreign Relations, 1900*, p. 160.

93. *New York Sun*, August 10, 1900; Adee to Hay, July 24, 1900, JHP:LC; Choate to Hay, August 1, 1900, Joseph H. Choate Papers, Library of Congress (hereafter cited as JCP:LC:LB I; Kasson to Hay, August 8, 1900, JHP:LC; H. White to Hay, August 11, 1900, HWP:LC; Adee to Pauncefote, August 14, 1900, "Notes to British Legation"; Pauncefote to Hay, August 22, 1900, JHP:LC.

94. McCormick, *China Market*, p. 163; Clymer, *Hay*, p. 151.

95. Clymer, *Hay*, p. 151; in the late summer, McKinley decided that the United States should consider taking its own sphere. Hay was incensed and vigorously protested in a strong note to McKinley. The President reconsidered and backed down. See Hay to McKinley, September 19, 1900, WMcKP:LC; also see Adee to McKinley, September 17, 1900, ibid.

96. Hay to Adee, September 14, 1900, JHP:LC.

97. Hay to Reid, September 1, 1900, WRP:LC.

98. See for instance, *New York Sun*, August 10, 1900.

99. Hay to Adee, September 14, 1900, JHP:LC.

100. Examples of this view are to be found in Kennan, *American Diplomacy*, pp. 23–37; Clymer, *Hay*, p. 156; Paul A. Varg, *The Making of a China Myth: The United States and China, 1897–1912* (East Lansing, Michigan, 1968), pp. 36–53; see also Marilyn B. Young, *The Rhetoric of Empire: America China Policy, 1895–1901* (Cambridge, 1968), pp. 230–31, for a more sophisticated analysis.

Chapter Seven

1. For a discussion of the Clayton-Bulwer Treaty of 1850 see Charles S. Campbell, Jr., *From Revolution to Rapprochement, The United States and Great Britain, 1783–1900* (New York, 1974), p. 81. Also see Hay diary, May 7, 1861, JHP:LC; Hay to Adams, June 15, 1900, ibid., LB:I; Hay to White, September 7, 1900, Henry White Papers, Library of Congress (hereafter cited as HWP:LC). A good survey of the recent scholarship concerning diplomatic events of this period is found in Robert L. Beisner, *From the Old Diplomacy to the New, 1865–1900* (New York, 1975), especially pp. 107–39.

2. For instance see Tyler Dennett, *John Hay, From Poetry to Politics* (New York, 1933), especially chapters 18–26; Kenton J. Clymer, *John Hay, The Gentleman as Diplomat* (Ann Arbor, 1975), chapters 6–9; Charles S. Campbell, Jr., *Anglo-American Understanding, 1898–1903* (Baltimore, 1957); A. E. Campbell, *Great Britain and the United States, 1895–1903* (London, 1960, reprint Westport, Conn.,1974), chapters 3–6.

3. Campbell, *Anglo-American Understanding*, pp. 88–119.

4. John A. Kasson to Hay, October 3, 1898, JHP:LC. For background of United States interest in Alaska see Howard I. Kushner, *Conflict on the Northwest Coast: American-Russian Rivalry in the Pacific Northwest, 1790–1867* (Westport, Connecticut, 1975).

5. Herschell to Hay, December 20, 1898, JHP:LC; H. White to Chamberlain, December 26, 1898, HWP:LC); Hay to White, December 3, 1898 in William R. Thayer, *The Life and Letters of John Hay*, 2 vols. (Boston, 1915), II, 204; Hay to Roosevelt, February 11, 1899, Theodore Roosevelt Papers, Library of Congress (hereafter cited as TRP:LC).

6. White to Chamberlain, December 26, 1898, HWP:LC.

7. White to Hay, December 30, 1898, HWP:LC.

8. Hay to White, January 3, 1899, JHP:LC.

9. Ibid.; in 1899 Sir Julian became Lord Pauncefote. See also Hay to White, February 14, 1899, ibid.; Campbell, *Anglo-American Understanding* outlines the issues in chapter 3 and discusses the diplomacy of the Joint High Commission in chapter 4.

10. William McKinley, "Second Annual Message," December 5, 1898, *The Messages and Papers of the Presidents, 1789–1905,* 11 vols. ed. James D. Richardson (Washington, 1907), X, 100–102.

11. Olney to Hay, December 12, 1898, Richard Olney Papers, Library of Congress (hereafter cited as ROP:LC); Olney to Pauncefote, December 13, 1898, ibid.; White to Hay, December 21, 1898, December 30, 1898, HWP:LC.

12. Olnev to Pauncefote, January 29, 1977, NA "Notes to British Legation".

13. Ibid.

14. The first treaty is described and analyzed by Hay in a letter to Pauncefote, December, 1901, JHP:LC; also see Campbell, *Anglo-American Understanding,* p. 128, for Pauncefote to Lansdowne, April 11, 1901 on drafting the convention. Also see Lodge to Roosevelt, February 14, 1909, TRP:LC. Lodge told Roosevelt that Hay had written the treaty.

15. Hay to White, December 7, 1898, National Archives, Record Group 59, Instructions, Great Britain (hereafter cited as "Instructions, Great Britain"); Hay to White, December 9, 1898, JHP:LC; Hay to Reid, February 7, 1900, WRP:LC; John Bassett Moore to Hay, February 12, 1900, John Bassett Moore Papers, Library of Congress (hereafter cited as JBMP:LC); Hay Memorandum for release to press, February, 1900, JHP:LC.

16. Hay to Cushman K. Davis, February 8, 1900, JHP:LC:LB I; Hay to Moore, February 14, 1900, JBMP:LC.

17. See notes 15 and 16 above.

18. Choate to Hay, January 27, 1900, JCP:LC; Hay to White, February 14, 1899, JHP:LC; see also Campbell, *Anglo-American Understanding,* pp. 56–87.

19. Hay to White, September 9, 1899, JHP:LC; Hay to Choate, October 2, 1899, "Instructions, Great Britain"; A. E. Campbell, *Great Britain and the United States,* pp. 101–3.

20. The fullest account of United States policy during the Boer War remains John H. Ferguson, *American Diplomacy and The Boer War* (Philadelphia, 1939).

21. See Hay to J. W. Forster, June 23, 1900, JHP:LC. For Hay's actions in regard to pressures upon him to mediate between the two sides, see Clymer, *Hay,* pp. 157–64.

22. Hay to White, September 29, 1899, JHP:LC; also see Hay to White, March 19, 1900, "Instructions, Great Britain."

23. Hay to Adelbert Hay, July 1, 1900, quoted in Clymer, *Hay,* pp. 160–61; and Hay to Adelbert Hay, October 1 & 5, 1900, JHP:LC; Hay to Adams, June 15, 1900, JHP:LC:LB I.

24. Hay to White, September 7, 1900, HWP:LC, includes Memorandum of January 8, which was enclosed in letter.

25. Hay to Adams, June 15, 1900, JHP:LC:LB I.

26. Hay to White, January 13, 1899, ibid.; Hay to Morgan, December 27, 1898, cited in Clymer, *Hay*, pp. 175–76.

27. Hay to Morgan, January 21, 1899, ibid.

28. Clymer, *Hay*, p. 176.

29. Choate to Hay, February 2, 1900, JHP:LC:LB I.

30. Ibid.

31. Pauncefote to Salisbury, January 19, 1900, in Campbell, *Anglo-American Understanding*, p. 190. Also see Bradford Perkins, *The Great Rapprochement: England and the United States, 1895–1914* (New York, 1968), pp. 174–85.

32. Hay to Choate, December 21, 1900, JHP:LC:LB II.

33. Ibid.

34. Ibid.

35. Hay to Pauncefote, December 1901, JHP:LC; Choate to Hay, January 30, 1901, ibid.; Hay to White, December 26, 1901, Hay Papers, BU.

36. Hay to White, February 27, 1900, in Allan Nevins, *Henry White, Thirty Years of American Diplomacy* (New York, 1930), pp. 150–51.

37. Dennett, *John Hay*, pp. 261–63.

38. Hay to Shelby M. Cullom or Pauncefote, December 1910, in JHP:LC and JHP:LC:LB II, 227–47. This letter is twenty pages long and is a history of the Isthmian canal controversy from the 1840s to 1901. See also Lodge to Roosevelt, March 10, 1900, TRP:LC.

39. See Campbell, *Anglo-American Understanding*, pp. 218 ff.

40. Hay to Pauncefote or Cullom, December, 1901, JHP:LC; see also Lansdowne to Pauncefote, January 14, 1901, in Campbell, *Anglo-American Understanding*, p. 218.

41. A. E. Campbell, *Great Britain and the United States*, pp. 64–70.

42. Hay to Choate, April 27, 1901, JHP:LC:LB II.

43. Pauncefote to Lansdowne, April 25, 1901, A. E. Campbell, *Great Britain and the United States*, p. 64; Campbell, *Anglo-American Understanding*, p. 230.

44. Choate to Hay, July 24, 1901, JCP:LC; Lodge to Hay, March 28, 1901, Hay Papers, BU.

45. See the *New York Sun*, November 20, 1900, p. 6, quoting Roosevelt interview. Lodge to Roosevelt, March 10, 1900, TRP:LC; Roosevelt to Hay, February 18, 1900, JHP:LC; Choate to Hay, September 25, 1901, JCP:LC.

46. Hay to White, December 26, 1901, Hay Papers, BU.

47. Ibid.; also see Campbell, *Anglo-American Understanding*, pp. 128 ff.

48. The Alaskan Boundary Treaty was not ratified until February 17, 1903. See Hay to Choate, February 17, 1903, JHP:LC:LB II.

49. Ibid. Also see A. E. Campbell, *Great Britain and the United States*, pp. 89–126.

50. Hay to Choate, February 17, 1903, JHP:LC:LB II.
51. Hay to Lodge, October 21, 1902, JHP:LC:LB II; Hay to Roosevelt, October 16, 1902, JHP:LC; see also Hay to Lodge, October 17, 1902, ibid.; Hay to John C. Spooner, July 15, 1902, ibid.
52. Dennett, *John Hay,* pp. 438–39.
53. For Hay on arbitration treaties see Hay to Moore, September 1, 1898, JBMP:LC; Hay diary, November 2, 8, 23, 28, 29, 30; December 2, 10, 13, 14, 15, 1904; January 20, February 3, 1905, JHP:LC; for Lodge's assessment of Hay see Lodge to Roosevelt, February 14, 1909, TRP:LC.
54. Dennett, *John Hay,* pp. 341, 337; Thayer, *The Life of Hay,* II, 262.
55. Hay to Reid, July 22, 1901, and August 31, 1901, WRP:LC; Adams to Hay, July 25, 1901, JHP:LC. That Adelbert took his own life cannot be entirely ruled out. His maternal grandfather, Amasa Stone, died by suicide and his uncle, Adelbert, for whom he was named, had also died at the threshold of his career under circumstances which could be interpreted as suicide.
56. Hay to Reid, July 22, 1901, WRP:LC.
57. Hay to Lady Jeune, September 14, 1901, JHP:LC.
58. Hay to Adams, August 9, 1901, Thayer, *Hay,* II, 265; also see Dennett, *John Hay,* pp. 336–37.
59. Roosevelt to Hay, December 25, 1901, JHP:LC.
60. Hay to Roosevelt, September 15, 1901, JHP:LC:LB II; Roosevelt to Hay, October 5, 1901, JHP:LC.
61. Hay to Adams, September 19, 1901, Thayer, *Hay,* II, 268.

Chapter Eight

1. Roosevelt to Lodge, July 11, 1905, *The Letters of Theodore Roosevelt,* 8 vols., ed. Elting E. Morison (Cambridge, Massachusetts, 1951–1954), IV, 1271; see also Roosevelt to William Howard Taft, July 3, 1905, ibid., IV, 1260.
2. Roosevelt to Hay, February 7, 1899, *Letters of Roosevelt,* II, 934.
3. For instance see Theodore Roosevelt, *Theodore Roosevelt: An Autobiography* (New York, 1926, reprinted and abridged, 1958), pp. 282–85.
4. Roosevelt to Mahan, February 14, 1900, *Letters of Roosevelt,* II, 1185.
5. Hay to Roosevelt, February 12, 1900, John Hay Papers, Library of Congress (hereafter cited as JHP:LC). See also Roosevelt to Nicholas Murray Butler, February 15, 1900, *Letters of Roosevelt,* II, 1186; and Roosevelt to Hay, February 18, 1900, in William R. Thayer, *The Life and Letters of John Hay,* 2 vols. (Boston, 1915), II, 339–41.
6. Hay to Adams, June 15, 1900, Hay Papers, BU. Thayer, *Hay* II, 342 incorrectly cites this letter as Hay to White.
7. Hay to Roosevelt, June 21, 1900, Thayer, *Hay,* II, 343.

8. Hay to Adams, November 21, 1900, in Tyler Dennett, *John Hay: From Poetry to Politics* (New York, 1933), p. 341.

9. Hay to Roosevelt, September 18, 1901, ibid, pp. 341–42.

10. Hay to Adams, September 19, 1901, Hay Papers, BU.

11. For instance he wrote to Taft about Hay's leadership of the State Department, "What I did'n't [sic]do myself was'n't [sic] done at all." Roosevelt to Taft, July 3, 1905, *Letters of Roosevelt,* IV, 1260.

12. Roosevelt to Albert J. Beveridge, July 11, 1905, ibid., IV, 1269.

13. Hay to Adams, September 19, 1901, Thayer, *Hay,* II, 268; Lodge to Roosevelt, September 19, 1901, in *Selections from the Correspondence of Theodore Roosevelt and Henry Cabot Lodge, 1884–1918,* 2 vols., ed. H. C. Lodge (New York, 1925), I, 505.

14. Roosevelt, *Autobiography* (abridged edition), pp. 282–85.

15. Ibid.

16. See for instance, Roosevelt to Taft, July 3, 1905, *Letters of Roosevelt,* IV, 1260. Also see David Healy, *U.S. Expansionism: The Imperialist Urge in the 1890s* (Madison, 1970), pp. 110–26, for Roosevelt's foreign policy views prior to his ascension to the presidency.

17. Hay to Adams, September 19, 1901, Thayer, *Hay,* II, 268.

18. Dennett, *John Hay,* pp. 345–46.

19. For a discussion of the Venezuela issue see Dennett, *John Hay,* pp. 388–94. Also see Paul S. Holbo, "Perilous Obscurity: Public Diplomacy and the Press in the Venezuela Crisis, 1902–1903," *Historian* 32 (April, 1970), 428–88 and Edward B. Parsons, "The German-American Crisis of 1902–03," *Historian* 33 (April, 1971), 436–52; Bradford Perkins, *The Great Rapprochement, England and the United States, 1895–1914* (New York, 1968), pp. 187–92.

20. Dennett, *John Hay,* p. 346.

21. Hay to Clara Hay, July 14, 1903, Hay Papers, BU.

22. See Hay to Clara Hay, January 24, 1903, JHP:LC; Charles S. Campbell, Jr., *Anglo-American Understanding, 1898–1903* (Baltimore, 1957), p. 302; Kenton J. Clymer, *John Hay: The Gentleman as Diplomat* (Ann Arbor, 1975), pp. 191–92.

23. U.S. Department of State, *The Foreign Relations of the United States, 1903,* pp. 488–93.

24. Hay to Root, February 22, 1904, Thayer, *Hay,* II, 324.

25. White to Hay, April 1, 1903, Henry White Papers, Library of Congress (hereafter cited as HWP:LC).

26. See Henry Cabot Lodge, "Memoir of Henry Cabot Lodge," edited by Charles G. Washburne, *Massachusetts Historical Society Proceedings* (April, 1925), p. 340.

27. Hay to White, April 10, 1903, JHP:LC.

28. Roosevelt to Lodge, January 28, 1909, Theodore Roosevelt Papers, Library of Congress (hereafter cited as TRP:LC).

29. Hay to Roosevelt, July 21, 1903, JHP:LC.

30. Roosevelt to Hay, July 29, 1903, *Letters of Roosevelt*, III, 532.

31. Campbell, *Anglo-American Understanding*, pp. 315–17.

32. See A. E. Campbell, *Great Britain and the United States, 1895–1903* (London, 1960, reprint Westport, Connecticut, 1974), pp. 112–16; Campbell, *Anglo-American Understanding*, pp. 319–45.

33. Roosevelt, *Autobiography* (abridged edition), p. 277. For more on the Panama situation see Charles D. Ameringer, "Philippe Bunau-Varilla: New Light on the Panama Canal Treaty," *Hispanic American Review* 46 (February, 1966), 28–52. Also see Ameringer, "The Panama Canal Lobby of Philippe Bunau-Varilla and William Nelson Cromwell, *American Historical Review* 68 (January, 1963), 346–61.

34. Hay to Root, February 22, 1904, Thayer, *Hay*, II, 324.

35. N. T. Bacon to Hay, October 6, 1904 in Dennett, *John Hay*, pp. 378–79; also see Hay to Roosevelt, September 13, 1903, TRP:LC.

36. For Hay's action in the abrogation of the Clayton-Bulwer Treaty, see chapter 7.

37. For Hay's view on reciprocity treaties in the 1890s see Hay to Adams, October 9, 1890, Hay Papers, BU; also see footnote 2, chapter 6.

38. Newfoundland was a separate British colony with its own Royal Governor. See Dennett, *John Hay*, pp. 422–29; Campbell, *Anglo-American Understanding*, pp. 259–68.

39. Campbell, *Anglo-American Understanding*, pp. 262–64.

40. See Dennett, *John Hay*, p. 424; Campbell, *Anglo-American Understanding*, pp. 265–66.

41. Lodge to Hay, October 16, 1902, JHP:LC; also see Campbell, *Anglo-American Understanding*, p. 265.

42. Hay to Roosevelt, October 16, 1902, in Dennett, *John Hay*, pp. 424–75; Hay to Lodge, October 21, 1902, ibid., pp. 426–28. Also see Hay to Robert L. O'Brien, January 14, 1905, Hay Papers, BU.

43. See Dennett, *John Hay*, p. 425.

44. Roosevelt to Lodge, January 3, 1905, *Roosevelt-Lodge Correspondence*, II, 128.

45. See Dennett, *John Hay*, p. 429.

46. Roosevelt to Lodge, November 12, 1904, *Roosevelt-Lodge Correspondence*, II, 110.

47. Hay diary, quoting Roosevelt, November 24, 1904, JHP:LC.

48. Hay to Reid, September 12, 1900, Whitelaw Reid Papers, Library of Congress (hereafter cited as WRP:LC); Brooks Adams to Hay, July 17, 1901, JHP:LC.

49. Hay to Roosevelt, September 17, 1903, JHP:LC; Adee to Leishman, September 9, 1903, ibid.

50. Spencer Eddy to Hay, August 28, 1903, JHP:LC; Hay to Roosevelt, August 31, 1903, ibid., LB:III, Hay to Roosevelt, September 7, 1903, ibid.; Adee to Hay, September 10, 1903, ibid.

51. Hay diary, May 28, 1904, ibid.

52. Hay diary, June 22, 1904, and June 24, 1904, ibid.

53. Hay diary, June 19, 30, July 1, 1904, ibid.

54. Hay to Horace Porter, February 12, 1904, National Archives, Record Group 59, Instructions, France.

55. Hay diary, July 1, 1904, JHP:LC.

56. Hay diary, July 1, 8, 14, 1904, ibid. The Senate, however, voted to refuse to allow Hay to accept the medal. See Dennett, *John Hay*, pp. 438–39.

57. Hay diary, May 19, 20, June 9, October 21, 24, 27, 1904, JHP:LC.

58. Hay diary, November 9, 1904, ibid.; see also Roosevelt, *Autobiography*, pp. 419–20.

59. Hay to Reid, December 22, 1881, WRP:LC.

60. For examples see: *New York Times*, August 10, 1898, editorial, "Secretary Hay," p. 6; Hay To Reid, September 14, 1898, WRP:LC; Charles H. Grosvenor to Hay, October 24, 1898, JHP:LC; Reid to Hay, November 5, 1898, December 31, 1898, JHP:LC; Paul Dana, to Hay, March 15, 1899, JHP:LC; Reid to Hay, February 9, 1900, WRP:LC; Edward Carey to Hay, July 15, 1900, September 29, 1900, JHP:LC; Charles A. Boynton, Superintendent, Associated Press, to Hay, September 3, 1900, JHP:LC; A. Maurice Low to Hay, October 19, 1900, JHP:LC; Hay to St. Clair McKelway, July 12, 1900, quoted in Dennett, *John Hay*, pp. 308–9.

61. Hay to Adams, June 15, 1900, Hay Papers, BU.

62. Roosevelt to Hay, July 22, 1902, quoted in Dennett, *John Hay*, p. 141; Hay diary, October 23, 1904, JHP:LC.

63. Hay diary, January 14, 1905, February 7, 12, 15, 1905, JHP:LC.

64. Ibid., February 15, 1905.

65. Hay to Roosevelt, September 8, 1903, JHP:LC.

66. Hay diary, March 4, 1905, JHP:LC; Thayer, *The Life of Hay*, volume II, facing p. 364, contains a facsimile of Hay's letter to Roosevelt enclosing the ring, March 3, 1905.

67. Hay diary, March 8 [1904], JHP:LC; Roosevelt to Hay, April 16, 1903, ibid.

68. Hay to Clarence King, October 27, 1901, copy in JHP:LC. It should also be noted that, after reporting at John Hay's dinner table and under his urging, Roosevelt wrote up his impressions of his tour of the country in a letter to Hay published in Elting E. Morison ed., *Cowboys and Kings*, (Cambridge, Mass., 1954), pp. 1–27. The letter is provocative, revealing, and astute. It is among the abler reports on social, political, and economic conditions which a Secretary of State could have received.

69. Hay to Roosevelt, May 20, 1905, JHP:LC; Hay diary, May 20, 21, 22, 25, 30, June 7, 1905. Beginning in 1900 Hay had been plagued, in addition to his other illnesses, with complications arising from an enlarged prostate gland.

70. Henry Adams, unsigned preface to *Letters of John Hay and Extracts*

from Diary, 3 vols. (Washington: Privately printed, 1908), I, xxi. For the differing view that Adams himself was the primary influence upon Hay see Thayer, *Hay*, II, 54; Herbert Edwards, "Henry Adams: Politician and Statesman," *New England Quarterly* 22 (March, 1949), 19–60; and Ernest Samuels, *Henry Adams: The Major Phase* (Cambridge, Mass., 1964), pp. 406–11. Much of the argument rests upon the premise that Adams was the stronger man and Hay the weaker and ignores Adams' own testimony in the *Education* which casts himself as the antihero and his father, Charles Francis, and Hay as the heroes who both think *and* act. Our own study of both men has supported Adams' conclusion. What we must add was Hay's self-perception that he needed intellectual stimulus and conflict. For these, he could always depend upon Adams.

71. John Hay, "President Roosevelt," July 17, 1903, in *Addresses of John Hay* (New York, 1907), pp. 219–20.

72. Hay diary, June 13, 1905, JHP:LC.

Appendix

1. John Hay Papers, John Hay Library, Brown University, Providence, Rhode Island (hereafter cited as Hay Papers, BU).

2. Ibid.

3. Caroline Ticknor, ed., *A Poet in Exile: Early Letters of John Hay* (New York and Boston, 1910), pp. 21–25.

4. Hay Papers, BU; also in William R. Thayer, *The Life and Letters of John Hay*, 2 vols. (Boston and New York, 1915), I, 58–60.

5. Hay Papers, BU.

6. Tyler Dennett, ed., *Lincoln and the Civil War in the Diaries and Letters of John Hay* (New York), 1939), pp. 34–35.

7. John Hay, "Speech to Floridians" (written but not delivered), spring, 1864, John Hay Papers, Library of Congress.

8. Dennett, ed., *Civil War Diaries*, pp. 211–12.

9. William H. Seward Collection, Rush Rhees Library, University of Rochester, Rochester, New York.

10. Ibid.

11. Hay Papers, BU.

12. Ibid.

13. Ibid.

14. Ibid.

15. Ibid.

16. Rutherford B. Hayes Papers, Hayes Memorial Library, Fremont, Ohio.

17. Hay Papers, BU.

18. Thayer, *The Life of Hay*, II, 120–21.

19. Hay Papers, BU.

20. Ibid.

21. Whitelaw Reid Papers, Library of Congress, Washington, D.C.

22. *Letters of John Hay and Extracts from Diary*, 3 vols. (Washington: Privately printed, 1908), III, 350.

A Note on the Sources

The most important sources used in this study were manuscript collections. John Hay's correspondence and private papers are scattered throughout the country. Two collections, however, proved to be essential: The John Hay Collections at Brown University in Providence, Rhode Island, and at the Library of Congress in Washington, D.C. The Brown University holdings include a significant amount of Hay's personal and public correspondence as well as those diaries and journals he kept from 1861 until 1870. The Hay Collection at the Library of Congress mainly covers Hay's post-1897 career, including a personal diary which he kept in 1904 until his death in 1905. Other John Hay manuscript collections of lesser and more limited importance are found at the Houghton Library of Harvard University and at the New York Public Library.

Of particular importance to Hay's family background is the collection of Hay family papers at the Illinois State Historical Library in Springfield. This collection includes various letters to and from Hay's father Charles, his uncle Milton, and other family members. Along with a collection of Dr. Charles Hay's letters at Brown University, the Illinois holdings provide an important, but generally neglected, perspective on John Hay's life and family relationships.

Of course, the State Department Papers at the National Archives in Washington, D.C., were important for our preparation of Hay's diplomatic career as well as for an evaluation of United States diplomacy at the turn of the last century. The published *Foreign Relations* volumes for the years 1896–1905 proved generally reliable so long as private correspondence and unprinted materials were used along with those volumes.

There are several published volumes of Hay's letters and diaries, none of which, of course, is complete. The *Letters and Extracts From Diary*, 3 vols. (Washington, 1908) were privately printed and compiled by Henry Adams and Hay's wife Clara. The collection is edited in a manner which makes its use risky. All names of persons have been deleted, and many important passages were edited out. A key to the deletions is in the Library of Congress. Two collections of Hay's early letters are more useful: *A Poet in Exile: Early Letters of John Hay*, edited by Caroline Ticknor (Boston, 1910), presents Hay's letters to Nora Perry and *A College Friendship: A Series of Letters from John Hay to Hannah Angell*, edited by A. C. Montague (Boston, 1938) reprints a series of letters from young John Hay to Hannah Angell, with whom Hay may have had one of his early romances. William R. Thayer's two-volume work, *The Life and Letters of John Hay* (Boston, 1915), reproduces many of Hay's letters and diary entries. In 1939 Tyler Dennett substantially printed the first three journals of Hay's Civil War Diaries entitled *Lincoln and the Civil War in the Letters and Diaries of John Hay*. In 1961 Brown University Library issued a small sample from its collection of Hay's letters and diaries in *The Life and Works of John Hay, 1838–1905: A Commemorative Catalogue* (Providence, 1961). George Monteiro's *Henry James and John Hay: The Record of a Friendship* (Providence, 1965) contains Hay's correspondence with Henry James. More recently Monteiro has compiled and published Hay's views on the Union's generals in "John Hay and the Union Generals," *Journal of the Illinois State Historical Society* 69 (February, 1976), 46–66.

Manuscript collections of Hay's friends and associates have been crucial in the preparation of this book. Particularly important were the following: The Library of Congress: Joseph Hodges Choate Papers, Grover Cleveland Papers, William McKinley Papers, John Bassett Moore Papers, Richard Olney Papers, Whitelaw Reid Papers, Theodore Roosevelt Papers, Edwin M. Stanton Papers, Henry White Papers, John Russell Young Papers. Massachusetts Historical Society: Henry Adams Papers, Theodore Freylinghuesen Dwight Papers, Lodge Family Papers. Houghton Library, Harvard University: Charles Sumner Papers, William Woodville Rockhill Papers, Brooks Adams Papers, William Dean Howells Papers, James Family Papers. Olin Library, Cornell University: Jacob Gould Schurman Papers, Andrew D. White Papers. Rush Rhees Library, University of Rochester: William H. Seward Collection. Butler Library, Columbia University: William Holls Papers. New York Public Library: John Bigelow Papers, George E. Jones Papers, Henry J. Raymond Papers, R. R. Stoddard Papers.

Many of the published collected letters of Hay's friends and associates are also available. The most useful include: *The Collected Works of Abraham Lincoln*, 9 vols., edited by R. Balser (New Brunswick, 1953); *Life in the Letters of William Dean Howells*, 2 vols., edited by Mildred Howells (Garden City, 1928); *Letters of Henry Adams, 1845–1891*, and *1892–1918*, 2 vols., edited by W. C. Ford (New York, 1930–1938); *Henry Adams and His Friends A Collection of his Unpublished Letters*, edited by Harold D. Cater (Boston, 1947); *Selections from the Correspondence of Theodore Roosevelt and Henry Cabot Lodge*, 2 vols., edited by H. C. Lodge (New York, 1923); *The Letters of Theodore Roosevelt*, 8 vols., edited by E. E. Morison (Cambridge, Mass., 1951–1954); and *The Letters of Mrs. Henry Adams, 1865–1883*, edited by Ward Thoron (Boston, 1936).

John Hay's own published poems, essays, as well as his novel *The Bread-winners* (1883) have been an important source and are discussed throughout the book and especially in chapter 3. In our text and particularly in our notes we have discussed, at length, the various published works concerning the life of John Hay and we refer our readers there. The same holds true for the many secondary books and articles we employed. In our citations we discussed the contributions and implications of these works. To do so again here would be redundant.

Index